Rethinking Leadership

NEW HORIZONS IN LEADERSHIP STUDIES

Series Editor: Joanne B. Ciulla
Professor and Coston Family Chair in Leadership and Ethics,
Jepson School of Leadership Studies, University of Richmond, USA

This important series is designed to make a significant contribution to the development of leadership studies. This field has expanded dramatically in recent years and the series provides an invaluable forum for the publication of high quality works of scholarship and shows the diversity of leadership issues and practices around the world.

The main emphasis of the series is on the development and application of new and original ideas in leadership studies. It pays particular attention to leadership in business, economics and public policy and incorporates the wide range of disciplines which are now part of the field. Global in its approach, it includes some of the best theoretical and empirical work with contributions to fundamental principles, rigorous evaluations of existing concepts and competing theories, historical surveys and future visions.

Titles in the series include:

Rethinking Leadership
A New Look at Old Leadership Questions

Donna Ladkin

Senior Lecturer, Cranfield School of Management, Cranfield University, UK

NEW HORIZONS IN LEADERSHIP STUDIES

Edward Elgar
Cheltenham, UK • Northampton, MA, USA

© Donna Ladkin 2010

Published by
Edward Elgar Publishing Limited
The Lypiatts
15 Lansdown Road
Cheltenham
Glos GL50 2JA
UK

Edward Elgar Publishing, Inc.
William Pratt House
9 Dewey Court
Northampton
Massachusetts 01060
USA

A catalogue record for this book
is available from the British Library

Library of Congress Control Number: 2009938387

Mixed Sources
Product group from well-managed
forests and other controlled sources
www.fsc.org Cert no. SA-COC-1565
© 1996 Forest Stewardship Council
FSC

ISBN 978 1 84720 935 1

Printed and bound by MPG Books Group, UK

For Robin

Contents

Preface

I came to the field of leadership studies as something of a sceptic. Certainly, the fascination with 'leadership' within management studies – as well as the more general public – was a fad. Sooner or later it would go the same route as 'Total Quality Management' or 'Organizational Learning'. The allure of leadership, (or more importantly, of leaders) seems to retain its pull however, as evidenced by our collective willingness to put hope into new political, community or business leaders while demonizing others. The varieties change; from transformational to servant, from charismatic to quiet, but the concept itself still seems to command our attention. Why is that?

On delving more deeply into that question, I have found myself becoming increasingly intrigued by the phenomenon. 'Leadership' is at once the providence of the rare individual even as it is democratized in the pronouncement 'Everyone can be a leader!' The salve for every organizational difficulty, on close examination leadership seems to be both 'everything' and 'nothing'. Although I have been critical of the notion that 'good' leaders can make a significant difference to organizational outcomes, I have also watched as 'bad' leaders have propagated destructive practices and politics resulting in strife within groups, communities and even countries. Perhaps something with such far-reaching effects was worthy of re-examination.

I wanted to take a different tack in that examination however. One of the aspects of leadership which began to attract my attention was its largely invisible nature. Leadership seems impossible to catch. I began to wonder about how we might start to notice the invisible, yet powerful aspects of the phenomenon which often mean 'we know it when we see, or, more likely *feel* it'. Were there new questions which would shed light on its lived experience, rather than on the mere traces that remain once it has occurred?

This book represents a journey into both discovering, and dwelling with, those questions. As I point out in the final chapter of the book, 'question' itself is rooted in the word 'quest'. A quest is a journey into the unknown. It is often embarked upon for its own sake, without a clear goal or outcome in mind. What heroes and heroines discover when they embark on a quest is that it is the questing that counts, the journey which makes a difference.

In a similar way this book is grounded in the notion that it is the questions that matter, for they open new possibilities for engaging with this fleeting, but nonetheless powerful aspect of communal life, leadership.

D.M. Ladkin
Kingsbridge, Devon, UK
June, 2009

Acknowledgements

One of the key themes of the book is that 'leadership' is a collective process, in many ways not reducible to 'the leader' – although much of the traditional literature does so. In a similar way, although I have been the author of this book, many of the ideas and arguments it contains have been collectively generated. Without the many colleagues, students and clients with whom I have spoken over the years the questions which are explored here would have remained hidden. Certainly, without their stories, insights and curiosity this book would be much the poorer.

In particular thanks go to the people who have walked alongside me as I have formed and tussled with the text. Thanks go to Joanne Ciulla, the editor of the New Horizons in Leadership Studies Series, who first encouraged the idea of the book and who provided invaluable feedback on early drafts. Bob Pickens, Francine O'Sullivan and Jennifer Wilcox at Edward Elgar were careful guardians of the editorial and publishing process. At Cranfield School of Management, thanks must go to my colleagues who were forgiving of the time I have spent on this endeavour, including Susan Vinnicombe and Kim Turnbull James. I must also say a special thanks to members of my Cranfield Writing Group, David Buchanan, David Denyer and Colin Pilbeam, who read multiple versions of several chapters and provided insightful comments.

A number of my students and colleagues have generously allowed me to represent parts of their own stories and read parts of the book in various stages of its development; for their generosity I am grateful. They include Ashley Braganza, Andy Cook, Stephen Evans, Ed Humpherson, Anne O'Brien, Colin Owen, John Pillay, Patta Scott-Villiers, Lesley Seymour, Steve Taylor, Caron Thompson and Martin Wood.

There are four people who must be singled out for particular mention because without them the text would be much weaker and probably not even here. My good friends and colleagues Ralph Bathurst and Patricia Gaya Wicks were meticulous in their reading of the entire manuscript, offered many of their own insights and thoughts, directed me to useful references and often provided the perfect word of encouragement at the right time to keep me going. My PA at Cranfield School of Management, Alison Cain, has provided invaluable assistance of all kinds. Without her eagle-eye for detail the book would be much less polished and her generosity and enthusiasm for the project have been enormously helpful. Finally, to my husband Robin, for his care, support and forebearance throughout the writing process (as well as through my life more generally!) go more thanks than I can say.

1. Why study leadership from a philosophical perspective?

> I would like to beg you, dear Sir, as well as I can to have patience with every-
> thing unresolved in your heart and to try to love the questions themselves as if
> they were locked rooms or books written in a very foreign language . . . Live
> the questions now. Perhaps then, someday far in the future, you will gradually,
> without even noticing it, live your way to the answer.
>
> Rainer Maria Rilke
> *Letters to a Young Poet*
> (1929 [2009], p. 35)

Why are there so many different theories of leadership? In fact, what *is*
leadership? Sociology, anthropology, political science and psychology are
among the disciplines which have addressed these questions. Definitive
answers, however, remain elusive. Rather than attempting to provide such
answers, this book questions the very questions perennially asked about
leadership. In it ideas from the branch of philosophy known as 'Continental
philosophy'[1] are applied to interrogate habitual ways of thinking about
and inquiring into this much studied phenomenon. For instance, rather
than asking 'What is leadership?', the question, 'How might we understand
leadership as a phenomenon?' is posed. Instead of pondering 'What is charisma?', you will be invited to consider 'How do followers make judgements
about the aesthetic quality of a leader's performance?' Through 'living the
questions' differently and living different questions, this book aspires to
breathe new life into the way scholars, teachers and students intrigued by it
might re-conceptualize leadership and its role in human communities.

Continental philosophy has never been wary of engaging with the significant questions of purpose and meaning central to human life. In this
book I employ ideas primarily drawn from the branch of Continental philosophy, known as 'phenomenology,'[2] to address similarly fundamental
questions about leadership. For instance, we will consider how concepts
such as 'The Lifeworld', 'ready-to-hand' and 'flesh' can offer insight into
the inner workings of the leader-follower dynamic. From the viewpoint of
aesthetic philosophy a novel way of conceptualizing charismatic leadership will be introduced. Concepts drawn from hermeneutics such as the
'fusion of horizons' and 'attunement' are explored for their potential to

enrich our understanding of the meaning-making aspect of leadership. Process philosophy will be used as a lens to reconsider organizational change and the role of leadership in facilitating it. Finally, the book suggests ways in which philosophical practices themselves, can assist those taking up leader roles to do so wisely.

The book is designed for readers who are eager to explore alternative ways of thinking about leadership and the questions we ask about it. You do not need to have been philosophically trained to follow the arguments made here but you will need to engage with an open and curious mind. This introduction serves both to sketch the terrain the book covers, and to orient you to a way of thinking and reflecting which will be echoed throughout the text. To start, let us address the questions, 'Why yet another book about leadership?' and, 'How is this one different from the hundreds of other books you could choose to read?'

WHY ANOTHER BOOK ABOUT LEADERSHIP?

One thing that is clear about the leadership literature is that there is relatively little that is clear about leadership![3] Rather than despairing about the lack of definitional clarity however, this book differs from many texts in that it invites you to consider the very 'indefinability' of leadership as significant. Does the lack of agreement amongst the hundreds of scholars who have written about this phenomenon itself hint at something essential about it? Considering leadership as a socially constructed phenomenon constituted by different people in particular circumstances provides some explanation for its lack of definitional edge. Rather than being satisfied with this explanation, this book interrogates such terrain more deeply and introduces ideas and modes of reflection which push the limits of current conceptualizations of both 'leaders' and 'leadership'.

In fact, the importance of drawing a distinction between 'leaders' and 'leadership' is a theme which runs throughout the book. Whereas many texts conflate the two terms, from a phenomenological perspective the difference between them is argued to be highly significant and even more noteworthy than the traditionally accepted polarization between 'leaders' and 'followers'. Similarly, rather than regarding leaders as central to organizational activities such as 'managing change' or 'sense-making'; these processes themselves are closely examined and re-conceptualized, resulting in a different understanding of the role of 'leadership' in their occurrence. These are just a few examples of how this text aims to de-stabilize and reposition some of the more habitually-held notions within this arena to propose a truly radical view.

First and foremost then, this book challenges us to re-examine the very questions we ask about leadership. In doing so, it aspires to stretch the leadership debate into areas not often considered within current theorizing. It is born largely from my own dissatisfaction with much that is currently written about what I see to be a fascinating and critical aspect of social life. As an organizational studies academic working in a UK-based School of Management, I am often called upon to design and deliver 'leadership development' interventions for commercial and public sector organizations. In my experience there is an earnest hunger from many of those working in organizations to understand more about leadership and how they might employ it to 'make a difference' in their organizations. In its enacted form, they know leadership to be an exciting, vibrant force; something quite different from the often sterilized accounts encountered in the literature. Although this book is primarily written for students of leadership, my hope is that much of what is offered here has practical implications for those who find themselves questioning how they might lead more effectively as part of their organizational roles.

WHY DO THE QUESTIONS MATTER?

As mentioned above, pursuing leadership from a philosophical standpoint invites us to reformulate the way we inquire into it. For instance, the question 'What is leadership?', shifts into the more philosophically oriented query, 'What kind of phenomenon is leadership?' This may seem only an inconsequential matter of semantics. However, if you pause and think about it, you will notice that each question evokes a different kind of response.

The question, 'What is leadership?' assumes the possibility of defining leadership in an objectively-determined, clear-cut way, perhaps as one might be able to define a 'bird' or a 'fork-lift truck'. Such a question suggests that we can 'report it as we see it' and that doing so is a straightforward endeavour. The lack of agreement from so many scholars, leadership developers and organizational theorists who offer different (although often similar) definitions of the term, would seem to indicate the task of defining leadership is not so easy.

By posing the query, 'What kind of phenomenon is leadership?', the certainty that leadership is the kind of thing which can be described in a definitive way loses some of its power. Depending on the kind of phenomenon leadership is, the way we go about defining it may be altered. For instance, phenomena such as 'love' or 'justice' may be difficult to define and do not lend themselves to the same kind of analysis as objects such as a 'bird' or a 'fork-lift truck' do. Lack of definitional clarity does not imply that 'love' or 'justice' do not exist. However, because of their nature as phenomena, the way we go about defining them needs to be carefully considered.

Following from this, the query, 'What kind of phenomenon is leadership?' informs the question 'What *is* leadership?' Once we are clearer about its nature, we are better equipped to ponder what it might 'be'. The appropriateness of the question itself may come under scrutiny. As many philosophers have pointed out, the nature of the questions asked reveals different aspects of the phenomenon being examined. In this way, I am suggesting that philosophical preoccupation with questioning the questions offers a way of expanding thinking into previously unexplored territories. Attending to the questions also raises issues of how they might best be pursued once they are discovered.

What is the Relationship Between the Questions we ask and our Methods for Answering Them?

The great majority of Western-based leadership theories are derived from research methods based in positivistic ways of knowing. In particular, the assumption that the approach used in the physical sciences can apply to examining leadership is witnessed by the large number of studies aimed at identifying particular leadership characteristics, traits or competencies. In this way, leadership is 'broken down' into its component parts and then, taking this method to its logical conclusion, those traits, characteristics or competencies are measured using a variety of psychometric or ideographic indicators.

An ideal example of this is 'transformational leadership', a popular leadership theory since its introduction by James MacGregor Burns (1978). Bernard Bass developed Burns' ideas in particular by identifying four attributes of transformational leaders: charisma, inspiration, individualized consideration and intellectual stimulation (Bass 1985). These four components can then be measured through the 'Transformational Leadership Questionnaire', an instrument developed by Beverley Alimo-Metcalfe and Robert Alban Metcalfe (2001), which assesses aspiring leaders' transformational capacities based on self-report and 360 degree feedback measures. Having identified their strengths and weaknesses in terms of this quotient, potential leaders can create a 'development plan', to improve their performance on specific factors. There is a neatness about such an approach which is highly attractive. Like a car engine registering 'low' on oil or water, once identified deficient attributes can be 'topped up'.

Under closer examination, such an approach can be seen to have a number of limitations. Firstly, it collapses 'leadership', a collective process which encompasses not only leaders but their followers and the context in which they come into contact, into 'leaders', an individually-based unit of analysis. In particular, the assumption that the approach used in studying the physical sciences can be applied to leadership is demonstrated by the large number of studies devoted to identifying leadership's 'parts' and measuring them using psychometric or ideographic indicators. However a normalized amount of idealized consideration may not be appropriate in every situation or organizational culture. What might be the perfect amount of individual consideration in an automobile factory might be entirely inappropriate within a university department.[4]

Secondly, by isolating particular variables in this way, such approaches can fool us into thinking the ingredients which constitute an entity are all that are required to create the entity. A cake results from combining flour, sugar, butter and eggs but its production depends on the type of oven in which it is baked and even the altitude at which it is cooked. Although from a natural science standpoint it may be possible to identify and measure all such factors, those approaches would still not be able to account for the 'meaning' attributed to the cake by those who eat it. The significance of a cake used as the central focus of a birthday celebration differs from that of one tucked into a rucksack for sustenance on a hiking trip. Additionally, the 'success' of a cake will be judged differently depending on its purpose: the lopsided gift proudly offered by my six-year old niece will be judged differently from a misshapen delivery from a cake company I hired to produce the centrepiece at my wedding. Likewise, the effectiveness of any act of leading will be judged from within particular social and historical moments. Reductionist methods are ill-equipped to provide adequate insight into how leadership arises from such particularized instances.

There is a growing body of literature which similarly calls into question accounts which attempt to identify individually-based traits or even individually initiated actions which alone constitute 'leadership'. Building on the earlier work of Cecil Gibb (1954), Peter Gronn's (2000) ideas about 'distributed leadership' contest the possibility of identifying individual leaders and measuring the level of impact they have on any task's achievement. Writers such as Amanda Sinclair (1994, 2005) and Mary Uhl-Bien (2006) bring to our attention the more relational and 'invisible' aspects of leadership which do not lend themselves to clear identification and quantification. This book joins the emerging post-positivist conversation about ways of engaging rigorously with the leadership terrain and offers a distinctive voice by contributing insights from Continental philosophy to the debate.

WHY PHILOSOPHY?

How might philosophy contribute to our thinking about leadership in ways other disciplines have not already attempted? In her introduction to the special issue of the *Leadership Quarterly* devoted to 'Leadership and the Humanities', Joanne Ciulla (2008) suggests 'leadership is a human phenomenon embedded in culture, which includes art, literature, religion, philosophy, language and generally all those things that constitute what it means to live as a human being' (p. 393). As a philosopher herself, she then traces the line of philosophers from the classical thinker Giambattista Vico (1668–1744) through to post-positivists such as Michel Foucault (1926–1984), who have laid the tracks in developing humanities-based ways of developing and verifying knowing. Ciulla argues that both social sciences, with their focus on deconstruction and correlation, and the humanities, with their attention to holistic understanding and reliance on human capacities for story-telling, use of metaphor and image in their sense-making processes need to be incorporated to come to a fuller understanding of a phenomenon such as leadership.

Philosophy, like psychology or sociology, is not a unified body of ideas and approaches. As indicated earlier, in this book I draw from a range of ideas located under the broad umbrella of Continental philosophy developed largely in Europe from the beginning of the twentieth century. Although I will also visit ideas from aesthetics and process thought; phenomenology, a branch of Continental philosophy which has genesis in the work of Edmund Husserl (1859–1938) serves as the main source of ideas. As we will see in Chapter 2, one of phenomenology's key projects is to reclaim the validity of epistemologies more associated with philosophy than science, especially in developing truths about the everyday world of human beings.

In particular, phenomenology recognizes the subjective nature of knowledge and pays close attention to lived experience as a valid source of knowing. Many of the more traditional ways of exploring leadership attempt to describe it 'from the outside' in accordance with accepted social science methods and assumptions about validity and objectivity. In contrast, phenomenology embraces the significance of meaning within human sense-making processes. Concerned with aspects of quality rather than quantity, it reasserts the importance of felt experience as well as the cumulative effects of history on our ability to know. Additionally, it recognizes the impact of absent or invisible aspects of an entity as well as explicitly present ones and in so doing alerts us to the possibility that when exploring a phenomenon such as leadership, what one does not see may be as important as what one does see.

As the qualitative, experienced and absent aspects of phenomena are impossible to identify, measure and correlate, they have largely been ignored by social scientists intent on defining, assessing and manipulating leadership. Phenomenology provides a language and an approach which allows access into these emergent and obscure territories. In this way, it may not arrive at definitive answers to questions such as 'How much "individual consideration" it takes to produce a transformational leader?' However, it does offer a set of concepts which enable the experience of transformational leadership to be pondered in a more complex and multi-dimensional way. Particularly, phenomenology brings the experience of whoever is being led directly into the centre of what constitutes leadership. In this way its very aim prohibits thinking of 'leadership' primarily in terms of 'leaders'.

Stepping back from the specific concerns of phenomenology momentarily, let us consider the question 'Why engage philosophy to study leadership?' more broadly. The word 'philosophy' has its roots in the Greek *philosophia* which is often translated as 'lover of wisdom'. We have come to understand philosophy both as a body of writing which addresses the fundamental questions of the human condition (for example, 'What is the meaning of life?'; 'What is my purpose?'; 'How should I balance my own needs with those of others?') as well as a method for thinking about those questions. In this book, philosophy is used in both ways. Firstly, particular philosophical ideas will be introduced which I hope will provide you with new vantage points from which to regard and expand your habitually held views about leadership.

Secondly, throughout the book the use of a potent philosophical tool; inquiry, will be modelled. As I hope may already be apparent, philosophers take the business of asking questions very seriously. Forming 'good' questions, that is those which lead to opening of the territory under investigation and allow for an expansion in thinking, is an art. My hope is that in addition to the ideas you might take from the text, you may also develop something of the skill of inquiry by immersing yourself in a text which has an explicit intent of 'living the questions'.

To emphasize this intent, the book's structure itself is organized around questions perennially raised about leadership. In the background of these explicitly articulated queries which serve as the focus for each chapter, other, more shadowy ones lurk. 'Why in our contemporary context do we keep asking so many questions about leadership?' 'What does the asking of these questions themselves reveal about who we are in our particular socio-historic moment?' 'How does reflecting on the "questioner" and why he or she is posing the question offer further insight into the nature of the phenomenon being investigated?' Ideally, the text will provoke many more explicit and emerging questions of your own from which you may rethink leadership.

QUESTIONS TO RETHINK

The next three chapters address ontological[5] aspects about the nature of leadership. Rather than just taking for granted assumptions about the kind of phenomenon it is, they open this territory be exploring three key questions. Chapter 2 asks: why are there so many different theories of leadership?

This question is often directed towards leadership scholars by sceptical social scientists with the implied suggestion: 'given its lack of definitional clarity, how can leadership claim to be a "real" sort of thing, worthy of the large amount of scholarly attention paid to it?'

Where does this question come from in the first place? (Philosophy is very good at asking questions about questions.) I argue that this query arises from the concerns of a positivistic paradigm in which definitions can be 'objectively' agreed and component parts of things identified and measured. Furthermore, the chapter goes on to explore the possibility that the difficulty in defining leadership itself might be a helpful clue as to the kind of phenomenon it is. Ideas from phenomenology, such as the relevance of 'aspects' and 'sides' in describing entities as well as the distinction between 'wholes', 'pieces' and 'moments' are introduced to explain the lack of definitive accounts of leadership. In fact, the chapter ends by proposing that we may need more rather than fewer renderings of leadership in order to fully appreciate its impact on social systems.

Chapter 3 expands on this phenomenological exploration by wondering: why is it so difficult to study leadership?

A growing number of leadership theorists, including Peter Gronn (2002) in his study of distributed leadership within higher education and Mats Alvesson and Stefan Sveningsson (2003) in their study of leadership in high tech firms, highlight the difficulties in pinpointing where or how leadership occurs within communities. Alvesson and Svenningsson conclude that leadership has a curious way of disappearing, both for leaders and for those who understand themselves to be led. Although ubiquitous in the way we construct our experience of organizations, leadership proves to be elusive under close examination. The chapter draws on the phenomenological notion of 'identity' to examine why its very elusiveness may be essential to its nature as a phenomenon. This argument is further explored through reference to the distinction Martin Heidegger (1962) draws between 'readiness-to-hand' and 'present-at-hand'. These ideas challenge us to be curious about the way in which the very difficulties associated with studying leadership themselves provide useful insight into its essence.

Chapter 4 introduces key ideas from Maurice Merleau-Ponty's thinking to explore the question: what goes on in the relationship between leaders and followers?

We all know that leaders are not leaders without followers. The last ten years have seen a burgeoning of 'relational' leadership theories, the most prominent of which is probably Leader-Member Exchange theory (Gerstner and Day 1997; Graen and Uhl-Bien 1995). Although this theory has brought attention to the leader-follower dynamic at the heart of leadership, it does little to explore what really constitutes the 'in-between' space connecting leaders and followers. Mary Uhl-Bien (2006) in her article *Relational Leadership Theory: Exploring the Social Processes of Leadership and Organizing*, points to the lack of relational leadership theories which genuinely attend to this relationship as their focus. Is there a way to conceptualize this 'relation' itself, rather than the separate entities of 'leaders' and 'followers'? In this chapter, Merleau-Ponty's notions of 'reciprocity' and 'flesh' are introduced as constructions capable of providing a means for understanding the dynamic in-between space at the heart of leader-follower relations.

Having explored these more general questions about the nature of leadership, the book turns to re-examine questions concerning specific aspects of leading which have been perennially debated.

Chapter 5 focuses on the question: what is charismatic leadership?

Since Max Weber first introduced the nature of 'charismatic authority' (1924 [1947]) there has been no shortage of writing about charisma and the part it plays in leadership. Although follower perceptions are often seen to play a role in the attribution of charisma, how followers form those judgements is less developed in the literature. This chapter draws from the field of aesthetics to examine the experience of charisma as a 'felt sense'. In particular, the theory of the sublime developed by Immanuel Kant in *The Critique of Judgement* (1790 [2005]) is introduced as a way of understanding the power of charismatic leadership. This analysis also sheds light on the shadow side of charisma and the unease which often accompanies its expression.

This exploration of charisma positions its occurrence as completely dependent upon those who perceive the leader's performance and attribute this quality to them. The importance of perceivers within meaning-making processes is also emphasized in Chapter 6, in which Hans-Georg Gadamer's hermeneutic philosophy (1975 [2004]) is used to explore the question: what is so important about the 'vision-thing'?

With the rise of a socially constructed view of leadership, the ability of leaders to create and convey meaning and vision to those who would follow them is increasingly recognized. Linda Smircich and Gareth Morgan (1982) were among the first to write about leadership as the 'management of meaning' in their article in the *Journal of Applied Behavioural Science*. Their work conceptualizes this meaning-making as relatively unidimensional, with leaders seen as those with the power to 'frame and structure experience in meaningful ways' (p. 258). The branch of philosophy known as hermeneutics problematizes this construction suggesting that if understanding is truly to be reached between human beings, there must be a 'fusion of their horizons' between them. Hermeneutics challenges the pervasive notion that 'meaning' is something that leaders 'make' in some isolated fashion and then pass on to passive followers.

Chapter 7 addresses a question which is often equated with the process of leadership itself: how do leaders lead change?

Many definitions of leadership closely couple leading with the creation of change. However, we also know that despite the large amount of research that has been conducted into how organizational change occurs and the role of leadership in those processes, the vast majority of change initiatives do not achieve what they set out to achieve (Beer and Nohria 2000). Is this due to a failure of leadership? The field of philosophy known as 'process thinking', spearheaded by writers such as Alfred North Whitehead (1978) and Henri Bergson (1912), is brought to bear on the question of how change occurs and the role leadership might play in facilitating it. Process thinking offers a radical understanding of change itself, suggesting that rather than being an anomaly, change continually occurs. The chapter considers how such a conceptualization of change might alter the way we think about the role leadership plays in 'making' it happen.

Insights from this chapter bring us to the final aspect of leadership covered by the book in Chapter 8: how can individuals take up the leader role wisely?

Increasingly, the importance of the moral and ethical dimensions of leadership are appreciated. As I write this book, the world has been pitched into a global financial recession of grave proportions. Some interpret what is happening as the result of the loss of a moral compass on the part of many leaders in the world's financial markets. Rather than offering ideas from philosophy which might equip leaders to make wise ethical decisions in an increasingly complex world, the chapter offers philosophical practices which might enable wise deliberation. In it, the phenomenological practice of 'dwelling', the hermeneutic art of inquiry and the development of judgement offered by aesthetics are offered as routes to developing the enactment of wisdom.

Chapter 9 reflects on the journey the book has taken by posing the question: what has it meant to rethink leadership?

This chapter dwells on the key themes which have arisen from the juxtaposition of leadership and Continental philosophy. One of those themes, the distinction between 'leaders' and 'leadership', is worth introducing here as it will enable you to understand the starting point for the ensuing arguments.

A NOTE ON TERMINOLOGY, 'LEADERS' AND 'LEADERSHIP'

This book is primarily concerned with 'leadership', rather than 'leaders'. Leadership is seen to be a collective process, encompassing both those who would be known as 'leaders' and those who would be known as 'followers'. Additionally, I assume that these are not static labels and that leadership can readily pass between them so that leaders can act as followers and followers can act as leaders in certain circumstances. The experience of leadership is also assumed to emerge from particular social and historical contexts. This implies that individuals may enact very similar behaviours in different contexts and they may be interpreted as 'leaders' in some and not in others. In this way, just as leaders cannot operate without followers, they also cannot operate outside historical times and places. All of these ideas will be explained more fully in Chapter 2. However it is important to alert readers to these assumptions at the outset of the text as they inform so much of the thinking within it. To put it simply, this book does not focus on the qualities, traits or abilities which 'leaders' may or may not exhibit. Instead, I conceptualize leadership as a collective process and seek to understand that process through applying philosophical ideas which by their nature aim to explicate experience from the 'inside out' rather than from an objective stance.

Labouring this distinction is important because it speaks to a fundamental purpose at the heart of this book. What has often passed as leadership scholarship has, on closer examination, been dedicated to understanding 'leaders'; those individuals who grab our attention amidst what is perhaps a much more complex intersection of contextual and personal factors. This one-pointed focus, I believe, allows limited scope for comprehending the full range of options available to anyone in an organizational system wishing to influence it in particular ways. Too often I have heard the complaint from participants on leadership development programmes, 'I am only a middle manager, it is the senior managers who have the power to make this happen'. 'It is the leaders, over there, up there, who have the power to actually make a difference'.

One answer to this protest is represented in contemporary discourse by the idea that 'everyone can be a leader'. I suggest that understanding 'leadership' as a more complex interaction brings a more nuanced appreciation of that pronouncement. As a start, it means that the way in which the 'follower' role is taken up is highly implicated in the quality of leadership which emerges from collective action. More than that, the book aims to broaden our understanding of leadership as a phenomenon which goes beyond constructions of 'leader-follower'. In doing so, it seeks to alert all of us working within organizational territories as well as studying them to the variety of possibilities available to all actors within hierarchical systems to initiate, influence or create significant instances of leadership.

My aspiration is that the ideas offered here might provide leadership scholars with additional conceptual breadth to reconsider the often hidden intricacies interacting whenever leadership occurs. The book is also written with those engaged in the practice of leadership, whether that be in organizational, community or family settings in mind, in the hope that they too might find ideas to underpin thoughtful and wise enactments of this aspect of collective activity.

SOME IDEAS ABOUT ENGAGING. . .

As indicated above, this book is written for two audiences. The first is the growing number of people studying leadership as a phenomenon in its own right. You may be an organization theorist or management academic who teaches leadership and is looking for an approach which throws new light on questions you have pondered yourself. You may be a student on one of the increasingly popular 'Leadership Studies' degree programmes who is grappling with the myriad of leadership theories and how to make sense of them. Alternatively, you may be involved in leadership development in search of a way of deepening your understanding of some of the theoretical underpinnings of leadership as a practice and looking for alternative constructions to offer clients. The second audience comprises organizational or community leaders who are actively engaged in developing a depth of understanding about leadership. You may have already learned all you can through reading the victory narratives offered by successful corporate executives or autobiographies of exemplars such as Nelson Mandela or Mahatma Ghandi. You may be wondering yourself about the difference between what is written about leadership and your own experience of it.

Whatever your background, you do not have to be a philosopher or have philosophical training to follow the arguments that will be made in this book. The fact that you have picked up this text and read so far already indicates the requisite curiosity to experiment with a kind of thinking which might lead to a new comprehension of this aspect of organizational and community life. The resources you will need on this journey are a bit of inquisitiveness, the willingness to challenge your habitual assumptions about leadership, and perhaps most importantly, a sense of play. Although philosophy and philosophizing are often thought to be serious pursuits, in fact philosophers throughout the ages have engaged in 'mind play' to test the edges of their thinking possibilities. This is serious play, with the intention of exposing one's current limiting assumptions and expanding into new conceptual territories.

The book engages with philosophy in two manners. Firstly, it introduces key ideas developed by particular philosophers, such as Merleau-Ponty's notion of 'flesh' (1968) or Heidegger's work on 'dwelling' (1971), and suggests ways in which these concepts might enrich, challenge or reframe traditional understandings of leadership. Secondly, the mode in which the text is written itself reflects a method of philosophical inquiry. It often challenges the questions which are asked about leadership and wonders about the extent to which they can foster further insight. It calls into question the taken for granted assumptions which inform traditional ways of thinking about leadership. By these means I aim not only to provide new content relevant to understanding leadership but to encourage a radical approach to the very process of thinking about leadership.

Therefore, you will not necessarily finish reading this text with fully-formed ideas of how to restructure your next research study or with a clear view of how to run a new and innovative leadership development programme. Instead, I hope the ideas offered here will open up what has become a congested area of study and evoke a sense of spaciousness in those who read it. By introducing a novel way of engaging with existing leadership theory, the book will demonstrate how each rendering – whether it be 'distributed', 'servant', 'collective' or 'transformational' – contributes to illuminating an important (but not sole) aspect of leadership's identity.

The book aims to be both intellectually stretching as well as practically relevant. In order to make this link, examples and stories from published studies as well as my own experience as a leadership scholar and developer are incorporated throughout the text. I am not setting out to deconstruct leadership and pronounce it dead or philosophically unjustifiable. Instead, the ideas presented here and the way in which they are offered are ultimately intended to provoke questions about why leadership has become the organizational panacea for our times. What does our current fascination tell us not only about leadership but about our particular historical and social moment and who we are within it? Have the ways in which we have traditionally thought about this phenomenon outlived their usefulness given the difficulties and complexities to which leadership must respond today? In disturbing our habitual patterns of thinking about leadership, this book aspires not only to provide new ways of thinking about it but also to foster renewed appreciation for this phenomenon and suggest a rationale as to why it might just justify the many thousands of words which have been written about it.

NOTES

1. Continental philosophy is a school of philosophy developed largely in Continental Europe during the twentieth century. It differs from 'analytic philosophy', which develops and applies the laws of rational logic by focusing on issues of meaning and the nature of lived experience. Analytic philosophy was largely developed in the United States and the United Kingdom.
2. For some, Continental philosophy and 'phenomenology' are synonymous. I am distinguishing the two terms and conceiving Continental philosophy as thinking which encompasses phenomenology, existentialism, structuralism and other philosophical ideas primarily developed by European thinkers.
3. For a comprehensive review of the range of different definitions of leadership, see Rost, J.C. (1993), *Leadership for the Twenty-First Century*, Westport, CT: Praeger.
4. For instance, in his study of University Presidents, Birnbaum (2000) found that transformational leadership was a very inappropriate kind of leadership approach to use when leading academic communities see: *Management Fads in Higher Education: Where they Come From, What they Do, Why They Fail*, San Francisco: Jossey-Bass.
5. Ontological questions are questions about the nature of a thing's 'being'. Ontological questions about leadership are those concerned with the kind of thing leadership is, that is, is it something we can easily see, is it constructed from the interaction of people's perceptions, is it located within a person? All of these questions will be addressed more fully in Chapter 2.

2. Why are there so many different theories of leadership?

> Phenomenology . . . examines the limitations of truth: the inescapable 'other sides' that keep things from ever being fully disclosed, the errors and vagueness that accompany evidence, and the sedimentation that makes it necessary for us always to remember again the things we already know.
>
> Robert Sokolowski
> *Introduction to Phenomenology*
> (2000, p. 21)

Situational leadership, trait-based leadership, transformational leadership, distributed leadership, servant leadership, collaborative leadership, shared leadership, charismatic leadership, authentic leadership – the list goes on and on. It grows longer as ever more leadership consultants, developers and scholars add their observations and ideas about leadership. Is it just the fact that leadership has become a twenty-first century fad that accounts for the proliferation of writing about it? Or might something else be going on?

This chapter addresses that question by considering whether or not the very plethora of ideas and theories about leadership conveys something critical about it. Rather than adding yet another definition or theory to the mix, I turn to the philosophical approach known as phenomenology to gain insight into the nature of leadership as a phenomenon.

Why ponder the nature of leadership? Firstly, the nature of a thing indicates the most appropriate means by which it might be studied. If the nature of a thing is such that when removed from the environment in which it naturally occurs it alters radically, you will not glean an accurate account of it by examining it within laboratory conditions. If you are only accustomed to seeing it operate within such an artificial arena, you may not even recognize it when it is functioning in its normal context. Indeed, if you ever spot it in that environment you may think it is something else. Similarly, if you believe that leadership only takes the form of heroic men metaphorically charging in on white horses to save the day, you may neglect the many acts which contribute to their ability to be there. You may fail to see the importance of the grooms who care for the horses, the messengers who bring attention to the crisis or the role played by those cheering from the sidelines. You may miss the fact that without troops supporting them, any claims to leading on the part of these heroes would be rather hollow.

Additionally, knowing the nature of a thing provides clues about where we might find it and therefore, where we might most usefully look for it. It is no good conducting experimental research into 'skunk behaviour in the wild' in the United Kingdom where wild skunks do not live. Similarly, phenomenology indicates that the places where leadership is traditionally sought, for instance in the personal traits of 'leaders', may not be the most appropriate starting places for identifying and studying it. Understanding the nature of leadership as a phenomenon brings an appreciation of the landscape in which it occurs, encourages us to consider the air it breathes, the environment which feeds it, as well as its distinctive occurrence.

Phenomenology offers a number of concepts which can be helpful in illuminating aspects of leadership territory which are often ignored. These include the notion of 'The Lifeworld', initially introduced by the 'Father of Phenomenology', Edmund Husserl, the distinction between 'sides', 'aspects' and 'identity' and the distinction between 'wholes', 'pieces' and 'moments'. Before introducing these notions in more depth, however, I would like to familiarize you with the philosophical 'project' of phenomenology, in order that the ideas subsequently offered can be placed within their own philosophical and historical contexts.

A SHORT INTRODUCTION TO PHENOMENOLOGY

As a recognized philosophical approach, phenomenology has its genesis in the work of the German philosopher Edmund Husserl (1859–1938). Husserl proclaimed his 'new approach to philosophy' in the texts *Logical Investigations, Volumes One* and *Two* published in 1900 and 1901. Husserl was a mathematician by training and his earliest writings concerned the philosophy of mathematics. However, his disillusion with the route of positivist sciences, where he saw truths being based increasingly on abstractions of reality rather than the real world in which we operate, led him to explore other ways in which the truth of the world could be determined.

In particular, he advocated a return to acknowledging philosophy as the 'Queen of the Sciences', rather than logical positivism[1] holding that position. In 1935 he gave a key lecture, 'Philosophy in the Crisis of European Humanity', in Vienna which argued that the tools of modern science are not equipped to address questions of meaning and significance central to human lives. For instance, positivist science might be able to establish certainty about the chemical components of bread but it could not lead us to any conclusions about the ethics of wealth and what we might do about the fact that some human beings have more than their needs for bread, while others starve. He also reminded the scientists of the time that all of their laboratory-based formulations about the world, seen through abstract mathematical relationships and 'idealized' circumstances (for instance, in worlds of flat surfaces and in which lines can extend forever), had limited application to the three-dimensional world of human beings.

I do not think it is too far a jump to hear parallels between Husserl's critique of the limits of modern science to assist in the lived world of individuals and the applicability of theoretical management theories to the lived world of organizational leaders. How often do we hear practicing organizational members make similar pronouncements about the lack of relevance of much academic work to their concerns? In response, Husserl's solution was to 'return to the things themselves'. This meant that instead of studying things in abstracted and theoretical ways we need to engage with them in the actual circumstances in which they exist. In order to better understand a phenomenon such as leadership then, we must attend to it in the particular circumstances in which it arises rather than through abstracted theoretical frameworks. These particularized circumstances Husserl called 'The Lifeworld' (*Lebenswelt*), a concept which has important implications for how leadership might best be studied.

Central to understanding the significance of 'The Lifeworld' is appreciating how phenomenology aspires to operate as a 'way of knowing'. A key goal for proponents of this branch of philosophy was to reassert the validity of epistemologies other than those revealed by logical positivism. Of course to some extent all philosophy concerns questions of knowing and how it is we can know. Phenomenology offers a distinctive way into this territory (especially in relation to scientific ways of knowing) in its recognition of the subjective world of the knower in creating what is known.

Phenomenologists argue that the way any perceived phenomenon is known is entirely interwoven with the viewpoint of the perceiver. This includes the perceiver's actual physical proximity and placement vis-à-vis what is being perceived, as well as on their psychological predispositions and previous experience of what is being perceived. Additionally, any purpose they have in mind will also colour their perception. All of these factors will contribute to how a phenomenon is 'known'.

An important concept within phenomenology which speaks to the interrelationship between 'knower' and 'known' is that of 'intentionality'. This is not intentionality as an act of will. Instead, phenomenologists use the concept to indicate that all perception is necessarily a perception *of* something. We cannot perceive without there being something for us *to* perceive. In this way our ability to perceive is as determined by the

availability of things to perceive as by our own capacity for perception.
Additionally, those foci of our perceptions will always be perceptually co-
determined by their own actuality and the expectations and positioning of
those perceiving them.

That perception is coloured by how we are positioned vis-à-vis a phenomenon, our experiences of it and our purposes for it have important
implications for leadership and how it is known. It suggests that you
will know leadership differently if you are a passenger on a boat which is
sinking and you are looking for assistance in getting into a lifeboat, from
knowing it if you are a secretary in an office going about your day-to-day
routines of responding to e-mails, making phone calls and answering
customer queries. What you are wanting from leadership in those two different situations are different things and your recognition of it will be coloured by what you are expecting from it at a given point in time. This is an
important idea which will be developed more fully through the chapter.

A final point to raise about phenomenology itself is that it is not a
unified and consolidated school of thought. After Husserl, philosophers
such as Martin Heidegger, Maurice Merleau-Ponty, Jean-Paul Sartre and
Emmanuel Levinas developed Husserl's ideas in their own idiosyncratic
ways. This happened to such an extent that Husserl was noted to have
said in the later years of his life, 'I am the greatest enemy of the so-called
phenomenological movement'[2] as he observed the ways in which this
philosophical approach was unfolding. Even though there were vast differences between the ways in which subsequent thinkers developed this
approach, they all retained a core interest in how the knowing generated
from day-to-day engagement with the world could have its own validity
and claim to 'truth', a claim grounded in the phenomenological notion of
'The Lifeworld'.

'The Lifeworld'

An underlying thrust of the phenomenological approach is the assertion
that the lived world of human beings is where the 'truth' of how they
should best operate could be found, rather than in abstracted scientific
principles and precepts. Husserl saw 'The Lifeworld' as the 'universal framework for all of human endeavour' (in Briefwechsel IX, p. 79,
quoted from Moran 2003), and as such encompasses scientific as well
as philosophic endeavours. Within 'The Lifeworld', the way things are
used and the meanings they hold for the humans who interact with them
are vital aspects of their nature. For instance, the chemical constitution
of the wood which makes up a chair or the physical forces which keep it
from collapsing when you sit on it may, indeed, be very important ways

of knowing the chair. However such facts do not convey the entire truth about chairs and the significance they hold within human systems.

For instance, the physical forces which hold together a chair occupied by a Chief Executive Officer during a meeting are identical to those which hold the Queen of the United Kingdom's throne together. The chair in which the Queen sits as she opens Parliament each autumn has special significance to her subjects, even though it may be constructed of the same physical elements as a chair used by a secretary in an office block. The swivel chair I sit on as I type a document and the throne on which the Queen sits as she makes pronouncements have very different functions within the human systems in which they are situated. It would not be 'right', somehow, for a secretary to bring an elaborate throne into work to sit on, as we would indeed think it odd were the Queen to open Parliament from a common office chair. In our 'Lifeworld', chairs have significance which go beyond their material constitutions. Phenomenology reminds us that those meanings are important aspects of the truth of any entity's being in the world.

The function which a physical entity such as a chair or a car or a banana plays within 'The Lifeworld' is an important aspect of knowing it as a phenomenon but when the 'thing' being considered is non-material, such as leadership, its place within 'The Lifeworld' is perhaps even more important. In fact, such 'things' can be seen only to exist within the socially constructed human communities in which they operate. Therefore, would it not make sense for them to be best studied as they are enacted in 'The Lifeworld'?

Social Construction and 'The Lifeworld'

The notion of 'The Lifeworld' reasserts the importance of meaning in human systems and ways of operating. Although meaning is not an objective, scientifically verifiable thing, phenomenology recognizes its central role in the day-to-day way in which humans live their lives and interact with one another. Shared meanings allow human beings to collaborate and live together in productive and potentially harmonious ways. However, shared meanings are not objectively 'given' entities, they are created by the human communities who engage with them. In this way, they are socially constructed; developed over time through culture, historical events and meaning-making systems of interpretation and dissemination across generations.

Social construction is particularly apparent in the way in which non-material concepts influence human ways of operating and being in the world. Concepts, such as liberty, freedom, wealth and leadership are fundamentally socially constructed. These are not material entities that exist independently of the human beings for whom they have conceptual meaning. 'Freedom' does not exist in a material form, it does not have substance or shape (although it may be symbolized by material artefacts such as flags). Social construction is also a unique human process. It is hard to think, for example, that sparrows have a notion of 'economics' (although they may well experience the scarcity of food, they will not think of this scarcity in economic terms). These are human constructions which are culturally determined and normalized.

For instance, as a child growing up in a rural part of Northern Maine on the Eastern seaboard of the United States, I regularly took part in the annual potato harvest which involved most of my schoolmates and their families. I experienced the weeks I spent picking potatoes as a community-based activity which was part of the rhythm of living in that place. It was only when I went away to university and began reading sociological accounts of 'child labour' in Aroostook County that I ever conceptualized what I had been involved in as indicative of a poverty stricken part of the country as these articles characterized it. (I was shocked to think about it in that way!) The same activity was perceived very differently, depending on the viewpoint from which it was observed. To academic observers, my community engaged in oppressive child labour practices. To me and my friends the harvest certainly demanded hard work, but it also provided ample time to play in the fields as well as the opportunity to contribute to a vital and vibrant part of our region's livelihood. Reading the sociologists' accounts was probably the first time I began to realize that concepts such as 'child labour' or 'poverty' are not objectively determined 'facts'.

Such constructs can create a significant impact on those people operating within their reach. The power of concepts arises from the way in which they remain unquestioned and remain generally accepted. In phenomenological terms, 'The Lifeworld' – the day-to-day reality of how these concepts operate – is central to their very existence. People who travel from one culture to another will recognize the veracity of this idea. I was told the story of a Western business setting up operations in China. Part of the induction process was to explain the ethical codes of the business including introducing the notion of 'sins of omission' as well as 'sins of commission'. The Western-based translator anticipated that there might well be difficulties in translating the words 'omission' and 'commission'. However, he was very surprised when the question which came back to him was, 'Sorry, we do not understand what it is you mean by the word, "sin"?' The Chinese culture which is more communally-based, sees transgressions based in 'shame' – which is something that is created through others' judgements of you – rather than 'guilt' – a concept based more in individualized notions of "sin". Such concepts have their very existence grounded in socially constructed views of reality.

Here I am joining the raft of other leadership theorists who consider leadership to be a socially constructed phenomenon.[3] As such, it is highly context dependent. However, what this actually means is somehow much weightier than what the term 'context dependent' seems to convey. Without 'The Lifeworlds' of human beings who would recognize, look for and respond to this phenomenon they agree to call 'leadership', there would be no leadership. Therefore, in order to understand leadership it is essential to understand 'The Lifeworlds' from which it springs. Studying it as 'something' which operates independently of those 'Lifeworlds' ignores the very 'stuff' from which it arises. It is like trying to comprehend 'love' abstracted from the people who feel and enact it. You may be able to capture a trace of it but it is virtually impossible to really appreciate its full impact and significance as a detached observer.

This understanding implies that approaches to understanding leadership from a logical positivist position will only ever be able to capture a trace of leadership in its experienced and socially significant form. However, because of its commitment to including 'meaning' in what constitutes an entitiy, I argue that phenomenology can get a bit closer to an apprehension of leadership which takes account of its socially embedded nature. It is able to do this through particular concepts which underpin a phenomenological way of knowing. The first of these is the distinction between 'sides', 'aspects' and 'identity'.

'Sides', 'Aspects' and 'Identity': Ways of Describing the Leadership 'Cube'

The importance of where a person is physically situated in terms of how they will perceive something is amplified through the phenomenological distinction between 'sides', 'aspects' and 'identity'. Robert Sokolowski elaborates on this distinction in his book an *Introduction to Phenomenology* (2000). Along with many phenomenologists, Sokolowski refers to a 'cube' when illustrating these notions and I will start by doing the same. You will remember that in Chapter 1 I suggested that one of the capacities which would aid you on the journey through the book is a sense of play? This is the first opportunity to play with your thinking in that way. After experimenting with different ways of perceiving a cube, I will consider how these ideas might apply to leadership.

Start by bringing into your mind's eye the image of a cube. Even better if you can find one, place a three-dimensional box in front of you as you read these next few paragraphs. At the most basic level of perception when you look at the cube you will be aware that it has six different sides. As you turn the cube over in your hand, at any one moment in time, you can see some sides of the cube and not the others. For instance, when you can see the front face of a cube, you can not simultaneously see its back or its sides. Phenomenologists point out that at any one point in time, when you are seeing one side of the cube you 'co-intend' the other sides. That is you hold them in your imagination; you know them to be there completing the entirety of the cube even though you can not see all of the sides at once.

To give another similar example of the way in which sides work, when you see someone walking down the street usually you can perceive only one side of them at any given time: their front, their back or indeed their side. However, you will 'co-intend' the rest of their bodily form by filling in the details of the sides you can not see. This is not a guaranteed route to perfect perception as evidenced from the occasions on which you might have walked up behind someone thinking they are an acquaintance only to discover a complete stranger when they turn around.

Similarly there are many different 'sides' to the phenomenon of leadership. There is, of course, the person who is perceived as 'leader' – and in this way the 'leader' role could be seen as one 'side' of leadership. However, 'followers' provide another essential 'side' and the community or organizational context in which leadership happens constitute another 'side', as will the historical situation which has brought all these factors together at a given point in time. All of these dimensions can be seen as different 'sides' of leadership and its description would depend on the side which is being perceived.

Many more traditional theories of leadership only attend to the 'leader' side of the phenomenon. The rest – the followers, the organizational culture, the particular market circumstances, are often 'co-intended' – assumed to be there and to act in unquestioned ways. The phenomenological idea of 'sides' points out that all of those co-intended sides of leadership are vital to its occurrence, they are the always present other 'sides' of the leadership 'cube'. In order to gain a full appreciation of the phenomenon of leadership all of these sides must be taken into consideration.

The phenomenological notion of 'aspects' builds on that of 'sides'. 'Aspects' are the specific angles or orientations through which something is perceived. Returning to the example of the cube, as you turn the cube in your hand you may also notice that its sides take on different appearances. For instance if you look at the cube straight on it will appear to be square but if you tilt it downward slightly it will look more like a trapezoid. These different appearances disclose different 'aspects' of the cube. You are still viewing one and the same cube but its appearance alters according to the different aspect which is being disclosed at any point in time.

To give another example, if you walk around the outside of a building you will be aware of each of its different sides and you will perceive each of those sides from a particular vantage point. If you are standing at street level looking up at a skyscraper in Tokyo, the side of the building will appear as a great looming rhomboidal form whereas if you look at the side of the same skyscraper from an adjacent skyscraper, you will be more aware of its horizontal span. From an airplane flying over the building, the vertical walls may be completely invisible and you may only be aware of the building's roof and have to co-intend the walls stretching down to the street. Each way of perceiving the skyscraper has its own validity from the particular vantage point from which it arises. No one aspect is more truthful than another.

Similarly leadership can be viewed from a variety of aspects. If you are the Receptionist in the headquarters of a Blue-Chip international company, you will perceive the leadership of that company and your role within the leadership of the company differently from if you are the Finance Director for the company. Your perceptions will be informed by the daily interactions you have with customers and colleagues which will not be shared by the Finance Director. In your role as gatekeeper to senior organizational members, your insight into the firm's leadership will be coloured by close and possibly more informal proximity to them. You may understand, for instance, that the reason the CEO is abrupt on a certain day is because their spouse is seriously ill, rather than attributing their mood to just bad temper.

Furthermore, through its location the receptionist role is available to customer reactions and other aspects of the external world in ways that more internally focused roles cannot be. As a member of the senior management team, the Finance Director would interact daily with other director-level people and would probably be privy to information about the informing ideas behind strategic decisions. Through those interactions, he or she would form different perceptions of the firm's leadership than the Receptionist would. Interviewing the receptionist and then the Finance Director about the leadership of the firm would probably elicit very different accounts. Which version is 'correct'? This question will be addressed through reference to a final distinction in this trio of phenomenological ideas; that of identity.

Returning to the cube for one last time, we can see that all of the different sides and vantage points from which those sides can be perceived (aspects) are distinctive yet they all relate to one phenomenon, the cube. At the same time, the cube's identity is more than a collection of its sides and aspects. What it 'is' includes its internal mass which cannot be viewed from the perspective of an outside onlooker, its colour, weight and form as well as the material from which it is constructed. More than the solely physical characteristics of the cube, phenomenology suggests its identity also takes account of its non-material aspects. The totality of its identity includes factors such as who made it, what purpose it serves and the meaning it holds for those who use it. A cube which acts as a die and in being thrown determines whether or not a gambler wins thousands of dollars has a very different identity from the cube which a two-year-old fits into a puzzle or a cube-shaped diamond exchanged between lovers. In such cases it is easy to see that the cube's identity is based on much more than solely its physical manifestation.

The notion of 'identity' offers its own frustrations however, particularly for positivist scientists who attempt to define and categorize phenomena. From a phenomenological perspective, an entity's identity always remains elusive. As much as we can perceive the sides which make it up, as much as we can be aware of the different aspects from which it can be viewed, as much as we can know about its internal workings, its history and its significance within human 'Lifeworlds', we can never know the totality of something which would constitute a definitive 'identity'. This is a key ontological assumption which underpins phenomenological investigations: that a 'thing's' identity will always be beyond the reach of human apprehension. In holding this position, phenomenology takes a radically different orientation to knowing from that assumed by logical positivism.

Applying the logic of 'sides', 'aspects' and 'identity' to leadership, if you want to understand how leadership functions in a particular firm how might you go about it? Whose perspectives would you collect? Perhaps a better place to begin such an inquiry would be to articulate the purpose behind your wish to understand 'leadership'. Would you be doing so in order to try to alter the way leadership is enacted in the firm? Or would you be doing so in order to add to theoretical knowledge about how leadership is perceived within an organization of a certain structure? Recognizing that leadership consists of different 'sides' and that people will experience those sides from particular aspects alerts you to the importance of identifying which of those sides and aspects might be most useful in addressing the particular purposes you are pursuing. For instance, if you are interested in understanding the way in which leadership fosters a firm's perception in the marketplace, you may find the receptionist who deals with external calls and visitors all day of more help than the Finance Director.

From the concept of 'The Lifeworld', phenomenologists see 'purpose' as key in what can be known about things and how such knowing might most appropriately be pursued. If I am asking the question 'What is leadership?' because I am an academic scholar attempting to plot the historic development of the concept, the way I will do so will be very different from the approach I would take were I an executive trying to understand how I might take up my leadership role in a manner that would halt the failing fortunes of my firm.[4] The purposes of the questions are very different; therefore it only makes sense that the choice of which sides or aspects you might focus on in order to answer them would also be different. Phenomenology highlights the existence of these distinctions and encourages us to be transparent about which we are focusing on and why at a given point in time.

'Sides', 'aspects' and 'identity' are not the entire story. The next group of phenomenological distinctions broadens our appreciation of the nature of a phenomenon such as leadership even further.

'Wholes', 'Pieces' and 'Moments'

When considering the nature of a particular phenomenon, another phenomenological categorization Sokolowski (2000) offers is that between a 'whole', a 'piece' and a 'moment'. 'Wholes' are clearly distinguishable, independent and separate things. A chair can be a 'whole', as can an art work, a bridge, a rug, a pencil or a trash compactor. Each of these things can be identified as a distinct entity and serves its own purpose, without reference to something else. 'Wholes' are comprised of 'pieces'. For instance, a rug is comprised of many coloured strands of wool. Each strand can still exist as a separate entity but in relation to the rug, it is a 'piece'. The chair's leg can exist on its own and in fact chair legs can be interchangeable but in relation to a particular chair, it is a 'piece' of the 'whole' chair.

The colour of the strand of wool in the rug or the weight of the leg of the chair are different kinds of things. A colour cannot exist independently of the strand of wool it infuses; the weight of the leg of the chair is inextricably determined by the chair leg. A quick thought experiment will show this to be the case. Try to think of the colour 'turquoise' without it occupying space. I hope that you will find it impossible to do so! Colours, weight, size are all things which cannot exist independently. Their 'beingness' is dependent on the things of which they are part. Phenomenologists call such things 'moments'. It is important to emphasize that a phenomenological moment is not a time related concept. Instead it indicates that this sort of phenomena is wholly dependent on other phenomena for its expression in the world.

In these terms, what kind of phenomenon is leadership? Is it a 'whole', a 'piece' or a 'moment'? Many leadership theories are based in an assumption that leadership is a 'whole'. It is studied outside of reference to the particular context from which it arises; as though it can be abstracted and still exist in an identifiable way. However, as has been suggested throughout this book already, I am arguing that leadership cannot exist apart from the particular individuals who are engaged and involved in any leadership dynamic. Leadership does not exist without people who are in some way identified as 'leaders' or people who are identified as people who they will lead. Neither can it exist outside of a particular community or organizational culture or history. For these reasons I argue that rather than being a 'whole', leadership can best be described as a 'moment' of social relations.

What does this imply about how we might come to understand leadership? Recognizing leadership as a 'moment' suggests that we can never arrive at the reality of leadership as separated from those particular contexts in which it arises.

Additionally, I am proposing that this conceptualization provides an explanation for the plethora of existing leadership theories and definitions. In fact there could be as many descriptions of leadership as there are situations in which it arises because it will always be subtly different depending on the 'pieces' and 'wholes' from which it emerges. Leadership that arises from a crisis situation, such as a forest fire in which there is a clear desired outcome and firefighters who have been trained to deal with such events, will look very different from entrepreneurial leadership in which someone generates an innovative idea and nurtures it to market. Leadership amidst professional groups, such as higher education teachers engaged in implementing a new curriculum, will be enacted differently from that in a call centre populated by large numbers of young workers who may not be very motivated and who do not see being call centre operators as their vocation in life.

Those who are part of the leadership event in each case may report they have experienced leadership happening but from an external perspective, its physical manifestations, the behaviours used and interrelationships enacted, may appear very different. Even if there are similarities between the behaviours perceived between contexts, there will be nuances and subtleties of expression which may be appropriate to one context but not to another. 'Leaderly' behaviours enacted by firefighters struggling to extinguish a blaze would look silly expressed in an academic environment and despite their noisiness would probably produce limited impact. I am suggesting that the distinction between 'wholes', 'pieces' and 'moments' helps to explain why this is the case. As a 'moment', leadership necessarily arises out of particular 'wholes' and its experience is interwoven with and dependent on those 'wholes'.

These three sets of ideas: 'The Lifeworld'; the distinction between 'sides', 'aspects' and 'identity'; and the distinction between 'wholes', 'pieces' and 'moments' have important implications for understanding leadership as a phenomenon. Firstly, the notion of 'The Lifeworld' suggests that in order to understand leadership as a lived experience, it is important to study it within the particular worlds in which it operates. As a phenomenon which arises from constructed social realities, the meanings it has for those engaged with it, either as leaders, followers or academic theorists, impacts significantly on how it is experienced or viewed.

This is further underlined by the ideas of 'sides', 'aspects' and 'identity'. Phenomenology points out that every 'thing' does have different sides and that at any one point in time we can only view one of them with the others implied. Additionally, a side will always be viewed from a particular aspect. The 'follower' side of the leadership dynamic could be perceived from the position of the 'follower', the leader or a researcher standing outside of the relationship but who may have a vested interest in what the leader and follower are trying to achieve. From each perspective, a different aspect of leadership's identity is potentially revealed.

Finally, the distinction between 'wholes', 'pieces' and 'moments' offers philosophical justification for the intertwining of leadership and context proposed by a number of leadership theories. For example, Mary Parker Follett's work (1949 [1987]) highlights the dynamic nature of leadership as it responds to changes in context. Keith Grint (2001) writes about the 'constitutive' nature of leadership; and Martin Wood (2005) coins the phrase 'leaderful events' in an effort to capture the interplay of individual agency and context which is constructed as leadership. As a 'moment' of social relations, leadership is wholly dependent on the historical, social and psychological context from which it arises. Just as the colour turquoise cannot be separated from the space it fills, leadership can only be expressed through particular localized conditions and the individuals who take part in both creating it and making sense of it. One way of conceptualizing the interactive and context-dependent nature of leadership is through a model I think of as the 'leadership moment' represented in Figure 2.1 below.

Rather than attempting to add yet another definition to the plethora of those already in existence, the leadership moment identifies the 'pieces' of leadership which interact in order for leadership to be experienced. Leaders must relate to followers and together they interact within a particular context and work towards an explicit or implicit purpose. These pieces also interact dynamically, with the consequence that the way in which followers perceive the context will affect the way in which they interpret the leader's pronouncements, the follower's behaviours will affect the leader's and together leader's and followers' actions will demonstrate how a purpose is being understood and embodied.[5]

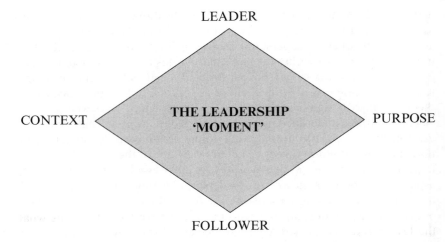

Figure 2.1   The leadership 'moment'

WHAT DOES THIS IMPLY ABOUT THE IDENTITY OF LEADERSHIP?

Does this all mean that leadership is anything and everything? Not quite. After all, the colour pink is still the colour pink, regardless of whether it appears in a geranium or in a plume of cotton candy. It is still distinctive from orange or blue or green. Likewise, although leadership may manifest itself differently within different contexts its energetic trajectory shares a common feature: collective mobilization towards an explicit or implicitly determined purpose. As the British leadership scholar Keith Grint argues, '. . . don't trace the leader, don't even trace the followers; trace the mobilization' (1997, p. 17).

How such mobilization is accomplished can appear very different depending on the circumstances. From the view of phenomenology, each expression of leadership – whether in the way it is embodied by firefighters trying to clear blazing buildings or by peace campaigners in dialogue with politicians – contributes to our understanding of its identity. Striving to provide a 'once and for all' definition for such a phenomenon is an impossible task. Understood as a moment of social relations, leadership's complete identity will necessarily always remain elusive.

This might best be illustrated by reference to another phenomenon which could be understood as a moment of social relations, the concept of 'justice'. Within human communities there is an appreciation for a phenomenon which balances ideas of rights and responsibilities (these too are social constructions!). What is considered to be 'just' differs radically from culture to culture. In some cultures it is considered just to subject perpetrators of extreme crimes such as murder to capital punishment. In other societies capital punishment itself is seen as morally unjust. The way justice is enacted manifests itself very differently even though both societies are enacting their way of balancing rights and responsibilities. Similar to leadership a common intentionality can be identified between acts aimed at achieving justice. However, the many and sometimes contradictory ways that it appears means that determining its total identity remains beyond our grasp.

You may at this point be thinking, 'What good is that? Is phenomenology's claim to knowing a phenomenon so limited that it is virtually useless?' On the contrary, I propose that through the specific way it encourages us to engage with leadership, it can assist us in clarifying what it is we are seeking in the first place. In pursuing leadership's identity, what problem is it we are hoping to solve? Are we actually more interested to know how to make sense of a confusing context and communicate that sense to others who are equally confused? Or instead are we interested to know more about why a model of leadership seems to have such good results in a particular context? Are we interested in leadership's identity because we are studying it as an abstract feature of organizational life or are we seeking an answer to the question because we are teaching first-year undergraduate business studies students the material they need to fulfil the requirements of their programme? Alternatively, have we recently been appointed 'line manager' and want to know how to best lead the members of our team? Depending on the purpose behind the question we might focus on a particular aspect of the leadership moment.

I hope this brief excursion into phenomenological ideas has demonstrated the importance of the questions we ask in bringing insight to a phenomenon like leadership. What particular aspect of this phenomenon are we trying to gain insight into? Given that, what are the most helpful sides of leadership's identity to investigate? What aspects of the 'whole' from which it arises, should we be paying attention to? Perhaps more importantly it highlights the importance of researchers recognizing the way in which their own perspective colours and shapes their experience of leadership. A phenomenological approach demands greater transparency on researcher's parts about their own positioning vis-à-vis the phenomenon and how that influences their interpretations and theoretical insights.

Finally, because phenomenology is concerned with the way things operate in 'The Lifeworld' regarding leadership from this perspective always retains a pragmatic orientation. We may not be able to establish leadership's abstract 'identity' but we can say something about how it

functions in a particular prescribed circumstance. Having introduced
these ideas, let us use them to reconsider why there are so many different
theories of leadership.

WHY ARE THERE SO MANY DIFFERENT THEORIES OF LEADERSHIP (AND WHY DO WE NEED MORE)?

From a phenomenological perspective, there are at least three answers to
this question.

Firstly, if we consider the role of leadership in 'The Lifeworld' from the
perspective of those who recognize it, it becomes clear that the very apprehension of leadership is a socially determined phenomenon. Influenced by
the dominant culture in which they operate certain behaviours will be read
as leadership and others will not be.

The story of Chris, a Royal Air Force officer, illustrates this point. Chris
explained to me how he realized his conception of leadership had changed
as a result of undertaking a Masters in Leadership Studies. In his job Chris
was responsible for high-intensity training activities for young cadets. His
role largely consisted of preventing them from doing anything dangerous
as well as assessing their teamwork and leadership behaviours. One day
his commanding officer (CO) visited his unit to observe how a cohort of
cadets was progressing. After a morning watching the young recruits in
action, the CO said to Chris, 'This is frustrating; I haven't witnessed a
single act of leadership all morning'.

Chris was somewhat surprised by this pronouncement, especially in light
of the reading and thinking about leadership he had been doing as a result
of undertaking the Masters programme. He said he found himself slightly
startled by his own response to the CO, when he said, 'I'm sorry Sir, I beg
to differ; I've been seeing acts of leadership all morning'. Apparently what
then ensued was a lively conversation between the two men in which Chris
expressed the view that leadership did not necessarily have to be enacted
through high profile 'commands' from the front. For the kinds of tasks
being undertaken by the recruits, leadership could move between people
depending on who was best equipped, either through expertise or experience, to take the lead at any given moment.

The CO had been operating from assumptions about leadership
informed by the Air Force culture. This view had largely remained
unquestioned especially among more long-serving members. From this
viewpoint, leadership is a phenomenon which is held by one person, 'the
man' (in the Royal Air Force it is still more often than not 'the man') who
is 'in front', often shouting orders. Chris' view of leadership allowed for a

much more distributed understanding of the phenomenon, something that can move around among those engaged in a task. Was Chris 'right' and his CO 'wrong'?

The notion of 'The Lifeworld' alerts us to the possibility that this may not be such a helpful question. Asking 'What is trying to be achieved in these circumstances and what would leadership look like which best fulfilled that purpose?' might provide a more fruitful response. The latter question helps to identify the most appropriate leadership response for a given context. Through addressing that question, a more appropriate definition for the leadership requirement of that context might be identified. What and how goals were accomplished was what Chris focused on as he assessed the leadership activity within his team of cadets. Identifying the 'leader' and assessing his or her performance was the CO's pre-occupation.

The example of the CO visiting Chris' unit demonstrates how 'aspects' also interact with definitions of leadership. In this context, the CO, Chris and the cadets involved in the task all had different viewpoints about the 'leadership' operating amongst them. Chris' aspect on leadership was coloured by his further study and his willingness to accept that leadership can operate collectively. The COs viewpoint was influenced by his own personal history and training as well as the situations in which he had encountered the need for a more individualistic approach. The actual cadets involved would have apprehended yet another aspect on the leadership process. It would be interesting to inquire about their experience of leadership as they engaged in tasks. Did they perceive particular individuals' inputs as 'leaderly'? How aware were they of the way in which the leader role moved amongst them? What insights could they offer about how they achieved tasks and the role leadership played in that success?

The notion of aspects demonstrates that leadership will be viewed from different perspectives and that each perspective can potentially provide a new insight into its identity. Depending on where one is situated vis-à-vis any leadership activity, a very different view of it will emerge. Although no one viewpoint can appreciate the totality of leadership, each contributes a distinct facet of leadership's identity.

Finally, this brings us to the categorization of leadership as a 'moment', rather than a 'whole' or a 'piece'. If leadership were a 'whole', a phenomenon which can operate independently of its context or social construction,[6] then perhaps achieving a more definitive rendering of it would be possible. As a 'moment' however, like the colour pink which cannot exist without extension, leadership can not exist without those who would enact it, the context from which it arises, as well as the socially constructed appreciation of it as a particular kind of interaction between human beings. The colour pink has an identity but the form of that identity differs depending on the chemical combinations which create the pigment, the textures and surfaces of the materials of which it is a part, the way the light shines on it at a particular time of day as well as my capacity to see 'pink' because of the range of colour my optic nerve can detect.

Similarly, leadership arises out of different and specific social constructions. Sometimes it can look forceful and outspoken and other times it is appreciated for its steady ability to hold a psychological space in which dialogue between people who hold vastly different views can safely occur. At times it can be concentrated within the charismatic power of an individual and their mesmerizing ability to capture the imaginations of followers. Suddenly, however, those charismatic individuals can find themselves toppled by the collective movement of those they have led who in turn replace the leader role with somebody else.

From a phenomenological perspective, each of the many leadership theories currently in existence could be seen to be addressing a particular side of the phenomenon from a particular aspect. For instance, transformational leadership concentrates on the 'leader' side and speaks from an interest in organizational change. More relational theories, such as distributed or collaborative leadership, attempt to capture much more of the 'follower' side, often from the viewpoint of de-centralized organizational structures. Servant leadership again attends to the leader but seeks to reveal an aspect of leadership which positions itself in support of followers rather than 'from the front'.

Each theory provides another 'piece of the leadership puzzle'. By considering leadership through the lens of phenomenology, we can appreciate that there will be as many different descriptions of leadership as there are situations in which it arises. In contemporary times, for instance, we see the need to understand how leadership works within virtual communities – a situation early leadership theorists could never have anticipated! We see the need for new theories which can inform how leadership might be constructed within globally distributed organizations, within communities and companies trying to reduce their negative impact on the environment, within organizations which span private and public domains. These are all new contexts in which leadership arises and, in providing ways of responding to each, leadership reveals new sides of its identity.

The phenomenological analysis presented here raises something of a conundrum for those seeking to understand leadership better. How can a phenomenon constituted by so many different and disparate factors be studied? Is it possible to say anything useful about such a thing? Furthermore, if leadership's identity is continually unfolding, how might it be approached at one given moment in time? The next chapter approaches these quandaries by addressing the related question, 'Why is it so difficult to study leadership?'

NOTES

1. Logical positivism is a way of investigating reality which assumes notions of objectivity, reductionism and the ability to verify knowledge through the testing of hypotheses. Largely associated with 'the scientific method', it largely grew from Enlightenment rationality and has been widely used in the study of the physical world.

2. Quoted in Moran, D. (2000), *An Introduction to Phenomenology*, London: Routledge, p. 2.

3. For a key text on social constructionism itself, see: Berger, P. and T. Luckman (1966), *The Social Construction of Reality: A Treatise on the Sociology of Knowledge*, Garden City, NJ: Doubleday. For leadership scholars writing about leadership as a social construction, see Meindl, J.R. (1995), 'The Romance of leadership as a follower-centric theory: a social constructionist approach', *Leadership Quarterly*, 6 (3), 329–41, Grint, K. (2005a), 'Problems, problems, problems: the social construction of leadership, *Human Relations*, 58 (11) 1467–94, and Sjostrand, S.E., J. Sandberg and M. Tyrstrup (eds) (2001), *Invisible Management: The Social Construction of Leadership*, London: Thompson Leary.

4. The mismatch between these different purposes for understanding leadership is revealed when executives come to business schools wanting to know about how they might 'do' leadership differently, and instead they are given historical accounts of different ideas about leadership by the academics who teach them.

5. These particular interactions will be considered in more depth in subsequent chapters of the book: for instance, Chapter 5 which looks at the way meaning-making occurs between leaders and followers will consider the link between leaders-followers and purpose in more depth; and Chapter 8 about how leaders might take up their role wisely, focuses on the interaction between the leader and how he or she makes sense of their particular context.

6. It is of course questionable as to whether or not anything can indeed act as a 'whole' which is completely independent of its context or social construction. For the purposes of the argument here, 'wholes' might be those things which are relatively more independent of their contexts – so for instance the physical being of a teapot would still exist as a 'thing' whether the teapot in question were a standard clay pot or an exquisite art object, the latter descriptions being determined by social construction.

3. Why is it so difficult to study leadership?

> When something 'ready-to-hand' is found missing, though its everyday presence has been so obvious that we have never taken notice of it, this makes a break in those referential contexts which circumspection discovers. Our circumspection comes up against emptiness, and now sees for the first time what the missing article was ready-to-hand *with*, and what it was ready-to-hand *for*. The environment announces itself afresh.
>
> Martin Heidegger
> *Being and Time*
> (1962, p. 105)

In the previous chapter I made the case that one of the reasons for the plethora of leadership theories is that its enactment has as many different expressions as contexts from which it arises. This alone makes it a very difficult phenomenon to study but the problem is exacerbated by its socially constructed nature, implying that leadership is held in the invisible, constructed and cognitive worlds of those who experience it. Rather than being content with its social construction as the primary cause for its elusiveness however, this chapter considers insights phenomenology brings to the difficulties associated with researching it. Why is it that on close examination leadership often seems to 'disappear'? (Alvesson and Sveningsson 2003). Given this aspect of its nature, how might those aspiring to study leadership do so appropriately? As a starting point, let us consider the 'disappearing' nature of leadership a bit more closely.

THE CLOSER YOU GET TO IT, THE MORE QUICKLY IT DISAPPEARS

Although many researchers have highlighted the difficulties with studying leadership, this chapter focuses on two approaches which draw particular attention to this issue: distributed leadership, as championed by Cecil Gibb and Peter Gronn and critical theory, as proposed by writers such as Mats Alvesson and Stefan Sveningsson.

Distributed Leadership

The concept of distributed leadership has its roots in the work of Cecil Gibb, an Australian psychologist working both within the Australian education field and the US Army during the 1950s and 1960s. In a chapter from the *Handbook of Social Science Research* published in 1954, Gibb was among the first to highlight the problems associated with attributing leadership to the sole efforts of a lone, individual 'leader'. Gibb devoted much of his research to analysing the 'inside' of leadership processes particularly in terms of the relations between leaders and followers. He undertook a number of studies in which he observed work groups tackling problems together and attempted to trace how leadership happened amongst them.

Gibb defined leadership as a process of influence in which leaders exercised higher levels of influence over followers than followers did over them. The results of his empirical research into leadership within small groups contradicted this understanding. Instead of resting with one person for the duration of any work task, he noticed that the influencing process he recognized as leadership moved around the group depending on the stage of the task. In the most successful work groups, leadership – defined in terms of influence – followed the task rather than being held exclusively by one individual. One of the outcomes of his research was to distinguish between 'headship', held by the person in a group with the highest level of hierarchical power and authority; and leadership, recognized as a process of influence which readily moved between groups of individuals focused on completing a task. In practice the two are often conflated but Gibb's research indicated that 'headship' can exist independently of 'leadership' and vice versa.

Peter Gronn, another Australian leadership scholar working in the education sector, develops these aspects of Gibb's work in his own formulation of 'distributed leadership' (Gronn 2000, 2002). In his way of understanding how leadership works, activity is a key feature, serving as the mediating factor between the individual agency of the person designated as 'leader' and a more systemic and contextually-based ground from which leadership arises. Specifically, Gronn draws from a notion of 'socially distributed activity theory' to explain the way in which he conceptualizes leadership operating in organizations. He notes that by focusing on what gets done and how the networks of interactions serve to achieve tasks, it is possible to track the 'leadership' moving amidst people dedicated to accomplishing shared purposes.

Like Gibb, Gronn notes that, 'If leadership is an instance of influence, then, like influence it need not be expressed by ways that are obvious to

the naked eye' (2000, p. 330). In this way, Gronn articulates a view Gibb
only hinted at: the realization that in studying leadership, it is only ever
possible to identify a 'proxy' for it. In the first instance, such a proxy
might be located in the reported descriptions of how leaders construe their
own performance. Alternatively it might be found in the reports followers
make about what their identified leaders 'did' to initiate, enable or make
things happen. Their studies highlight at least three aspects of leadership
which contribute to the difficulty in studying it:

- The suggestion that leadership, as defined by power to influence,
  emerges over time and is part of the historical experience of people
  working together and thus cannot be captured in finite moments.
  Even those who are part of a leadership relationship may not appreciate the historic instances which have contributed to the resulting
  experience;
- The fact that leadership does not rest with a single, appointed
  'leader' but that it moves around groups of people in ways that can
  not necessarily be predicted (therefore, if you are studying it, where
  exactly do you look to find it?); and
- That the task to which leadership is applied acts as an 'invisible'
  leader, guiding the way in which activities are undertaken in often
  unspoken and unacknowledged ways.

Gibb's and Gronn's work begins to reveal the extent of the invisible
factors which constitute leadership as a phenomenon, including historical
events, the emergent nature of group activity and the assumptions about
purpose and goals which are so often implicit, rather than explicit aspects
of collective action. These certainly play a role in the difficulties associated
with studying leadership. We will return later in the chapter to explore
how a phenomenological rendering might enrich our understanding of
how they occur and how we might account for them when conducting
research. For now, let us turn to a second explanation for 'disappearing'
leadership found in the literature.

'Critical' Approaches to Leadership

Mats Alvesson and Stefan Sveningsson are two Swedish leadership
researchers working from the critical studies tradition, who question the
very existence of leadership as an explanatory variable within organizational life. Their 2003 article 'The Great disappearing act: difficulties
doing "leadership"' in *Leadership Quarterly*, illustrates the complications
of pinpointing behaviours which either leaders or followers recognize as

'leadership'. In this particular study, conducted in an international biotech company, they interviewed over 40 organizational members ranging from senior managers to scientists. In addition to the interviews, Alvesson and Sveningsson undertook ethnographic research observing management team meetings. The study aimed to discover what leaders did which constituted leadership from their own perspective.

In their six reported case studies, those investigated were vague about the behaviours and ways of interacting with others, which they recognized as expressions of leadership. Alvesson and Sveningsson point out that initial claims were aligned with 'fashionable views' about the nature of leadership with responses focusing on behaviours such as 'setting direction' and 'communicating purpose'. However, on closer scrutiny, when their research subjects were asked to give examples of how they went about 'getting people to think', for instance, the responses were not completely indicative of what we might think of as 'leaderful'. For instance, one senior manager reported, '[If a subordinate] needs reassurance, you can say, "well there's two ways of doing this, I favour this way and you do that and what do you think?"' (2003, p. 371).

Alvesson and Sveningsson conclude that in the six cases they observed, 'there [was] not much leadership produced' (2003, p. 376). However, could it be that their method for discovering leadership failed them, rather than there being a lack of leadership present? I wonder, for example, whether senior managers were best located to describe their 'leaderly' actions? Would it have been more illuminating to have asked those they 'led' about their experiences? Rather than attributing the difficulties associated with describing leadership to the lack of its existence, is another explanation possible? Perhaps there are ideas from phenomenology which might provide additional insight into this situation.

Invisible Leadership: 'Absences' and 'Presences'

Rather than explaining the difficulties associated with studying leadership by reference to the emergent nature of influence or, indeed, by suggesting that leadership does not really exist at all, let us recall the notion of 'identity' introduced in the previous chapter. There the case was made that from a phenomenological perspective the full identity of any phenomenon cannot ever be completely known.

Part of the reason for this is that there are so many contributing factors to identity. Even an object as mundane as the wooden desk upon which my computer sits embraces a history which stretches back to include the people who manufactured it, the type of tree it was cut from, the soil in which the tree's roots grew, the weather conditions which influenced its grain, the choices which were made about how the tree was cut – a table's story can go on and on! How many more factors go into one human being's story or, indeed, how much more complex are the ideas which inform human actions? When identity is conceptualized to include a phenomenon's cultural history as well as the totality of its intellectual heritage, it is clear that knowing its complete identity extends beyond human capabilities.

Furthermore, the endless aspects of a phenomenon's identity are rarely actually present at the point of its apprehension. Returning to my wooden desk, the soil from which it grew is most certainly not in my office. However, without it my desk would not have an identity; in fact it would not exist at all. Using the metaphor of people declaring their love through the gift of a ring, the person who extracted the diamond from a mine is not present when the ring is given. His or her contribution to the diamond's existence however, is crucial. Both the joiner who made my desk and the miner who located and cut the diamond are key to the identity of those objects and phenomenology suggests that both are present within their identities: as a 'negative' presence.

Phenomenology calls this kind of negative presence, not surprisingly, an 'absence'. As 'absences' are not immediately apparent, we may not be aware of the forces they are exerting on our apprehension of an entity. However, absent presences can indeed exert forces and influence. For instance, the type of wood from which my desk is constructed has a very slow pattern of growth and only reluctantly releases its moisture to the air. Although I have now owned the desk for six years, it is continuing to shift and change and I find I have trouble sliding a drawer open this year which fitted perfectly last year. The negative presence of the tree's natural pattern of growth, though 'invisible', is exerting a significant impact on my ability to use the desk drawer. Furthermore, I am cautioned by the joiner who built the desk against making any alterations before the wood more completely settles in another few years.

Similarly there are 'absent' aspects of leadership which powerfully exert influence on the experience of leadership but which may be virtually impossible to explicitly perceive. Here I will focus on three in particular:

- The expectations of leadership held by all of those engaged in a leadership dynamic;
- The stories which are told about leaders and the way all those engaged in a leadership dynamic make sense of them; and
- The invisible role played by the multi-layers of culture which will influence what is perceived as leadership and what is not.

Absent but present: expectations

It is perhaps relatively easy to see how 'absences' can exert influence over socially constructed ideas such as leadership. A significant absence which always underpins leadership is the expectations of those engaged in any leadership dynamic. This includes both those taking up the 'leader' role as well as those who see themselves as 'followers'. For instance, 'followers' very rarely say to the person taking up the leader role, 'this is what I expect of you: I expect you to sort out the interpersonal difficulty I have with the guy who sits next to me in the office, I expect you to notice everything I do well and always praise me for it and I expect you to negotiate me a substantial raise in the next year. In short, I expect you to make my life so much better'. In fact, on a conscious level followers themselves may be unaware they hold such desires but such unexpressed wishes may still influence and colour their own, as well as their 'leader's' experience of the relationship. More importantly to those who research leadership, these often unacknowledged expectations will influence any assessment research subjects make of their experience of leadership.

Similarly, a person taking up the 'leader' side of the leadership dynamic will hold absent expectations of the role which will colour how they enact it. They may hold an unconscious view that if they are going to be 'leader', they must know all of the answers to any question anyone in their organization might pose to them. When, inevitably, something happens or a question arises to which they do not have a ready response, they may feel vulnerable and exposed. In fact they may feel themselves to be failing as a leader. They may not even realize why it is they feel so uncomfortable – but it can be because of this invisible 'absence', their expectation of themselves in the role.

The notion of 'absences' suggests that in any situation there will be such invisible factors influencing what occurs. Being aware that these 'negative presences' are always there, like watchful shadows playing in the background of leaderly engagements, may encourage students of leadership to be sensitive to indications that there is more going on than meets the eye in any leadership interaction. Attempting to uncover those absences might provide a means by which difficult or confusing interactions might be explored more consciously. New interpretations and possibilities for action could result from such deeper investigations.

The influence of such 'absences' on the experience of leadership, both from 'follower' and 'leader' perspectives, goes some way to explain why it is so difficult to study this phenomenon. After all, the absent aspects of leadership's identity are rarely explicitly articulated. How can an externally-based researcher know that the slight awkwardness in an interchange between a 'leader' and their 'follower' is due to an unexpressed hostility between them because the leader is not living up to the 'follower's' expectations? The 'follower' may not even know this him or herself. Similarly, what sense can a researcher make of a leader's espoused commitment to encouraging followers to search for their own solutions to dilemmas – is the leader abdicating responsibility or trying to enact a more shared form of leading? (And more importantly, how do their followers interpret such a pronouncement?)

A further complication is that the expectations of what constitutes leadership will not only be individually-based but will also be communally determined and, again, this communal determination occurs invisibly. Unspoken communal expectations will be historically influenced and will also be influenced by national and organizational cultures. When an individual summarizes the thoughts from a meeting and then suggests a way forward, this may be construed as taking up the leader role effectively within the USA but may not be perceived in the same positive light in China. Such an observation might, indeed, question the validity of the concept at all – but bear with me for a little longer while I develop this argument. The point is that leadership's identity is multi-dimensional and that many aspects of those dimensions are invisible. As such, they may not even be apparent until one 'trips over them'.

Absent but present: stories
There is another way in which leadership operates through 'absence'. Drawing momentarily from a model of leadership which recognizes the 'leader' as the source of leadership, it is apparent that in many organizations people recognize someone as their 'leader' without ever coming into physical contact with him or her. Instead, their 'leader's' 'presence' is conveyed through media such as photographs and video, public statements and, perhaps most powerfully, through the stories that are told about him or her. Stories can be compelling means by which 'leaders' are known to their 'followers', yet they act through 'absence'. The 'leader' is seldom present when the story is told and, in fact, has very little control over which stories are conveyed or how they are spread. Though made of no material substance, whether they are true or false, a 'leader's' 'leadership' can be strengthened or diminished by the stories told about him or her.

One organizational leader who clearly recognized the power of such stories was Greg Dyke, the Director General of the British Broadcasting Corporation (BBC) from 2000 to 2004. The BBC is the largest broadcasting organization in the world and employs more than 28 000 people in the UK alone. It is also an organization steeped in British culture and history, renowned globally for its broadcasts to war-torn parts of the world during times of conflict.

Taking over the post of Director General, Dyke promised to 'cut through' much of the bureaucracy which was seen to be hampering the effective running of the Corporation. One of the platforms upon which he built his role was in empowering employees throughout all hierarchical levels of the organization. A key way in which this was enacted was through an ambitious commitment to visiting broadcasting stations throughout the country, especially ones in far off corners of the UK which had never before been visited by the Director General. His success in fostering a sense of personal relationship between himself and his large staff was evidenced by the fact that so many people physically protested – left their offices and went out on the street – the day Dyke resigned from the role. His resignation came after allegations of mishandled reporting concerning the way in which the BBC had questioned the verdict delivered by the Hutton Report. This report investigated the suicide of David Kelly, a senior Military of Defence employee who had advised the government about the possibility of discovering weapons of mass destruction in Iraq. Dyke's decision to leave the BBC generated a good deal of controversy. Speculation ranged from questions about the extent to which he had been pushed, to suggestions that he had only tendered his resignation in the belief that it would not be accepted by the Board of Governors of the BBC.

I once heard Dyke give a talk entitled, 'The Ten Lessons of Leadership'[1] in which one of the key points he made was that the leader should recognize the power of stories that were told about him or her. To illustrate this, he told his own tale. Early in his time as Director General, he had planned to visit a small station in a rural part of the South East of England. The night before the visit, his house caught fire and burnt down. The next morning his personal assistant contacted him, saying she would cancel his visit to Kent. 'Don't do that,' he told her, 'of course I'll go.' 'But your house has just burned down!' she protested. 'I know, but I promised I'd make this trip.' Dyke confessed that one of the factors which contributed to his decision was the nature of the story it would foster – that despite having lost his house he still honoured his commitment to visiting the radio station. Such a story would impress upon his 'followers' his commitment to meeting them and hearing their stories and concerns, no matter what impediments were put in his path.

Dyke also reflected on another aspect of this 'absent' part of leadership; that the stories told about a 'leader' are usually out of their control. Although from time-to-time a leader might be able to do something in the hope that it will initiate a certain kind of story, stories are also interpreted, socially constructed things and the sense people make of them is out of the control of the leader. Yet they still have power in terms of their ability to shift the leadership dynamic and to influence how leadership is experienced by their followers. Of course, such 'absences' are highly problematic in terms of how one might go about researching them. Certainly they do not lend themselves to quantitative, 'tick in the box' behavioural surveys.

Absent but present: culture
As a container for the values, beliefs, norms, expectations and taboos of collectives, culture effects the enactment of leadership in ways that are not readily apparent. This might be most usefully seen through a comparison of cross-cultural leadership. For instance, let's consider the case of Western companies doing business in China and trying to develop local Chinese leaders. Generally, Chinese culture differs dramatically from that in the West in terms of its emphasis on collective, rather than individualistic ways of operating. This cultural assumption about the primacy of collective action, over the desirability of individual agency feeds into Chinese enactments and expectations of their leaders. Western expectations of leaders who direct 'from the front' with little pause to consult others, do not suit Chinese assumptions about appropriate 'leader' behaviour.

Such differences in cultural expectations raise interesting conundrums for globally-operating organizations, such as Shell, when they try to recruit local senior managers. A study currently undertaken in the UK[2] which compares the ways in which Western senior managers are perceived by locals with the way Chinese senior managers are perceived by locals, illustrates this difficulty. Preliminary findings suggest that when Western senior managers go about doing 'leadership' in the way that is individually focused and highly individualistic, this behaviour is accepted by Chinese locals as being appropriate. However, when Chinese managers use the same kinds of behaviours as their Western counterparts, Chinese locals are not happy to accept their individualistic ways of operating.

Simultaneously, if Chinese senior managers enact leadership behaviours more attuned to the local expectations, these ways of operating are not perceived as being appropriate to the Western-based company. It would seem that Chinese locals, wanting to occupy senior positions within Western global companies, may find themselves in an impossible situation in which however they lead, they are not seen to be effective.

This is a similar version of the way culture can influence gendered experiences of leadership. Researchers such as Amanda Sinclair and Joyce Fletcher[3] have highlighted the 'double bind' of being a female leader within many organizational cultures. The kinds of behaviours which 'followers', be they men or women, perceive to be indicative of the person holding the 'leader' role, may not look 'right' when enacted by a female.

The difficulty faced by Hillary Clinton in her bid to win the Democratic party's nomination for USA President in 2008 illustrates this. The media often reported on her 'toughness' as a reason that people did not warm to her and yet on the few occasions when she expressed emotional fragility, she was berated for not being 'tough enough'. The point is that the culture will carry certain, often unarticulated, assumptions about what leadership looks like. For those researching leadership, it can be very difficult to bring to the surface such informing assumptions and to appreciate fully the role they will be playing within a particular leadership dynamic.

In summary, one cause of the difficulties associated with studying leadership is that as a socially constructed phenomenon, it operates largely through its absence. This includes the absent expectations carried by both the 'leader' and the 'followers', through the stories that are told about the 'leader and through the culture from which leadership arises. The growing number of organizations which rely on information communication technologies to maintain contact between geographically dispersed members offers a new arena for exploring the way in which leadership operates through absence. It will be interesting to see how leadership operates within ever more virtual encounters.

Phenomenology offers another set of concepts which might be helpful in explaining the difficulties associated with studying leadership; 'presence-to-hand' and 'ready-to-hand'. These are rather more complex ideas than that of identity. However, I believe them to be worth introducing because they potentially offer a significantly novel way of conceptualizing the 'disappearing' nature of leadership.

'Present-at-Hand' and 'Ready-to-Hand': What can be Learned from Failed Leadership?

Let us return to the notion of 'The Lifeworld' for a moment. As you will recall, 'The Lifeworld' is the day-to-day world in which we live and in which knowing is very much grounded in our practical realities and desires. If I want to have a cup of tea I boil water, put tea bags into a pot, pour the boiling water over the tea bags, wait for awhile, then pour the liquid into a cup. As I do these things, I do not stop at each step and think, 'Now I am going to heat this water by exciting electrons to the point that they reach a temperature of 100 degrees centigrade and I am going to pour the water over these tea bags which are constituted of paper and pour it into this china cup which is held together by these forces of physics.' No; I merely engage in the practical steps required to make a cup of tea. I do not think about the science involved in making it happen. That way of engaging with the world of 'things', in which they are almost extensions of us and we do not really think about their identity, is called 'ready-to-hand' in phenomenological terms.

Likewise, my computer was 'ready-to-hand' this morning when I sat at my desk to begin working. I did not think, 'This is my computer, this is the way I turn it on, it requires electric power to work and it functions through a system I'll never completely understand which involves digital technology.' On the contrary I turned it on, waited for the screen to light up and more or less began typing. I engage with the things in my life, my computer, my desk, my chair, the cup of tea which I am drinking, in a habitual, almost unconscious manner. That is, until something goes wrong.

We all know the feeling of pressing the 'on' button of the computer and rather than the familiar whirring sound indicative of the system booting up, a blank screen stares back. When that happens, we start to engage differently with the computer. Instead of just beginning to type on the key-board, we have to stand back and examine it differently. We notice whether or not the power cable is attached properly, we wonder whether the hard drive has corrupted, we begin to consider the computer's inner workings and what might be wrong. Rather than engaging with it in a 'ready-to-hand' way, we step back from it and consider it as a piece of equipment which has its own way of working, which we now must try to understand in order to enable it to do what we want it to do. This shift, from the habitual way of engaging with the world, to one in which we look closely at 'what has gone wrong' phenomenologists call moving from 'ready-to-hand' engagement, to 'present-at-hand' engagement.[4] This involves interacting with the 'thing' as it 'presents' itself, rather than as we use it.

One of the key differences between these two modes of operation is that when we are engaged with something in a 'ready-to-hand' mode, the something we are engaged with 'disappears'. Think about it for a minute. When you are typing on your computer, do you really think about each keystroke you hit? Unless you are a beginner typist, the answer is probably not. You think about the message you want to convey and how you might put it into words. If you are a skilled touch typist, you unconsciously tap the correct keys to spell the words you want to write. The keyboard and the computer become extensions of your body in enabling you to express yourself. In 'ready-to-hand' engagement with the world, the 'things' we use 'disappear' into the purposes for which they are being used.

What happens if we think of leadership as working in a similar way? When people are undertaking a task of some sort, if they are really engaged in the task and its completion, I would suggest that they very rarely step back and think, 'Where is the leadership now?' They go ahead and do the task. Certainly, at different phases in an activity's unfolding, the necessity for a different mode of leading may become more apparent. For instance, consider the example of emergency services working together to rescue stranded climbers from a mountain cliff. Each person in the rescue team may have a different form of expertise and will take the leading role depending on what is needed at a given point in time. The helicopter pilot might take the lead in identifying the right spot to attempt the pick-up and then a technical person who knows about wind currents and how they work in terms of rescue equipment may take the lead in positioning the helicopter and the crew vis-à-vis the stricken climbers. Once the climbers are safely on board, a medic, who might know nothing about helicopters or rescue equipment, will take the lead in deciding what kind of care the walkers need and the kind of treatment they require before they are brought to a hospital.

While the rescue effort is being undertaken, in highly functioning teams the role of leader probably passes between those involved in an effortless manner. An outsider would probably not be able to recognize how this occurs and, in fact, those taking part might themselves not be able to identify the exact moment in which the leader 'baton' passes between them. Certainly, transitions between team members would not be as clearcut as I might have depicted here because of overlaps in expertise and the need to consult with one another. For instance, although the medic would take the lead in terms of treatment, that decision might also be taken in consultation with the helicopter pilot, who will have a view about how long it will take to get to a hospital and the nature of the journey there. The leadership, in terms of the influence in making decisions, will also overlap and coincide. If this team has worked together before, they may not consciously think about how they manage this process. They will just go ahead and do it. Additionally, much of their way of working together in a given moment will also be informed by their history of working together before; that is the invisible absence of their prior experience of these kinds of situations.

In highly integrated and well-functioning teams with experience of these kinds of scenarios, the leader role would pass amongst individuals in a seamless and unconscious manner. Were a researcher to come along to interview team members about how leadership operated between them, it would not be surprising if the responses were vague and inarticulate. Team members would have been engaging in leadership processes in a 'ready-to-hand' mode; in which leadership itself 'disappears' and is not visible and distinctive from the purpose to which it is put. The fact that those involved in 'doing' leadership have difficulty articulating what they do does not mean leadership itself does not exist. The difficulty arises when attempting to move from a 'ready-to-hand' engagement with leadership, in which it is seamlessly enacted and thus not consciously available, to a 'present-at-hand' examination of it, whereby it 'freezes' for an instant and can be subjected to closer scrutiny.

A situation which calls for 'present-at-hand' attention to leadership, as with any phenomenon, is when it goes badly wrong. Just as when the computer fails to boot up and its malfunction demands questioning into how it works, examining what is missing when leadership fails may glean new insights into its 'ready-to-hand' mode.

Simultaneously, such an analysis provides another opportunity to explore the possibilities offered by the notion of absence: we can understand more about what leadership is by thinking about what is missing when it is not there. Put another way, the ideas of 'ready-to-hand' and 'presence-to-hand' suggest that when leadership is serving its purpose, it is actually very difficult to 'see'. Then it operates in a 'ready-to-hand' mode and disappears into its purpose. Perhaps when leadership goes wrong it is easier to identify what it is that has failed. By articulating what is missing in such instances, leadership might paradoxically reveal itself more explicitly, thereby gaining insight into the purpose it serves when it is there.

Let us test this idea by examining a situation in which it was generally recognized that leadership had failed to a significant degree, the case of the US Government's response to Hurricane Katrina in August 2005.

HURRICANE KATRINA: WHAT DOES ABSENT LEADERSHIP REVEAL ABOUT LEADERSHIP?

Amidst the hundreds of pages which have been written in the aftermath of Hurricane Katrina, the tropical storm which struck the city of New Orleans in August 2005, a recurring theme arises: 'It was a failure of leadership'; 'Too many leaders failed to lead'; 'Where were the leaders?' As noted in the US House Select Committee Report (2006) charged with investigating the Government's response to the disaster: 'We are left scratching our heads at the range of inefficiency and ineffectiveness that characterized government behavior right before and after the storm. Too many leaders failed to lead' (pp. 359–60).

Rather than add to the critical chorus bemoaning the ineffectiveness of leaders at every level of government during the perplexing week following Hurricane Katrina, here I take a different perspective. When a hammer I am using fails to work because its head falls off, I have to stand back and examine it more closely. I must ask myself 'What essential aspect of its effectiveness as a hammer has been breached?' Then I can repair it, or acquire a new tool. Similarly, perhaps by identifying the essential aspect of 'leadership' which was absent from the official response to Hurricane Katrina we can better understand something critical about the nature of leadership required within that context.

What Happened During Hurricane Katrina?

First, let's introduce the individuals who might have been expected to enact the 'leader role' as events transpired and recall some of the key aspects of the Hurricane Katrina story. Individuals holding significant roles of authority in the ensuing drama which have been criticized for their 'lack of leadership' include: the Director of the Federal Emergency Management Agency (FEMA), Michael Brown; Secretary of Homeland Security, Michael Chertoff; the Governor of Louisiana, Kathleen Babineaux Blanco; the Mayor of New Orleans, Ray Nagin; and the holder of the most senior authoritative post in the USA at the time, the President, George W. Bush.

Hurricane Katrina was classified as a Category 1 storm (out of a possible five-point scale, in which 'one' is the lowest and 'five' is the highest level of severity) on Thursday 25 August 2005 when she first hit the coast of Florida and began her journey westward. Despite the enormous technological advances in tracking weather systems, at this point in time it was still impossible to know exactly how severe the storm would become or what direction it would take. However, by Saturday 27 August, forecasters were convinced Katrina was going to be a big storm and was headed towards Louisiana.

A warning issued at 10.00 am Saturday predicted the centre of the storm would be very close to New Orleans, with winds approaching 130 miles per hour within the next day. Although the storm itself would be frightening, the more worrying aspect was the possibility of flooding, particularly if there was a breach in the levees which protect New Orleans. In his recounting of the events surrounding Katrina in the book, *The Storm* (van Heerden and Bryan 2006), Ivor van Heerden, Deputy Director of the Louisiana State University Hurricane Centre reports that by 12.45 pm on Saturday, a broadcast had been released from his office predicting that water 'would get into New Orleans from the airport side. [It would be] very close and likely to overtop from every side' (p. 43). Given the warnings his office were issuing, van Heerden admitted to having been alarmed when an evacuation order was not forthcoming.

In dealing with events such as Katrina, state governments are the first port of call for assisting their citizens. Only when state officials ask for help does the Federal Government intervene. On Saturday 27 August the Governor of Louisiana, Kathleen Blanco, asked for Federal

Assistance. From that point onwards the authority for action rested at the national government level and should have been assumed by the Federal Emergency Management Agency (FEMA) under the direction of Michael Brown.[5]

Katrina was a major hurricane, with winds reaching sustained strengths of 125 miles per hour after making landfall on Monday 29 August. However, the resultant loss of life (estimated to be 1836 people) was attributed primarily to the breach of the levees which should have protected the city from flooding. Although George Bush declared a State of Emergency for the region on Sunday 28 August, and at this point a mandatory evacuation was ordered, by then it was too late for many New Orleans residents to arrange transportation out of the city. People took shelter where they could. An estimated 15000 people made their way to the Convention Centre where they remained stranded for up to three days without adequate facilities, food or water.

As the storm abated, the scale of the flooding problem revealed itself. Literally thousands of people were homeless or stranded in what remained of their homes. The world watched on television as government at any level failed to respond. Among the distressing stories were accounts of aid agencies sending food for those in the Convention Centre but not being able to deliver it because 'FEMA had said not to go in unless they had the necessary paperwork from the state. The state knew nothing about such a requirement, nor was there any such paperwork' (van Heerden and Bryan 2006, p. 136).

An important aspect of understanding what went wrong during and after the Hurricane concerns the line of command which should have taken up the leader role at various points. In marked contrast to the imaginary mountain rescue team described earlier, no one stepped into a role of authority as the tragedy unfolded. The House Committee Report entitled 'A Failure of Initiative' (2006) clearly outlines the points at which necessary leadership was absent, from the White House's failure to verify information about the severity of the storm and the threat to the levees; to the delay in ordering a mandatory evacuation of the city. Co-ordination of the rescue effort was sorely lacking, with the FEMA Director, Michael Brown, often appearing uninformed about the state of the situation or whose role it might be to respond to particular aspects of the crisis. This was plainly apparent as the media reported day after day of non-response in their coverage of people left without food, water or rescue from the rooftops of their submerged houses.

In terms of the subsequent media reports and articles written about the many failures that happened, the following seem universally agreed upon:

- From the onset of the crisis, there seemed to be lack of clarity about leaders' responsibility and who would take charge of addressing problems as they arose. The investigation carried out in Katrina's aftermath revealed that Michael Brown still held the view that New Orleans was exempt from FEMA aid during natural disasters of this kind (van Heerden and Bryan 2006, p. 141).
- There is some question as to the extent to which the populace understood the nature of the problem. However, later reports indicate that the vast majority of those who died were in fact not able to leave New Orleans. This was because either they did not have transport, as no central evacuation plan for them had been put into place, or because they were in institutions (nursing homes, prisons) which did not enable them to leave the city.
- The rescue event lacked central co-ordination; there seemed to be little understanding of the interconnections between different agencies and how they might best support one another. This was in sharp contrast to what occurred after the 11 September attacks in New York, when Mayor Guilliani took up a very prominent co-ordinating and figurehead role.

There were also invisible 'absent' factors which contributed to the unravelling of this event:

- Two years prior to Hurricane Katrina a scenario planning exercise had been undertaken which revealed many of the difficulties New Orleans would face in the event of a hurricane of this magnitude. This exercise (staged as 'Hurricane Pam') revealed numerous failures in the city's response system, including lack of transport resulting in up to 10 per cent of the city's residents being unable to evacuate. The probability that the levees would be breached was also recognized. Yet, nothing was done to prepare for the onslaught of a storm like Katrina. In this way, the 'failure of leadership' attributed to Katrina actually had its genesis long before August 2005. This raises the issue that in order to understand the nature of leadership failure 'in the moment', one also has to understand its history.
- Finally, prior to Hurricane Katrina, out of 120 different government agencies, FEMA had been identified as the very worst to work for by employees and managers alike. FEMA suffered from the highest level of staff turnover of any government agency and, at the time of Katrina, at least 50 per cent of senior managerial positions were either vacant of filled by individuals temporarily in their roles. Its

Director, Michael Brown, had no prior experience of disaster management. If FEMA was the organization charged with dealing with emergencies, it was not in itself best fit to do so.

These two factors alone indicate the extent to which the seeds of the failure of leadership apparent during and in the aftermath of the hurricane were planted well before Katrina made landfall. In the moment when apparent leadership needed to be enacted, these deficiencies came to light. Their 'absences' became 'presences' within the tragedy of Katrina.

What does the Absence of Leadership During Hurricane Katrina Reveal about Leadership?

It is beyond question that there was something missing in terms of the leadership response to Hurricane Katrina and its aftermath. The images of people swimming through the waters carrying their belongings on their heads, the overcrowded and chaotic conditions in the New Orleans Conference Centre as well as the tales of victims of the flooding who were without food and water for days, indicate that *something* could have been done differently. For many commentators, analysts and people who lost homes and livelihoods in that storm, that something was 'leadership'. Can we get closer to this slippery phenomenon by probing what was missing during those weeks in August and September 2005?

In keeping with the argument posed in earlier chapters, it is important to emphasize that whatever is revealed about leadership through its absence during Hurricane Katrina it is particular to the kind of leadership required for that particular situation. Hurricane Katrina was a crisis, certainly one that had been predicted and to some extent planned for, but nonetheless a natural disaster with attendant uncertainties. One of the reasons subsequently given for the late order to evacuate New Orleans was the habit that tropical storms have of suddenly changing direction. Ordering an evacuation and then having the storm shift would cause unnecessary chaos, something city officials were keen to avoid.

In this specific situation, two aspects were clearly absent from the government's response. Firstly, there was a lack of perspective on the entire situation. We often talk about the need for leaders to have a 'vision', a purpose to which they are leading their followers. I would argue that in the case of Katrina, even more than 'vision', what was needed was a way of 'seeing' the entire scenario and its attendant intricacies and complexities. Rather than the skill of looking forward, this situation called for the capacity to deeply perceive what was going on in the here and now. More than a vision, Katrina required a perspective large enough to encompass the entire context with its critical interdependencies and from that perspective to create a plan for effective action.

It is generally recognized that during and after Katrina such an integrating perspective was lacking. Instead, responsibility seemed to heave from one government agency to another without any apparent co-ordination. In the subsequently produced government report which detailed the lessons learned from Hurricane Katrina,[6] there is much written about the need for a match between 'responsibility and authority' of those acting to respond to the crisis. In order to make this match however, both the ability to see the interconnections and then the authority to exercise power in co-ordinating a cross-agency response had to be present.

A second aspect of leadership which became obvious through its absence during the response to Hurricane Katrina was the absence of a leadership 'face'. Although I do not want to fall into the trap of equating 'leadership' with an individual leader, an individual who actually takes up the 'leader' role is an important aspect of the leadership moment. Within crisis situations such as Katrina, perhaps the need for an individual to visibly take up the 'leader' role is even more pronounced. The faceless government agency, FEMA, did not adequately serve that purpose.

The importance of the leader 'face' in times of crisis is apparent throughout Western history. A sizeable proportion of the UK population still reminisce fondly about King George and Queen Elizabeth's presence on the streets of London following the bombing blitzes of the Second World War; John F. Kennedy's very public response to the Cuban missile crisis; Rudy Guilliani's active presence at Ground Zero in the aftermath of the World Trade Centre strikes – each provides an illustration of visible 'leading' in times of national difficulty.

Although these failures of leadership were apparent both during and in the aftermath of Hurricane Katrina, the crisis revealed ways in which the absence of leadership in the years and months prior to the storm also played its role in the crisis. For instance, the government agency charged with responding to emergency situations was itself in a state of emergency and not capable of co-ordinating an effective plan. No one or no agency took responsibility for attending to the deficiencies revealed by the trial scenario of Hurricane Pam, thus problems noted then had not been rectified. Van Heerden and Bryan (2006) suggest that the city's decisions to allow building developments in crucial wetland areas surrounding New Orleans contributed to the scale of the flooding and in this way a lack of leadership to protect these crucial areas long before 2005 came home to roost in the wake of the storm. All of these factors, invisible and forgotten as they might have been, played their role in the 'leadership moment', or 'lack of leadership moment', apparent in New Orleans in the autumn of

2005. Where does one factor start and another stop in creating the 'leadership moment'? That question itself indicates something about the difficulty inherent in studying leadership.

WHAT IS A LEADERSHIP RESEARCHER TO DO?

Phenomenology introduces the concept of 'absences': the powerful, invisible forces which can impact on the way leadership is enacted and experienced. These include more obvious influencing factors such as the expectations of 'leaders' and 'followers' as well as the quality of connection and trust between them but they also include more elusive factors, such as historical relationships and long-established patterns of interactions.

These absent facets of leadership's identity mean that anyone trying to study this phenomenon is faced with the challenge of uncovering a multitude of impacting factors which are difficult, if not impossible, to identify. Furthermore, because they often operate at unconscious levels for both leaders and followers, they are very hard to elicit. Perhaps it is only in the incongruities, the unexpected disconnects between what a researcher might expect and what actually happens, which enable such forces to be apprehended. The fact that the FEMA was populated by demoralized people and that many of those in senior roles were not adequately prepared to undertake the responsibilities associated with those roles severely limited the agency's ability to respond in a 'leaderful' manner to the unfolding drama of Katrina. Although it may be much easier to blame individual 'leaders' for the emerging disaster, factors such as the ill-equipped Federal Agency were undoubtedly invisibly present throughout the handling of the crisis. Spotting such factors requires leadership researchers to penetrate behind the easy answers available at a surface level of analysis.

Additionally, researchers need to be aware of the limits on their ability to generalize about 'leadership' from particular cases or situations. The example of Hurricane Katrina only reveals something about the nature of leadership required in that particular situation. The kind of leadership which would have enabled lives to have been saved and which would have fostered a sense of greater security from those too old or sick to help themselves as the levees broke, is different from that required by a high-tech company faced with the threat of a technologically superior market rival. I am not suggesting that lessons learned about leadership and how it operates in one situation can never bring insight to other contexts, only that such lessons must be applied with caution. The invisible factors which contribute to one leadership moment may be entirely different from those constituting another, even when the surface appearance is very similar.

Due to this, leadership researchers are encouraged to interrogate the terrain below the surface level of apparent perceptions. Actively seeking the invisible, absent factors which contribute to any experience of leadership is vital. They are always there. It might be helpful to assume that anything which appears to be obvious about the way in which leadership is operating is underpinned by currents that are not obvious. This is especially true of the historic and cultural factors which are taken for granted by those involved in a leadership dynamic. In this way it is important for leadership researchers to acknowledge and gain insight into the part organizational history plays in the experience of leadership. What is the story of how someone came to see themselves or others as 'leaders' in certain contexts? How do either national or organizational cultural expectations inform perceptions of what constitutes leadership? Such questions can begin to shed light on how those involved in leadership, either as followers, leaders or even observers make sense of the phenomenon.

Although a raft of studies regularly relies on self-report type psychometric instruments or interviews as methods for gaining insight into leadership, the concepts introduced here would suggest expanding the methodological palette might enable deeper insight into this phenomenon. Ethnographic methods in which the researcher embeds him or herself in a particular culture in order to experience leadership 'from the inside' could reveal new sides and aspects, as would action research approaches. In order to gain insight into the contextual aspects of the leadership moment, longitudinal studies might be employed.

The implications for researching leadership which emerge from the book as a whole will be re-examined in Chapter 9. For now, I will end this chapter by suggesting that the notions of 'absence', 'ready-to-hand' and 'presence-to-hand' encourage leadership researchers to attend carefully to their own experience when engaging in leadership research. When data just 'does not add up', when a situation evokes a feeling of disquiet, curiosity or unease, when you hear those you are interviewing telling you one thing but your gut is telling you something else; pause. One of the invisible, intangible, negative presences at the heart of the particular 'leadership moment' you are investigating might be trying to reveal itself to you.

One of the elusive aspects of leadership which is increasingly coming under scrutiny within leadership studies is the relationship between 'leaders' and 'followers'. A raft of theories broadly identifying themselves as 'relational leadership' or 'follower-centred leadership' have emerged, which begin to highlight the paradoxical nature of this key relationship. Of course, the awareness that this relationship is not completely straightforward is not new; as recounted earlier, Cecil Gibb wrote about the way in which leadership moves between 'followers' and 'leaders' in the 1950s.

However, there has been a marked revival in 'relational' leadership theories since the 1990s. What transpires in the space between leaders and followers which contributes to the experience of 'leadership'? The next chapter examines this question more closely, particularly by drawing on the idea of 'flesh' offered by the French phenomenologist, Maurice Merleau-Ponty.

NOTES

1. This event occurred at the Centre for Leadership Studies, University of Exeter's annual forum in London in January 2006.
2. This is a study being undertaken by Lake Wang in pursuit of his Doctorate in Business Administration at Cranfield School of Management, Cranfield University in the UK.
3. See Sinclair, A. (1994), *Doing Leadership Differently*, Carlton, Victoria: Melbourne University Press, or Fletcher, J. (2004), 'The paradox of post heroic leadership: an essay on gender, power and transformational change', *Leadership Quarterly*, **15**, 647–61.
4. Although a number of phenomenologists worked with the notions of 'presence-to-hand' and 'ready-to-hand', these concepts were probably most strongly developed by Martin Heidegger and are elaborated in his (1962) book, *Being and Time*.
5. This was actually contested by Michael Brown in a subsequent statement to the House Investigating Committee when Brown suggested that New Orleans was exempt from a request for Federal Aid.
6. Townsend, Frances Fragos (2006), 'The Federal Response to Hurricane Katrina: Lessons Learned', Washington DC Office of the Assistant to the President for Homeland Security and Counterterrorism, www.whitehouse.gov/reports/katrina-lessons-learned (accessed 15 September 2008).

4. What goes on in the relationship between leaders and followers?

> There is a circle of the touched and the touching, the touched takes hold of the touching; there is a circle of the visible and the seeing, the seeing is not without visible existence . . .
>
> Maurice Merleau-Ponty
> *The Visible and Invisible*
> (1968, p. 143)

The last three chapters have addressed some of the broader questions perennially asked about the nature of leadership itself. This chapter acts as a pivot point between those ontologically-based concerns and more specific questions about how leadership gets accomplished by attending to the dynamic at the heart of leader-follower interactions. In it, I introduce ideas developed by the French phenomenologist Maurice Merleau-Ponty in order to construct a radical way of conceptualizing this relationship.

Although much of the literature assumes 'followers' and 'leaders' to be distinct modes of operating, there are also hints that separating the two roles in real life may not be completely straightforward. You will recall the work of Cecil Gibb and Peter Gronn introduced in Chapter 3 which highlighted the way in which leadership, as indicated by level of influence, flowed amongst group members rather than being situated solely with one person. Their research indicated the difficulties associated with clearly identifying who might be following and who might be leading during any period of collective activity.

The apparent ambiguity inherent between 'leaders' and 'followers' has been noted and developed into more relationally-oriented leadership theories. Scholars such as the 'father of transformational leadership', Bernard Bass, have urged us to go beyond equating 'leadership' with 'leaders', to recognize the essential nature of the relationship between 'leaders' and those who would follow them (Bass 1985). In his landmark article of 1995, James Meindl[1] calls attention to the 'romance of leadership', suggesting that our over-reliance on ideals of individualistic leadership models is flawed. Instead, he argues that we need to examine the relationships involved to fully appreciate the leadership dynamic. These writers herald a more general trend in leadership theorizing away from 'heroic' models of leadership in which the 'leader' is recognized as the one person responsible for 'leadership' to more inclusive and complex perspectives.

This chapter investigates this territory further by posing the question, 'What is going on in the relationship between "leaders" and "followers"?' In particular, is there a way of getting beyond thinking of 'leaders' and 'followers' as separate independent entities, to examine the 'space between' them as a force in its own right? What does such an analysis imply? As a starting point, let us explore two key contemporary theories of relational leadership and consider the questions arising from them.

RELATIONAL LEADERSHIP

Probably the most well known theory of 'relational' leadership is Leader-Member Exchange, developed by writers such as Gerstner and Day (1997), Graen et al. (1982) and Graen and Uhl-Bien (1995). The hallmarks of this theory are that leadership occurs through one-to-one relations between a 'leader' and a 'follower', and that the quality of that relationship will differ between 'leaders' and individual 'followers'. This can result in the creation of 'in-groups', who will go above and beyond the call of duty to fulfil the requests of the 'leader', while those further from the 'leader's' favour (in out-groups) may not be so highly motivated to do so. Although Leader-Member Exchange theory describes this phenomenon of in-groups and out-groups, it does little to probe what occurs between leaders and followers to create the in- or out-group effect. What happens in the space between leaders and followers to create the experience of the exchange?

Building on Leader-Member Exchange theory, the social network perspective developed by writers such as Prasad Balkundi and Martin Kilduff broadens the scope of attention away from one-to-one relationships to encompass larger groupings. They propose that at its essence, 'leadership is the relationship which connects individuals so they experience themselves to be part of an extended network of people working together in some way'. (Balkundi and Kilduff 2005, p. 957). In this way their work calls attention to the span of people who create the experience of leadership, however it does not examine the internal mechanisms by which networks operate or the means by which they are held together.

Although Leader-Member Exchange theory and the social network perspective advance a conceptualization of leadership based primarily on the actions of individual 'leaders', the scholar Mary Uhl-Bien suggests a further step can be taken in understanding leadership as a relationship. She proposes that instead of remaining focused on the separate identities of 'leader' and 'follower' a truly 'relational' view of leadership would attend to the middle space; that is the relationship *between* those engaged in leadership itself. Such an approach would start from the 'relationship' as the unit of analysis, rather than from the individuals comprising the relationship. She argues that in order to truly understand what is happening in 'relational' leadership, we need to pay attention to the 'space between' 'leaders' and 'followers' (2006, p. 671). Doing so, Uhl-Bien suggests, focuses our attention on the 'place' where leadership actually occurs.

How might it be possible to perceive this seemingly invisible space operating between 'leaders' and 'followers'? Are there conceptualizations which might enable us to go beyond recognizing them as separate entities and bring our attention to the space between them as an active dynamic in its own right? I believe the phenomenologist, Maurice Merleau-Ponty, introduces a way of constructing intersubjectivity that could provide insight into this invisible, yet potent space.

MERLEAU-PONTY AND INTERSUBJECTIVITY

Born in 1908, Maurice Merleau-Ponty was Professor of Child Psychology and Pedagogy at the Sorbonne before taking up his post as Professor of Philosophy at the Collège de France. His philosophical work was influenced by his study of psychology, especially his understanding of infant development, along with his exploration of psychological pathologies. This practically-based engagement with human development is apparent in his philosophical works where he also demonstrates a keen understanding of the neurological, as well as psychological, aspects of perception.

Philosophically, Merleau-Ponty aligned himself early on with the German phenomenologist Husserl and was one of the first French philosophers to engage seriously with Husserl's ideas. Another key influence on Merleau-Ponty's thinking was through his long-term friendship with the existentialist Jean-Paul Sartre.[2] Merleau-Ponty's most well-known book, *The Phenomenology of Perception* published in 1945 (1945 [1962]), presents a radical formulation of the embodied nature of perception. However, the ideas presented in his final book *The Visible and the Invisible* (1968), which was incomplete at the time of his sudden death in 1961, are particularly relevant to exploring the 'in-between space' of human interactions.

Here, two ideas which inform Merleau-Ponty's thinking about intersubjectivity; 'reversibility' and 'flesh' will be introduced. In order to understand these concepts, two other foundational ideas are offered: 'immanence' and 'transcendence'. They serve as building blocks to understanding Merleau-Ponty's notion of intersubjectivity.

The Intertwining of Immanence and Transcendence

A basic understanding of the terms immanence and transcendence is needed in order to follow Merleau-Ponty's argument. Each of these terms has been extensively theorized itself. For the purposes of this chapter, immanence will be taken to refer to the embodied, present, material aspects of humanness. Human immanence is realized in its fleshy, material, physical aspect. Our corporeal bodies are immanent. Transcendence, on the other hand, refers to the aspects of humans which are seemingly unbound by material corporeality. The animating force of the human body, for instance, can be described as 'transcendent', as can the human capabilities of imagination, intention, rationality and consciousness. They seemingly move beyond and independent of the physical body.[3]

In the West since the time of René Descartes (1596–1650) a seventeenth century French philosopher, the cognitively-based, transcendent aspects of being human have been privileged over the more immanent, corporeal ones. This can be explained in part by the Enlightenment's pursuit of unquestionable truth. Enlightenment science noticed how the sensory awareness afforded to the body can sometimes be 'faulty'. We mistake ice on the road for glass, for instance; we perceive pools of water that deteriorate into mirages; we watch the sun set in the Western horizon and conclude that it circles the Earth. Moreover, our experience of qualities such as colour, weight, dimensions and taste are subject to individual interpretation. Our perceptual apparatus are not refined enough to hear certain pitches or to see tiny phenomena. Enlightenment science aspired to go beyond the abilities of our embodied constraints to discover immutable certainties about the world. The instrument for doing so was deemed to be our reasoning mind which through exacting training and the use of the scientific method could discover such absolute 'truths'.

Descartes' famous pronouncement, *Cogito ergo sum*[4] encapsulates the view of the mind split from matter championed since the seventeenth century. Although phenomenologists before him sought to re-conceptualize an integrated form of mind-body relationship inherent to the human condition and human knowing, Merleau-Ponty is recognized as presenting the most complete account of the intertwining of human immanence and transcendence. Merleau-Ponty argues that rather than being irreconcilably separated, immanence and transcendence mutually inform one another and it is only through their interaction that humans can know at all. This idea is radical in relation to the larger context of Western thought preceding him, in which the mind and rationality have been reified as that which makes us distinctly human.

The assumed primacy of 'mind' is apparent in the majority of writing devoted to leadership. For instance, throughout the canon the rational ways of being a 'leader' are emphasized. There is a great deal of focus on creating a 'vision', and the importance of logical decision-making is encouraged. Objectively determining followers' levels of commitment and ability is suggested as a means by which the leader can flex his or her style. Leading is characterized by 'thinking through options' and 'communicating objectives through the use of verbal language' rather than being associated with a physical, bodily way of being.[5]

In taking seriously the 'relational' dimension of leadership, however, it becomes apparent that a key way in which humans interrelate is through our bodily presence. We are not just attracted to a leader's ideas and visions; we are also attracted to their bodily way of being in the world. These ideas will be developed further in the next chapter which focuses on charismatic leadership. For now the important point is that Merleau-Ponty's philosophy not only recognizes the corporeal, material aspects of humanness; it makes it central to our very way of being in and knowing the world. He stresses that our curiosity about the world around us arises as we *move* through it, not just as we *think* about it. This idea is summarized in his statement, 'The world is not what I think, but what I live through' (Merleau-Ponty 1945 [1962], p. xviii).

'Moving' thus becomes an essential aspect of 'knowing'. It is the body which provides us with the mechanism for moving. It is not possible for us to know the world from a disembodied perspective, we live in and amidst the world, rather than distanced from it. Furthermore, our bodies constantly readjust themselves to accommodate being in the external environment. We shift position according to how cold or warm it is, where the sunlight is, how much space we have to stretch out into. We also position ourselves in physical relationships with other human beings. We do this largely without thinking about it and if someone invades the territory we feel is ours, we automatically move forward in an effort to shift them back or step back ourselves. These actions occur without conscious thought because of the body's way of knowing and being in the world.

Is it too large a leap to consider the ways in which this kind of bodily knowing informs the interactions between 'leaders' and 'followers', especially when the 'leaders' and 'followers' are within close physical proximity to one another? Our bodies naturally respond to others' ways of being in the world. For instance, sometimes when a person takes up the leader role they can have the effect of 'making your skin crawl with discomfort' whereas another might infect you with his or her enthusiasm. These reactions result from primal, physical exchanges between human bodies which might subsequently be rationalized as cognitive constructions. This recognition of the bodily or immanent aspects of human being in the world, particularly in regard to how we relate to one another, can give us a new way of understanding what goes on in the space between 'leaders' and 'followers'.[6] Instead of conceptualizing the leader-follower dynamic as a completely cognitive interchange consisting of well-posed arguments and mobilization towards aligned purposes, this middle space can be appreciated for its energetic and physical component, something that exists and is communicated below the surface level of rational apprehension.

There is another important point to make about how Merleau-Ponty sees the body in relation to the world. At a fundamental level, Merleau-Ponty understands the body to be a phenomenal 'thing' in a world of other phenomenal things. What does this mean? To understand Merleau-Ponty's meaning, one must momentarily leave aside the notion of the 'ego' which is so central to most of our understandings of what it is to be a person. Here 'ego', refers to the sense of self-consciousness about the existence of the 'self' and the attachment one naturally has to that 'self' as a unique and independent being.

For a moment, try to experience yourself as primarily a 'thing,' that is a 'form' which is unconnected to your sense of 'identity' in any particular way. Without an 'ego' attached to it, is it possible for you to think of the body as a 'thing', not too dissimilar from a 'chair', a 'tree', a 'pineapple' or a 'marble' (apart from having the kind of motility associated with a human body?). Thinking of the body as an egoless 'thing', the world becomes populated by a collection of entities, all of which have different properties and abilities but which interact in various ways. My body sits on this chair, which stands up from this floor, which is part of a building, which rests on the earth, which is teeming with insects, which breathe the same air that I do. This exercise perhaps allows you to approach Merleau-Ponty's idea; that at a phenomenal level – one which dismisses the 'ego' the body is a thing among a world of other phenomenal things. What is the significance of this way of thinking?

I see its significance in at least two respects. Firstly, through this construction Merleau-Ponty once again asserts the role our bodies play as phenomenal entities through which we know the world. Our minds are not capable of knowing without our bodies but our knowing is also fundamentally constituted by the world and what it presents to us. A more common assumption is that human beings are somehow privileged vis-à-vis the things of the world because of our rationality. By identifying so strongly with our transcendent consciousness, we forget that our bodies are constantly interacting with the world as objects interacting with other objects. These interactions are essential for developing knowledge and understanding of the self. It is because the chair that I sit on holds my body in a certain relation to the floor that I understand myself to be 'short' or 'tall'. It is because of the comparison I can make between my own girth and that of a tree that I understand my relative size in the world.

Additionally, the very way in which we interact with the world is determined by our corporeal presence. At a fundamental level, if we are short in stature, we will literally see a different perspective of the world from that viewed by someone who is taller. This recalls the notion of aspects introduced in Chapter 2. If we want to see a situation from a different viewpoint, adjusting our position, either metaphorically or literally enables us to do so.

Secondly, this construction hints at the central position Merleau-Ponty's philosophy gives to relationality itself. Relationality is at the nub of Merleau-Ponty's way of conceptualizing the world of things, including human bodies. It is not the separate entities which are of prime significance in his view but the relationships between them. This relationality is further elaborated upon in the philosopher's notion of 'reversibility'. This notion of reversibility has important implications for how the 'middle space' between leaders and followers operates.

Reversibility

The notion of reversibility is captured by Merleau-Ponty's term: 'percipient perceptible'. By this he means that as a 'thing' within the phenomenal world; in seeing other 'things' I am also 'seen' by them. In other words, according to Merleau-Ponty, part of being a human is defined by the fact that as I perceive, I am also perceived.[7] Although this may sound apparent, in fact, if you think about it deeply this notion holds significant implications for our way of understanding the nature of how human beings *are* in the world and thus for how leaders are in the world.

Further analysis of Merleau-Ponty's thoughts may be helpful before drawing the links between these ideas and leadership more fully. One of the significant aspects of this idea is that it highlights the importance of the world, or the context, within which an individual operates in terms of how they might know themselves. Merleau-Ponty stresses the complete embeddedness of being a human when he writes: 'Through the possibility of reversal, the little private world of each is not juxtaposed, to the world of others, but surrounded by it, levied off from it' (1968, p. 142).

Here Merleau-Ponty is pointing out that rather than being merely juxtaposed against the world, the self is continually constructed through interaction with it. This highlights the fundamental 'reversibility' which occurs between the self and other 'things' in the phenomenal world. For instance, I know myself to be a certain height because of how I stand in relation to the ceiling in my English cottage (and my stepson knows something about himself because he has to crouch beneath some of its low passageways). Notice how you adjust an office chair in order that it better accommodates the way in which your body rests in that space. Almost imperceptibly we note something about ourselves by the way in which we must adjust the world around us to 'fit' better.

More importantly for Merleau-Ponty's notion of reversibility is the realization that I cannot touch a 'thing', be it a piano, a caterpillar or a kumquat, without being simultaneously 'touched' by it. The smooth stone I hold in my hand may not have a consciousness through which it 'feels' me but if I put it into my hiking boot and try to walk for a while, I will certainly be aware of its touch on me! Through touching and being touched, I am aware not only of those phenomenal 'things' which populate my world but also of myself and who I am in relation to those 'things'.

Perhaps the significance of reversibility can be seen more clearly when it occurs between human beings. In confronting another's perceptions, I become more aware of my own predispositions and limits. There is a passage within Merleau-Ponty's *The Visible and the Invisible* (1968) which describes this experience in terms of its significance for the social relations between human beings:

> As soon as we see other seers, we no longer have before us only the look without a pupil, the plate glass of things with that feeble reflection, that phantom of ourselves they evoke by designating a place among themselves whence we see them: henceforth, through others' eyes we are for ourselves fully visible (1968, p. 143).

I recently found myself in a situation which threw the experience of reversibility into high relief for me. When I took up my post at the university where I teach, I was temporarily given an office without externally facing windows. My only window looked out into a large atrium, a public space through which my colleagues regularly walked in order to enter and exit the building. When people walked into the atrium, their line of sight immediately caused them to focus on the light shining in my office and consequently, on me working at my desk. I had the distinct feeling of being 'inside a goldfish bowl', on show for whoever might pass by.

On the occasions when I would look up and acknowledge the person looking at me, I started to notice something strange occur between us. Instead of just feeling that I was being looked at, I suddenly apprehended that just as I was being seen, I was also seeing the other. Somehow, the pane of glass and its frame served to accentuate the reversibility of perception between us. I noticed that people would often behave in quite unusual ways when we registered seeing one another. For instance the person on the other side of the window would begin pulling funny faces or waving wildly. Sometimes I would respond in kind. One way of interpreting this behaviour is that through encountering one another through my office window our mutual perception, which we normally take for granted, sparked into relief. I was conscious of myself and the other person's perception of me and they were conscious of themselves and my perception of them, in a distinct way. Perhaps this sudden realization would make us feel slightly uneasy and the antics which then transpired were our way of easing our discomfort.

I might add that the knowledge that people could look in and see me at work also affected my behaviours in the office. I refrained from having my lunch at the desk. I noticed that I did not relax and sit comfortably at times that I normally would, for instance when taking telephone calls. The absent presence of the possible 'eyes' that could view me at work meant that I altered what I did and how I positioned my body while at work there. I became more aware of 'who I was' in that space or, perhaps more precisely, who others might perceive me to be as they looked in on me in that space.[8] The window looking into the atrium made the reality of being 'perceived' real to me in a way which coloured my behaviour while occupying that space.

Merleau-Ponty's philosophy offers a way of understanding this experience. His notion of 'reversibility' suggests the self is fundamentally informed by how it understands itself to be perceived. In other words, I know my 'self' as much through my own agentic ability to touch starfish, acorns, mobile phones, other people's knees, as through the experience of being touched by starfish, acorns, mobile phones or other people's knees. I know I am made of flesh which feels pain if it is brushed too closely by a starfish, that my hand is the size that can hold eight acorns and that my ear feels warm after a long conversation on my mobile phone. I can interpret being touched by another person's knees as an indication of their perception of me as someone whose space can be readily invaded or as someone with whom the other would like to begin a romantic relationship.

How powerfully does reversibility play a role in relations between 'leaders' and 'followers'? The 'leader' role is highly visible; akin to occupying my goldfish bowl office. As the 'leader' acts and is observed by 'followers', the 'followers' engage relationally with the 'leader'. Through their gaze, a leader knows him or herself and through the leader's perception followers understand who they are. This mutually constructed give and take of perceptions constitutes and energizes the 'between space' of relational leadership. I have often heard those taking up leader roles say that they have acted a certain way because it was what they felt their followers needed from them at the time. The notion of reversibility suggests that although this experience may be interpreted as the exchange of

psychologically-oriented expectations, the means by which these expectations are exchanged is through perceptual engagement. Furthermore, this
dynamic is mutually co-constructed and as such subject to constant altera-
tion. Reversibility provides a precursor to and the foundation upon which
expectations are exchanged between those taking up the 'leader' role and
those who would follow them.

This philosophy also offers insight into how leaders and followers can
understand the impact they have on one another. Such empathy is made
possible through the notion of 'analogic apperception'.[9] Merleau-Ponty
argues that human bodies are 'isomorphic' in relation to one another, that
is; I can attribute to others' bodies there, what I experience in my body
here. I assume that just as I experience a field of sensation, a conscious
life, a capacity for reflection, so do others (Dillon 1997, p. 117). This iso-
morphism of our bodies provides a basis for mutual understanding. I can
understand what it is for you to be in a certain situation because you have
a human body which is like mine.

However, our bodies are also distinct. Although I know how my body
would feel in the situation in which I perceive your body to be, I cannot
know for sure that your experience is identical to mine. The important
point here is that all of this knowing is mediated through the body rather
than through the mind alone. In this way, our knowing of others is a
visceral, physical interconnection which provides the fundamental ground
for relationships between 'leaders' and 'followers'. The practical implications of this will be explored more fully later in the chapter. Now, however,
I would like to introduce the second of Merleau-Ponty's concepts which
builds on the idea of 'reversibility' and could provide the conceptual link
to a truly relational view of leadership.

'Flesh'

A concept which stretches the possibilities of intersubjectivity even further
is that of 'flesh'. Merleau-Ponty appropriated the notion of 'flesh' from
Jean-Paul Sartre (1943 [2002]), who defined it as the 'union' of contradictions. In Sartre's sense, 'union' denotes two aspects which come together
but are still fundamentally separated. Such a formulation could be seen as
analogous to where many 'relational' leadership theories arrive; in that, as
Uhl-Bien (2006) points out, they attend to separate follower-leader entities
rather than to the relationship between them. For Merleau-Ponty, 'flesh'
is instead the *unity* of contradiction. In his words it is: 'the concrete coin-
cidence of immanence and transcendence in the phenomenon of the lived
body' (quoted in Dillon 1997, p. 140). 'Flesh', for Merleau-Ponty is the
mechanism by which immanence, that is our corporeal way of being, and

transcendence, our animated way of being, are intertwined. I propose that the concept of 'flesh' might provide a way of conceptualizing the 'middle space' between 'leaders' and 'followers' which Uhl-Bien (2006) argues would be indicative of a truly relational view of leadership.

For Merleau-Ponty, as well as acting as a carrier of immanence and transcendence, 'flesh' has a progenitive sense. In other words, 'flesh' is at once the source of our being in the world as well as the medium through which we experience the world.[10] In that sense 'flesh' has an elemental and foundational dimension out of which experience springs. It might be helpful to return to Merleau-Ponty's idea of 'percipient perceptible' in order to further explicate the notion of 'flesh'. The link between them is articulated in the following:

> Thus since the seer is caught up in what he sees, it is still himself he sees; there is a fundamental narcissism in all vision. And thus, for the same reason, the vision he exercises, he also undergoes from the things, such that, as many painters have said, 'I feel myself looked at by the things, my activity is equally passivity, the seen and the visible reciprocate one another and we no longer know which sees, and which is seen. It is this visibility, this generability of the sensible that we have previously called 'flesh' (Merleau-Ponty 1968, p. 139).

This quote demonstrates that for Merleau-Ponty 'flesh' goes beyond the notion of perception as an individually experienced phenomenon. Instead, perception is more like a primordial quality of the world itself and 'flesh' is the 'stuff' of the world in which perception is embedded. Furthermore, through 'flesh', perception and the things of the world which are perceived are intertwined. Self-consciousness itself is similarly not possible without the mirror of other entities, be they human or be they rocks, terrain, trees, chairs or space rockets through which we see ourselves. 'Flesh' constitutes the means through which those perceptions occur; it holds both the materiality of separate entities and their field of interpenetration. With this notion, Merleau-Ponty offers a radical re-conceptualization of the 'body-world' relationship. My entire sense of myself is created through my perceptual interaction with the world.

Merleau-Ponty extends this notion by proposing that this construction reveals unexpected relations between the subjective and objective worlds in that, 'each calls for the other' (1968, p. 137). The idea of a mutual calling forth seems to offer a new way of understanding human relations with other humans, as well as human relations with other creatures and things of the world as being inherently and continually mutually constructing. I am who I am, not only because of my personality and the DNA which determines my physical appearance and potential, but also because of what my environment and those around me have evoked from me. Put simplistically, if my life has required courage and intrepidness from me, I will have practiced these qualities and will know myself to be courageous and intrepid. If, on the other hand, the circumstances of my life have required me to develop skills of sensitivity and empathy, these may similarly be qualities I attribute to my 'self'.

This may seem to echo Freudian constructions of the development of the self which place an emphasis on the role environment plays in determining an individual's capabilities. Merleau-Ponty's framing certainly overlaps with such theories but places interpersonal and interworld perception as the explanatory means for this development of a sense of 'self'.[11] How might the notion of flesh enrich our understanding of what goes on in the dynamic between 'leaders' and 'followers'?

'FLESH' AND LEADERSHIP: A WAY OF CONCEPTUALIZING THE SPACE BETWEEN 'LEADERS' AND 'FOLLOWERS'

One of the unanswered questions relational leadership theories pose is how the 'middle space' operating between leaders and followers might be conceptualized. I believe Merleau-Ponty's notions of 'reversibility' and 'flesh' can help us to approach this space in at least two ways. First, they point to the central role perception plays in leaders' and followers' understanding of one another. Second, they provide a means for understanding the way followers and leaders can remain distinctive and yet join in a co-constructed experience perceived as 'leadership'.

The Centrality of Perception

Through the notion of reversibility, we understand that 'leaders' and 'followers' not only continually perceive one another but also continually perceive themselves through the others' perceptions. The leadership dynamic is constantly in a process of co-construction occurring between these mutual perceptions. As 'leaders' see themselves through their 'followers'' gaze, they construct how they operate within the 'leader' role. Followers do likewise, creating their own ways of operating within the field of their perceptions and expectations of themselves intermingled with the way they experience themselves to be perceived through the gaze of those leading them.

Perhaps the strand of leadership literature which best speaks to this mutual construction of the dynamic between 'leaders' and 'followers' is grounded in social identity theory, introduced by writers such as Daan van Knippenberg and Alex Haslam.[12] An interesting notion at the core of their work is that 'leaders' must remain within a particular 'identity orbit' in order to remain viable as 'leaders' for particular groups. If a 'leader' moves outside of the bounds of a group's identity, they are no longer able to lead.

The manner in which Margaret Thatcher, Prime Minister of the UK from 1979–90, lost her role as leader of the Conservative Party illustrates this point. In opposition to many of her Cabinet members, Mrs Thatcher held a strong anti-European stance and wanted to maintain the UKs independence vis-à-vis European unity. Many commentators attribute the rather sudden way in which her leadership was challenged and toppled to the reluctance of her Cabinet in aligning themselves similarly with her anti-European views. She had moved outside their 'identity orbit' and could no longer effectively lead them.

The notion of 'reversibility' develops and extends a psychological explanation of how this occurred. If her Cabinet members had complied with Mrs Thatcher's stance, they would have had to accept self-perceptions of being 'anti-European'. This did not equate with their self-perceptions and thus they were no longer willing to accept Mrs Thatcher as their leader. 'Reversibility' suggests that 'leaders' know who they are through the eyes of 'followers' and, likewise, 'followers' can only know themselves as 'followers' through the eyes of their 'leaders'. When these perceptions jar against deeply held ego identities, the leader-follower connection can be severed.

The notion of 'reversibility' offers another reason for the difficulties associated with studying leadership explored in the previous chapter. The notion of 'reversibility' might also offer an explanation for the 'disappearance' of leadership noted by scholars such as Alvesson and Sveningsson in the previous chapter. We cannot hold *both* being perceived and perceiving at precisely the same instance. I can either experience my left hand touching my right hand or my right hand touching my left hand, I cannot perceive both simultaneously. Analogously, at the point where interactions between individuals constellate into 'leadership', there is a similar kind of 'slip' or disappearance.

'Leading hands'
The 'slip' that occurs between 'leaders' and 'followers' as they interact is illustrated by an exercise I regularly invite participants in leadership development programmes to try, called 'leading hands'.

In this exercise participants are invited to stand face-to-face with a partner. One person chooses to be 'A' and the other 'B' and they are given the instruction not to speak to one another for the duration of the activity.

In the first instance, 'A' is requested to act as 'leader' and 'B' as 'follower'. They are asked to place the backs of their hands together. Person 'A' is told to move the followers hand around, using only the back of their hands as their point of contact. Person 'B' closes their eyes and is told they should not lose contact from their partner's hand. At first the pairs often remain quite static and rooted to the ground but after awhile, people inevitably grow a bit more courageous and start walking with their partners, all the time maintaining contact through the backs of each others' hands. After a few minutes they are asked to reverse roles, so that Person 'B' now leads with their eyes open, and Person 'A' shuts their eyes and is led. When practicing this exercise, a hush often descends on the room as people pay close attention to their partners' movements and I often have to remind people to keep breathing!

After a while, when both people have had the opportunity to 'lead' and to 'follow', they are both invited to close their eyes. Now, neither 'A' or 'B' is the leader but the instruction is to continue to move around the room, keeping contact through the backs of each others' hands. This is always the most interesting stage of the exercise and the room often becomes even more silent as people concentrate on moving together despite both being 'blind'. In the many years in which I have used this exercise, no one has ever fallen over or even stumbled.

In their reflections on this activity, participants often talk about how in the third stage of the exercise, they are not sure who is leading and who is following. They talk about the relief they feel at no longer feeling responsible for the 'follower', and how instead, they felt themselves relinquish into something different from a sense of responsibility. Participants often remark on experiencing a flow of energy working between them, a kind of invisible exchange of leading and following. So far no pair has ever been able to articulate exactly how this happens. Somehow, the relationship has taken over, as a kind of mutually experienced and binding force. I wonder if it is this hard to articulate the kind of flow which is at the heart of a relational view of leadership?

I also wonder about the way in which the physical nature of the task foregrounds the field of energy which occurs between 'leaders' and 'followers' who might usually be more physically distant. In this exercise there is literally the reversibility of 'flesh' at play. Partners detect a myriad of sensory perceptions – nervousness, anxiety and excitement – through the way in which movement is executed. My guess is these perceptions are transmitted even when human beings are not touching and similarly contribute to the dynamic operating amidst the 'in-between space' of any relationship.

This simple exercise approaches the heart of 'relational leadership'. In the exercise, the relationship – the need to 'stick together' becomes the focus, rather than the enactment of distinct 'leader' and 'follower' roles. In this way the task becomes the 'invisible' leader, guiding how individuals relate to one another. How might these ideas inform the practice of leadership?

The story of Sacha

Sacha works for a professional services organization and had recently been promoted to the Board when he engaged me as his coach. The coaching was to focus on two particular areas in which he wanted to improve his performance: he wanted to feel able to make a more significant impact during Board meetings and he wanted to work on 'getting the best' from those who reported directly to him.

On first meeting Sacha, I was struck by the way he habitually held his body in what I perceived as a 'closed' manner. When he sat, his upper body often twisted slightly so that he did not look me directly in the eye but rather he met my gaze from a more sideways orientation. I remember thinking he appeared to be uncomfortable in this stance, as well as guarded. Interestingly, one of the ways he characterized his experience of being in Board meetings was that he often felt defensive and 'put on the spot'. However, he also knew himself to be someone who could 'pull the rabbit out of the hat' in his ability to conjure up truly innovative solutions to problems the Board was trying to solve. This self-perception was indeed confirmed through conversations with other Board-level members of the organization.

The challenges he was experiencing with his direct reportees largely concerned the under-performance of two key people. The majority of his staff were extremely able and conscientious about producing work to the necessary standard and on time, but these individuals habitually turned in work which needed re-working and which was also late. Sacha found his dealings with these two particularly frustrating and by the time we met, he felt he had exhausted his ideas about how to turn their performance around.

In coaching I often rely on my own 'felt sense' of how I might respond to the client were I in a work relationship with him or her. In this case I often experienced discomfort and ill-ease when with Sacha. His closed body position evoked the feeling that he might be withholding something from me. I also sensed that if I did not want to do something he was expecting, I would probably be able to produce enough excuses to avoid him confronting me directly about my underperformance.

Along with helping Sacha to find alternative ways of framing his involvement with the Board and his relationship with his reportees, we began to attend to the way in which Sacha habitually held his body. He experimented with a more open stance and he began practising breathing exercises which resulted in his feeling more secure and calm when in uncomfortable situations. From the new embodied vantage point, he began literally to 'see' the situations in which he was involved differently. From a more open physical stance, he could notice the power games playing out during Board meetings and he could see that they had little to do with him personally. He could perceive people's positioning and agendas as merely that, not personal attacks. This realization enabled him to relax and hold his own position with greater force and authority. As he began to present himself from a more grounded orientation, he noticed that the other Board members responded differently to him. They gave him more space to make his point and he began to feel that he could influence them without solely relying on his ability to produce stunning new ideas.

His more direct way of holding himself physically also impacted on his ability to interact effectively with his direct reports. Although this was not a 'magic bullet', just presenting himself differently altered his interactions with them. He reported that a number of them said that they had a better understanding of 'where he stood' and found it easier to work to his expectations. Significantly, he found himself more able and willing to inquire about how things were going during the course of work being prepared as well as to be more appreciative when good work was produced.

It could be argued that what is being highlighted here is merely a question of helping Sacha change his 'body language' and in a way that would be correct. However, the reason why body language is so important within interpersonal relationships is our bodies provide both the focus for perception and the conduit through which we perceive. The language of the body speaks to the critical role of perception in the intersubjective experience. The way we hold ourselves, our bodily reactions, our facial expressions, are critical because they convey the very basis of our means for understanding one another. Altering the way in which we use our body (as long as the change becomes 'who we are' rather than just being a 'pasted on' affectation) results in being perceived differently. As we are perceived differently, the notion of 'flesh' tells us that the dynamic between us and those who perceive us will also shift. This all happens subtly, at a level below conscious recognition.

Furthermore, without the accompanying shift in the language of the body, any cognitive reframing achieved will not result in substantive change in the interpersonal dynamic. If Sacha had reached the conclusion that political machinations during Board meetings were not to be taken personally but had continued to sit in a defensive stance, the 'in-between space' operating between him and the other Board members would correspondingly not have shifted. The 'in-between space' is substantially a product of the interplay of our physical perceptions of one another. This is the significance of the idea of 'flesh' as a concept for understanding the relationality at the heart of leader-follower dynamics. It highlights the fundamentally physical, perceptual dimension through which relationality occurs.

THE 'FLESH' OF LEADERSHIP

> Let us therefore consider ourselves installed among the multitude of things, living things, symbols, instruments, and men, and let us try to form notions that would enable us to comprehend what happens to us there. Our first truth – which prejudges nothing and cannot be contested – will be that there is presence, that 'something' is there, and that 'someone' is there. Before coming to the 'someone', let us first ask what the 'something' is (Merleau-Ponty 1968, p. 160).

So begins the final section of Merleau-Ponty's final work, *The Visible and the Invisible*. Prior to this point, he has taken us on a journey through a deconstruction of Cartesian ontology, he has demonstrated the intertwining of immanent and transcendent capacities within the human being and he has introduced a radical relationship between human beings and the world through his notion of 'flesh'. In the passage quoted above, he further illuminates the meaning of 'flesh' by indicating its progenitive capacity. 'Flesh' is that from which the possibility of experience itself springs. Without the interconnection which is made possible through the medium of 'flesh' a phenomenon like leadership could not exist.

The notion of 'flesh' additionally highlights the criticality of all three elements; 'leaders', 'followers' and 'the space in-between them' in constituting leadership. In this way, it offers a way of conceptualizing the relation created by the perceptual interpenetration of leaders and followers. Such a construction highlights that although the in-between space is completely dependent on the entities which constitute the relationship, that relationship has a dynamism which is more than just the combination of entities which comprise it. The interaction itself has a life of its own.

This idea points to the very sensitive and subtle nature of the 'in-between space'. By necessity it is constantly being co-constructed; constantly shifting as a result of the fluctuating perceptual field operating between leaders and followers. The idea of 'flesh' and how it operates within the leader-follower relationship poses the possibility of new questions concerning this relationship. For instance, from the perspective of a leader hoping to increase their power in a relationship, we might ask, 'How could leaders strengthen the "flesh" between themselves and their followers?'

It is interesting to hold this question in mind while thinking of the election campaign run by Barack Obama in the 2008 USA Presidential race. It is recognized that Obama used the Internet in unprecedented ways during his race for the White House. As a member of Democrats Abroad in the months running up to the election, I regularly opened my e-mail to find a message from the campaign with a link to a video featuring Obama seemingly speaking directly 'to me'! There he was at six o'clock in the morning telling me 'personally' about his plans for changing the way government is conducted in America. Many commentators noted the personal nature of the way in which the campaign was organized, with messages relayed to Democratic Party members at key points in the campaign, for example just before Obama accepted the Democratic Party's nomination and just after he had won enough electoral college votes to vanquish John McCain.

One way of thinking of this tactic was that it strengthened the 'flesh' operating between Obama and his supporters. He became a very present figure and this presence was further elaborated by 'behind the scenes' depictions of his family life and seemingly less-guarded moments on the election trail. Although these videos would have been carefully compiled and vetted, they gave the impression of letting us, his followers, 'know' him better. Similarly, our thoughts and ideas were canvassed through regular supporter questionnaires. The campaign was run in a way which continually worked to strengthen the 'in-between space' operating between Obama and his supporters.

Ways of strengthening the 'flesh' of leadership might be particularly useful in thinking about the leadership role during times of change. During periods of planned change 'leaders' must navigate a course between the unknown and the day-to-day realities of their 'followers' in a way which means 'followers' do not get left behind. The concept of 'flesh' provides a conceptual metaphor for understanding how 'leaders' might think about retaining connectivity between themselves and their 'followers' as they explore unchartered waters. If the 'flesh' is too thin, if it has not been built of stuff which will sustain the connection, they may well lose their 'followers' as they move forward. How might 'flesh' be 'fattened' so that it can maintain itself during testing times? This is perhaps where qualities such as 'trust' and 'inspiration' have a key role to play in building sustainable 'flesh' which links 'leaders' and 'followers'.

'Flesh' also alerts us to the way in which perception is completely embedded in particular places, historic times and cultures. Relationships arise out of the geographic, physical and energetic realms in which we operate as much as through interpersonal interactions. In this way, the 'orbit' which keeps 'leaders' and 'followers' in relationships to one another includes their history together, the culture in which they are embedded, as well as the particular moment in time in which leadership is enacted. All of these factors contribute to the 'flesh' of a particular leadership moment.

With this thought, we return full circle to the notion of the 'moment' introduced in Chapter 2. There I proposed that leadership might best be conceptualized as a 'moment' rather than as a 'whole' and as such is inextricably embedded in the specific context from which it arises. Perhaps 'flesh' provides an additional way of thinking of 'moments' and develops that concept further with its emphasis on constant co-construction. The 'flesh' of leadership is continually being created and disintegrated according to its location within time as well as within particularized cultural and historic contexts.

I like the concept of 'flesh' for two additional reasons. Firstly, the word itself connotes something material; something physical that one can touch and hold. In this way it locates leadership firmly within the physical realm of human relating. It encourages us to think of leadership as a 'fleshy thing', something that connects and arises between human bodies. I have experienced a visceral connection between myself and leaders I have followed which has seemingly enveloped all of us involved in a particular endeavour. Such an experience has fuelled my commitment to our project expressed through a willingness to work longer hours and give my best. The sense of electricity which passes between leaders such as Martin Luther King or Nelson Mandela as they address crowds is apparent. The connection is more than just rational; there is a visceral, bodily aspect to it. Maybe 'flesh' provides a construct which enables us to approach more closely what happens during such encounters. The book turns to precisely this area in the next chapter which looks at the question: 'What is charismatic leadership?'

NOTES

1. See Meindl, J.R. (1995), 'The romance of leadership as a follower-centric theory: a social-constructionist approach', *Leadership Quarterly*, **6** (3), 329–41.
2. The two philosophers are purported to have had somewhat of a tempestuous friendship and spent a number of years not speaking with one another at all towards the end of their lives. However, they are also thought to have had a deep respect for one another and one another's ideas. Some of the key ways in which Sartre's and Merleau-Ponty's philosophies differ are around their different ideas of embodiment and intersubjectivity. For further reading see Evans, F. and L. Lawlor (2000), *Chiasms: Merleau-Ponty's Notion of Flesh*, Albany: State University of New York Press, or Barbaras, R. (2004),

The Being of the Phenomenon: Merleau-Ponty's Ontology (T. Toadvine and L. Lawlor, trans.), Indianapolis: Indiana University Press.

3. There is a move in current neurological science which reduces these transcendent aspects of human capability materiality, see for instance: Armstrong, D. (1968), *A Materialist Theory of Mind*, London: Routledge and Kegan Paul; or Place, U. (1988), 'Thirty years on – is consciousness still a brain process?', *British Journal of Psychology*, **47**, 44–50.

4. Although this is often translated as 'I think therefore I am', a more accurate translation is probably, 'I know myself to be a thinking being'. This rendering is more consistent with Descartes' project within the larger project of his 'Meditations on First Philosophy' (1641 [1996], to identify knowing of which he could be completely certain.

5. This assumption is challenged by writers such as Amanda Sinclair and Arja Ropo, who recognize the embodied nature of leading in their work. For instance, see: Sinclair, A. (2005), 'Body possibilities in leadership', *Leadership*, **1** (4), 387–406; and Ropo, A. and J. Parviainen (2001), 'Leadership and bodily knowledge in expert organisations: epistemological rethinking', *Scandinavian Journal of Management*, **17** (1), 1–18.

6. For a fuller account of Merleau-Ponty's ideas about the intertwining of immanence and transcendence, see Dillon, M.C. (1997), *Merleau-Ponty's Ontology* (2nd edn), Evanston, ILL: Northwestern University Press.

7. This is perhaps straightforward to understand in human relations with other humans. Where it becomes more challenging perhaps, is to understand that Merleau-Ponty seemed to indicate that other 'things' perceive us as well. This is not, as Dillon (1997) suggests, to say that Merleau-Ponty believed that the trees had eyes. It is more that as a being in a world of beings, we stand in relation to other entities in such a way that they also become part of our way of knowing ourselves. Dillon explains: 'In the presence of trees, if I am sensitive to it, I can experience my being seen as I experience my being seen in the presence of an Other. The trees can function as the mirror that lets me experience my own visibility . . . the trees and I are made of the same stuff: flesh' (pp. 168–9).

8. This experience could similarly be explained by Michel Foucault's notion of 'disciplinary institutions' (1986) in which institutional structures and norms themselves exert influence over behaviors. Prior to Foucault's writing, the British philosopher and inventor Jeremy Bentham (1748–1832) had drawn on a similar idea in his conception of the Panopticon. The panopticon was a never-constructed spiral-shaped prison, in which all of the prisoners could be watched by a lone guard sitting on the ground floor.

9. Husserl introduces the notion of 'analogical apperception' in his *Cartesian Meditations* and this notion was subsequently developed by Merleau-Ponty in his own account of intersubjectivity. For a more thorough explanation, see Dillon, M.C. (1997), *Merleau-Ponty's Ontology* (2nd edn), Evanston, ILL: Northwestern University Press, pp. 116–17.

10. Merleau-Ponty believed there was not another concept within Western thinking that was like 'flesh' although subsequent writers have linked it to the 'Tao' in Confuscionism or 'Ma' in Japanese culture.

11. For a more detailed analysis of the overlap between Merleau-Ponty's ideas of flesh and human development, see Cataldi, S.L. (1993), *Emotion, Depth and Flesh: A Study of Sensitive Space,* Albany, NY: State University of New York Press.

12. For a further account of Social Identity Theory and its implications for leadership, see: van Knippenberg, D. and M.A. Hogg (2000), *Leadership and Power: Identity Processes in Groups and Organizations*, London: Sage; and Haslam, S.A. and S.D. Reicher (2007), 'Identity entrepreneurship and the consequences of identity failure', *Social Psychology Journal*, **70**, 125–47.

5.   What is charismatic leadership?

> The mind feels itself moved in the representation of the Sublime . . . whilst in aesthetical judgments about the Beautiful it is in restful contemplation. [The Sublime] is like an abyss in which Imagination fears to lose itself . . .
>
> Immanuel Kant
> *Critique of Judgement*
> (1790 [2005], p. 72)

Much of this chapter has been written during the USAs Presidential campaign of 2008. The final stage of that contest has been waged between a man acclaimed for the charisma of his oratory skills, Barack Obama, and an opponent whose appeal seems to rest more on his many years of experience and personal history as a prisoner of war, John McCain. Obama first appeared on the world stage as keynote speaker at the Democratic Convention held in Boston, MA, on 27 July 2004. His declaration, 'We are not white America, or Black America, we are the United States of America', excited the crowd and whispers of 'Presidential candidate' were first heard. Throughout the campaign, this young senator from Illinois was compared with other charismatic icons of American politics such as John F. Kennedy and Martin Luther King. Certainly, Obama's ability to attract record numbers of people to his rallies (200 000 in Berlin on 24 July 2008; 70 000 at the Democratic National Convention in Denver, CO in August 2008; where he took his party's nomination) has caused his opponents to liken him to a 'rock star' and celebrity, rather than as a serious politician.

That attribution itself expresses some of the ambivalence inherent in the experience of charisma. Is there real substance behind charismatic power? What about the dangers associated with it? After all, Adolf Hitler is also remembered as having charismatic presence. How essential is charisma to successful leadership? Questions such as these have been debated within the leadership literature since Max Weber first identified 'charismatic authority' as a source of power within bureaucracies. The organizational theorists who have developed Weber's ideas within managerial worlds have primarily analysed charisma as a behavioural or psychological phenomenon.

From the viewpoint of philosophy, we turn away from phenomenology to a different school of thought which focuses on the judgements we make about the quality of our perceptions and experiences; that of aesthetics. Aesthetics speaks to the 'felt sense' we have of interactions with other people and things. The philosophy of aesthetics concerns how human beings go about making judgements about what they perceive; for instance what makes us judge a rose to be beautiful but scrubweed ugly? Here I will explore the possibilities that thinking of leadership from an aesthetic perspective might offer.

In particular this chapter explores the notion of charisma as an aesthetic judgement. It begins by examining some of the current ways in which charismatic leadership has been theorized and highlights the questions these theories leave unanswered. It then introduces ideas from aesthetic theory drawn primarily from the Enlightenment philosopher Immanuel Kant and his *Critique of Judgement* (1790 [2005]). Kant's ideas about 'the sublime' are used to analyse charismatic leadership through comparing the election campaigns of Barack Obama and Hillary Clinton for the Democratic nomination in the USA General Election of 2008.

WEBER'S NOTION OF CHARISMA

Despite its psychological roots, much of the theorization which has been undertaken about charismatic leadership has occurred within the field of political science. Perhaps political leaders most visibly exercise charisma in the manner of taking up their role vis-à-vis large constituencies of followers. This work has its basis in Weber's theory of charismatic authority. It is useful to place this theory within the larger project in which Weber was engaged; that of analysing the role of authority in bureaucracies. In his books *The Theory of Social and Economic Organisation* (1924 [1947]) and *Economy and Society: An Outline of Interpretive Sociology* (1922 [1968]) Weber identified three pure sources of authority: the rational, the traditional and the charismatic.

In defining charismatic authority, Weber returns to the roots of the word charisma; 'gift'. In Weber's sense, charisma is literally a 'gift' from the Divine. This Divine endowment was seen to be 'extraordinary' and enabled its recipient to be perceived as having unusual abilities to influence and inspire others. For instance he writes:

> The term 'charisma' will be applied to a certain quality of an individual personality by virtue of which he is considered extraordinary and treated as endowed with supernatural, superhuman, or at least specifically exceptional powers or qualities. These are such as are not accessible to the ordinary person, but are regarded as of divine origin or as exemplary, and on the basis of them the individual concerned is treated as the 'leader' (Weber 1924 [1947], p. 241).

This definition is not far removed from the way charismatic leadership is described within leadership literature. In fact, much of the leadership literature tries to identify the particular behavioural characteristics which are indicative of the charismatic leader.

A second key aspect of Weber's theory of charismatic authority is the co-constructed aspect of it. Charisma is not charisma unless it is experienced to be so by *the other*. Furthermore, those recognized as having charismatic authority must continually prove to their followers that they retain the gift of the Divine, through the winning of battles and wars, and the general benevolence of Providence. As the conduit for Divine favour, if charismatic leaders somehow lose their power to meet followers' needs, likewise their charismatic power disperses. Although more contemporary theories of charismatic leadership may mention its co-constructed nature and the importance of followers in its attribution, there are rather fewer studies which explore this dimension seriously.

This leads to a final element of Weber's theory which is important here, that of the role of context. According to Weber, charisma arises out of specific contexts, namely those of crisis. Perhaps it is at these times that people acutely feel the need for Divine intervention. Throughout history it can be seen that such times almost 'conjure up' charismatic leaders. Examples such as Churchill's leadership during the Second World War or Gandhi's leadership as India fought for its survival as a nation independent of the UK illustrate the point. Once the situation becomes 'normalized', charismatic leaders are no longer needed and can be problematic in the routinized world of bureaucracy. In fact Weber pointed out the extent to which charismatic authority can be detrimental in the smooth running of organizations, be they nations or firms, once a crisis is past. Although this was a key aspect of Weber's rendering of charismatic authority, even less is seen within the broader leadership canon about the importance of context to the production of charismatic leadership.

Weber's ideas of charismatic authority do, however, inform much of the subsequent theorizing which has been done about charisma from an organizational studies' perspective. Some writers, such as Janice Beyer suggest that Weber's notions have been considerably 'tamed' within leadership literature, to the extent that charismatic authority is rendered 'much less extraordinary' than Weber's original accounts (Beyer 1999, p. 316). Beyer argues that maintaining a more accurate interpretation of Weber's theory implies that the occurrence of charisma within organizations is so rare that it probably should not even be a preoccupation of organizational theorists. The concept does, however, occupy a sizeable portion of the organizational leadership canon and it is worth outlining some of the key issues raised in that body of work.

CONTEMPORARY RENDERINGS OF CHARISMA

Since the 1980s there has been a wave of leadership theories which emphasize the inspirational aspects of leading epitomized perhaps by Bernard
Bass' theory of 'transformational leadership' (Bass 1985).[1] Charisma can
be seen to be at the heart of Bass' theory, in which the leader is seen not
only to influence followers to pursue idealized visions but also to alter the
way they see themselves as a result of aligning themselves with that vision.
The way in which this transformation occurs is through the four 'I's';
charismatic influence, inspirational motivation, individual consideration
and intellectual stimulation. In keeping with much of the theorizing about
charismatic leadership, Bass focuses most of his attention on the charismatic leader, him or herself, rather than considering in detail the roles
followers or, indeed, the context plays in the emergence of charismatic
leadership.

In fact, the preoccupation on the leader is common to the majority
of charismatic leadership theories, even those which note that 'followers' do have a notable role to play in the attribution of charisma. For
instance, two other theorists who have written extensively in this arena
are Jay Conger and Rabindra Kanungo, who agree that the assessment
of charisma is made by followers. However, they go on to identify four
behaviours enacted by charismatic leaders:

- Communicating a vision which has a high degree of discrepancy
  between the status quo and the future goals and vision of the
  leader;
- Utilizing innovation and unconventional means for achieving the
  desired change;
- Realistically assessing the environmental resources and constraints
  for change being achieved; and
- Articulating the message and using impression management in a
  way which inspires subordinates in pursuit of the vision (Conger and
  Kanungo 1987).

Here the focus of charismatic leadership remains on the leader, him or
herself. It is encompassed by behaviours: communicating in unconventional but inspiring ways, or differing from the status quo. But is that all
there is to it? Is it possible that leaders who articulate their purposes in
novel ways might not be considered charismatic?

In answer to that question there is a slim body of literature which
attends to the role followers play in the attribution of charisma as an
answer to this question. Writers such as Jane Howell and Boas Shamir

(2005) and Stuart Weierter (1997), pay particular attention to the role self-identity plays in the attribution of charisma on the part of followers. A notion proposed by Howell and Shamir is that if the leader is seen to match the followers' version of an idealized self, they are much more likely to attribute charisma to the leader (Howell and Shamir 2005).

Although such research makes an attempt to consider the complexity of the charismatic leadership dynamic, it remains based in a wholly rational psychologically determined realm of analysis. When I looked at the photographs of people gathered in Grant Park, Chicago to hear Barack Obama's Victory Speech in November 2008, it occurred to me that there might be something else going on between Obama and his supporters. There seems to be a visceral, embodied connection between the man and the crowds. More than that, the moment of his nomination seemed to resonate with strains from the past as well as anxieties of the present. It was almost impossible to watch Obama speak to the crowds without remembering Martin Luther King address similar crowds in Washington DC 45 years earlier. The present context too played its role in this moment. With two wars still being fought, unemployment rising and a number of major banks being bailed out by the Federal Government, citizens experienced a loss of confidence in their leaders on the world stage. Obama won the election on a ticket promising 'change', with the watchword of 'hope' always present. Could these contextual factors have a role to play in the election of the first mixed-race President? How might they contribute to the attribution of Obama as 'charismatic'?

Although I was pleased that Obama was elected, I felt uneasy as well. This was particularly true when I listened to people talking about why they had voted for Barack Obama and their expectations of his leadership. Their high hopes I found both inspirational and a little frightening. Could an aesthetic analysis bring insight into this experience?

WHAT DOES 'AESTHETICS' HAVE TO DO WITH LEADERSHIP?

The aesthetic dimension of perception is the physically-based 'felt sense' we experience of other people, things, entities or our surroundings. It is the immediate bodily apprehension of what we perceive, informed first and foremost by physical, rather than intellectual, perception. Considering charismatic leadership through the lens of aesthetic perception might offer new insights into the paradoxical nature of charismatic leadership.

As a philosophical discipline, aesthetics has a long history; Plato wrote about the nature of 'the beautiful', as did the philosopher Plotinus before him. The Greek *Aisthitikos* from which the term 'aesthetics' is derived meant 'perception by feeling' and the American philosopher Susan Buck Morss points out that 'the original field of aesthetics was not about art, but about reality, corporeal, material, natural. [It was a] discourse of the body . . . a form of cognition, achieved through taste, hearing, seeing and smell' (1992, p. 6). In other words, aesthetic perception is informed not only through the rational, conscious part of ourselves but also from a more bodily, physically based sensitivity. Grounded in bodily awareness, it also often includes an emotional reaction and in this way combines the total felt apprehension of an object, situation or person. As such, the aesthetic content of our experience often operates at a level below alert consciousness but nonetheless informs the ways we relate with one another and our contexts.

For example, when a person first walks into a room their body picks up a myriad of sensory impressions. It will note the way the room is lit (harsh fluorescent lighting or soft pools of candle glow), the texture of the flooring (plush carpet or gritty concrete), the room's temperature and level of humidity. Eyes register the colours of the walls and the presence or absence of flowers, paintings and other decorative artefacts. All of these sensory perceptions combine to create an aesthetic impression of the space which will in turn evoke an emotional and kinaesthetic response.

As well as sensing aesthetic qualities, human beings themselves project aesthetic qualities. Think about it for a moment. When you meet someone for the first time, before they have the opportunity to 'do' anything, just being in their physical presence provides a plethora of sensory data. Our aesthetic apprehension of another is the immediate perception unconsciously transmitted by subtle cues which provoke an emotional, as well as rational, response. We note one another's level of physical energy, emotional states and styles of self-presentation even before we hear one another speak. Delivered between bodies, I would like to suggest that the information exchanged at an aesthetic level goes beyond that is usually attributed to 'body language'.

Before exploring that notion further, it is important to distinguish between the way the term 'aesthetic' is used here and its more colloquial meaning. The word 'aesthetic' is often used interchangeably with the notion of the 'beautiful'. We often say that something has an aesthetic appeal meaning that we find it to be beautiful. In this chapter the term conveys a much broader interpretation. Here the 'aesthetic' is used to denote any qualitatively felt apprehension. The argument extends to suggest that every perceptual encounter has an aesthetic aspect to it. The aesthetic is not necessarily always 'beautiful'. Our aesthetic sense alerts us to the 'ugly' as often as it might tell us that something is beautiful. In this way, the aesthetic takes into account the ugly, the distasteful, the comic, the wanton, the authentic – as well as the 'beautiful'.

Perhaps the word 'anaesthetic' conveys more about the aesthetic and what it means. We know an anaesthetic to be something that puts us to sleep, that which stops us from feeling. Anaesthetics deaden our perceptual awareness; most often to pain, which is very helpful when visiting the dentist. The necessity of having an anaesthetic alerts us to the possibility that without such an intervention, we are always feeling something. That felt sense, whether it is of pain or of ugliness or beauty, is what I am referring to as the aesthetic.

In leadership terms, the aesthetic judgement we make of a person taking up the leader role would be informed by our 'felt sense' of him or her. Their 'aesthetic' contributes to that almost immediate apprehension of what the person is like. It is the invisible yet very powerful bodily-informed, intuitive feeling we have about other people. In fact, we use it all the time. It plays a key role in the judgements we make about who to trust in the world and who not to trust. Those taking up leader roles might therefore usefully consider the quality of their aesthetic presence and the impact this might have on followers.

Charismatic leadership has a particular aesthetic quality. Although highly inspirational, this aesthetic often carries with it a darker side. Is there a particular aesthetic category which can explain charisma's paradoxical nature?

ENTER IMMANUAL KANT

Immanuel Kant's (1724–1804) *Critique of Judgement* (1790 [2005]) is a seminal text in how aesthetic qualities can be judged. In particular, the *Critique* focuses on the distinction between the 'beautiful' and the 'sublime' and it is his ideas about the 'sublime' which are particularly relevant to the experience of charismatic leadership. Before exploring that connection, it might be helpful to introduce Kant's aesthetic theory more fully.

Kant was an Enlightenment philosopher whose over-riding philosophical project was to demonstrate the supremacy of logical reason as a way of knowing. Aligned with this larger preoccupation, Kant's aesthetic theory presents a way of understanding aesthetic judgement from the perspective of the person making the aesthetic judgement. Earlier aesthetic theories often focused on the object of perception as that which determined its own aesthetic. In contrast to these theories, Kant's philosophical project was to demonstrate the observer's critical role in aesthetic experience. This is an aspect of his philosophy which is particularly relevant to an aesthetic rendering of charisma.

The argument presented here is rooted in the distinction Kant made between the aesthetic categories of the 'beautiful' and the 'sublime'. For Kant, in line with other philosophers before him, the 'beautiful' does not reside in the eye of the beholder. Rather, independent of human judgement, that which is 'beautiful' stands on its own accord. A number of factors contribute to beauty, including its form, 'Here it is not what gratifies in sensation but what pleases by means of its form' (Kant 1790 [2005], p. 45); its lack of purpose, 'Now when the question is if a thing is beautiful, we do not want to know whether anything depends or can depend on the existence of the thing either for myself or for anyone else' (ibid., p. 28); and most importantly, the feelings it evokes from those who contemplate it, 'The "Beautiful"' brings with it a feeling of the furtherance of life, harmony and contentment' (ibid., p. 61).

According to Kant, it is we who must train ourselves to identify the beautiful, rather than that beauty should conform to our ideals. We do this through developing 'taste', the ability to identify that which is truly beautiful. An important human capability which plays a role in developing such taste is the 'free play of the imagination'. This is the capacity to connect with another entity and respond emotionally to its qualities. For Kant, the imagination plays an important role in our assessment of aesthetic qualities. When we apprehend something, be it an orange, a cherry tree or a potential Presidential candidate, our imagination is that which allows us to connect with it. There is a kind of dialogic space between our own rationality and the thing we perceive. It is the imagination, Kant argues, which enables us to step out of our own situation and engage with something other than ourselves. Through the free play of the imagination, we allow ourselves to notice how we are moved by a thing, how it speaks to us and in this way we become aware of its aesthetic qualities.

When we encounter something which is beautiful, our imagination responds through evoking feelings of peacefulness and happiness. This is very different from engaging with something that evokes the 'sublime' aesthetic experience. According to Kant, the experience of the 'sublime' occurs when we apprehend something, be it a snow-capped mountain or a ferocious mountain lion, and its very apprehension is somehow 'too much' for our imagination to cope with. We are momentarily paralyzed by its enormity, strength or its superhuman qualities.

Through such an encounter we experience emotional disturbance. We feel threatened or overwhelmed. In extreme experiences, our very life can feel endangered. However, just before we are overwhelmed by the feeling of being out of control, Kant suggests that our rationality steps in. Our reason declares that we can indeed cope with the overwhelming phenomenon in some way. This reaffirmation of our mastery is then experienced as a sort of 'negative pleasure'. It is this feeling of 'negative pleasure', produced from the apprehension of a near-death experience followed by the reassertion of our own mastery, Kant calls the 'sublime'.

In this way the experience of the 'sublime' produces a kind of emotional 'edginess' which is absent from our experience of the beautiful. In fact, there are three key ways in which Kant differentiates the aesthetic experience of the 'sublime' from that of the 'beautiful':

- Something is determined to be sublime by reference to the perceiver, rather than through reference to the thing itself;
- The entity which is deemed to be sublime cannot be held within the imagination of the perceiver. It is 'other-worldly', terrifyingly vast or magical in a way that does not 'make sense' to the perceiver. The beautiful, on the other hand, can be contained by the imaginal capabilities of the perceiver; and
- The experience of the 'sublime' involves a sense of disturbance or 'negative pleasure', whereas that of the 'beautiful' is wholly pleasant.

Are there significant similarities between the aesthetic experience of the 'sublime' and that of charismatic leadership? Let us examine each of the above distinctions as a way of considering that question.

Firstly, the 'sublime' is an apprehension that originates in the perceiver, rather than in the thing which evokes it. Kant elaborates on this when he writes:

> . . . we express ourselves on the whole inaccurately if we term any object of nature sublime . . . the object lends itself to the presentation of sublimity discernable in the mind. For the sublime, in the strict sense of the word, cannot be contained in any sensuous form, but rather concerns ideas of reason . . . [It is] the disposition of soul evoked by a particular representation engaging the attention of the reflective judgement, and not the object, that is to be called sublime (1790 [1952], p. 25).

In other words, it is because of the perceiver's ability to reason that the 'sublime' is experienced. The perceiver encounters something which is more than his or her imagination can deal with and at the point of feeling completely overwhelmed by it, reason steps in and reasserts that the person can indeed cope. A story I have recounted elsewhere (Ladkin 2005) tells of one of my favourite depictions of the 'sublime' in a cartoon strip known as 'Calvin and Hobbs' created by Gary Waterson. In the strip I am referring to, Calvin, who is a young boy, looks out into the vastness of the night sky over the first few frames. In the final frame, he shouts out into the darkness, 'I am TOO significant!!' In the moment of declaring his own significance in the face of the overwhelming experience of the night sky, Calvin is having an experience of the 'sublime'!

If we interpret charismatic leadership in terms of this analysis, this aspect of the 'sublime' (that its experience originates from the perceiver rather than from that which is perceived) places the follower in *the* critical position vis-à-vis charismatic leadership. The experience of charisma would analogically rest within the 'follower' rather than within the 'leader'. Analysing charisma in this way goes further than leadership theories which propose that charisma is attributed by 'followers'. Indeed it suggests that charismatic leadership is something experienced by followers and the leader who evokes such a response may necessarily share the felt sense of a charismatic encounter.

However, what is inducing the experience of the 'sublime' if the 'sublime' is equated with charisma? Is it the leader him or herself? Kant says that in order to experience the 'sublime', the perceiver must encounter something that is initially overwhelming. For instance, Kant writes:

> . . . the sublime . . . is ill adapted to our faculty of presentation, and to be, as it were, an outrage to our imagination, and yet it is judged to be all the more sublime on that account . . . it is rather in chaos, or in the wildest and most irregular disorder and desolation, provided it gives signs of magnitude and power that . . . excites the idea of the sublime (1790 [1952], p. 23).

Following on from this, in the case of a charismatic leader, is it the leader who is perceived as overwhelming or does something else evoke this response? Referring back to Weber's writings, we note the importance of context in the experience of charisma. Charismatic authority is not necessary when things are going well and there is no reason to alter the status quo. However, during times of overwhelming change when issues of life or death are uppermost, charismatic authority comes to the fore. Accordingly it is not only the gifts of the Divine which determine whether or not a leader is seen to be charismatic; context also plays a vital role.

In this way both the experience of the 'sublime' and the experience of charisma can be seen to be generated by circumstances which are perceived to be extreme. In much of the charismatic leadership literature, an often utilized behaviour of charismatic leaders during such times is to communicate high expectations and confidence in their followers. Theorists in the field such as Jane Howell and Boas Shamir (2005), note the extent to which charismatic leaders 'continually refer to followers' worth and efficacy in exemplary and symbolic behaviours' (p. 99). Through the lens of the 'sublime', such action could be used as a means of calling forth the reasoning capacity of followers to address the overwhelming situation in which they find themselves.

The 'yes we can' mantra of Obama supporters could be seen to fulfil precisely such a function. Throughout his campaign, Obama declared that the possibility of his candidacy was not just about him, it was largely about the times in which United States citizens found themselves. From the moment he won the first primary in Iowa, he told cheering crowds that 'this victory was not about me, it is about you'. From the point of view of charismatic leadership literature, this can be seen as fulfilling the function of communicating high expectations and confidence in his followers. From the lens of the aesthetic experience of the 'sublime', Obama's rhetoric could be seen as an attempt to call forth the rational powers of his followers to help them see that they did not have to submit to the seemingly overwhelming issues facing them. Although Kant explains the process as one in which rationality plays a key role, the *experience* is highly emotional, as can be gathered by looking at the photos of rapturous Obama supporters when they heard he had won the election.

Finally, it is important to consider the third way in which the 'sublime' differs from the 'beautiful' in Kant's rendering and see how it might apply to the experience of charismatic leadership. Kant claims that an important way in which the 'sublime' differs from the beautiful, is that in the experience of the beautiful, the emotion that is generated is wholly positive. It is one of contentment and happiness. In the experience of the sublime, although there may be a sense of relief or even a sense of 'thrill', this is also accompanied by a feeling of disquiet or unease. Similarly, there is a good deal of literature which suggests there is a corresponding feeling of unease which often accompanies the experience of charismatic leadership.[2] Does this feeling stem from the same source in both the experience of the 'sublime' and that of charisma?

Returning to Weber's account of charismatic leadership in his later writings (1924 [1947]), Weber draws attention to the alternation between states of pleasure and unease which accompany the charismatic encounter. He hypothesizes that this arises from the high degree of identification the follower has with the leader and the sense of self-annihilation this generates in the follower. In order to escape from this overwhelming and unpleasant feeling, the individual identifies even more strongly with the leader resulting in a renewed feeling of pleasure. However, this is short-lived as the sense of annihilation returns. Weber suggests that this sense of identity and loss of identity can vacillate in an ungrounded manner and is at the heart of the charismatic leadership dynamic. It also suggests that there is something inherently unstable about charismatic authority.

We have already examined the source of negative pleasure which Kant associates with the 'sublime'. However, on close examination this analysis suggests there is a different source from which the feelings of pleasure arise. In Weber's theorization of charismatic authority, the source of pleasure arises from identification with the leader which necessarily results in a loss of the sense of self. In contrast, with the experience of the 'sublime', pleasure arises as a result of the perceivers' realization that they can cope with the overwhelming situation. The experience of the 'sublime', as offered by Kant, empowers the perceiver whereas in Weber's theorization of charisma, the 'follower' necessarily loses a sense of his or her own agency and capacity and forfeits it to identify with that of the 'leader'.

This distinction might have an important explanatory role in distinguishing between generative and degenerative forms of charisma. For instance, Jane Howell (1988) has offered the ideas of 'personalized' and 'socialized' charisma as a way of distinguishing between charismatic leadership which is characterized by self-aggrandizement and self-centred ends and that which is used to serve generative purposes. Following from this, the analysis of charisma as a sublime aesthetic encounter suggests that if the leader works to awaken 'followers' to their own agency and sense of power, this is indicative of engagement with the 'sublime'. Whereas 'leaders' who use their power primarily to evoke identification from their 'followers' and their resulting lack of empowerment could produce a different aesthetic experience.

In summary, there are significant similarities between Kant's theorization of 'the sublime' and Weber's ideas of charismatic authority. Both are generated within circumstances which are experienced as overwhelming, chaotic or extreme to those involved. The encounter with both evokes feelings of discomfort and 'edginess'. Both Kant and Weber point to the experience being one that arises from extreme conditions. In the case of the charismatic leader however, an individual is recognized as being a channel for Divinely-bestowed gifts which enable his or her followers to deal with difficult circumstances. This differs from the realization of the 'sublime', in which an individual is faced with an overwhelming situation and finds through the power of their own rationality the ability to cope with it. The two experiences could work together if, when faced with a crisis situation, the leader would encourage his or her followers to access their own resources to overcome difficult situations.

Let us examine how the sublime and charisma could interact more closely. Seen as a manifestation of the 'sublime', the experience of charismatic leadership is clearly situated within followers' perceptual fields. They are the ones who judge a situation to be critical (either consciously or subconsciously) and experience a leader's response as providing a means of coping with it. This analysis also intimates how degenerative and more wholesome forms of charisma might be enacted. If the 'leader' uses his or her power to bring 'followers' to a greater appreciation of their own power and ability to deal with difficult situations, this is aligned with the 'sublime' aesthetic experience. If instead, the 'leader's' influence is used to encourage a loss of the 'followers' agency through over-identification with the 'leader's' power, this is not sublime but more akin to the aesthetic categories of the 'ugly' or in worst cases, the 'sadistic'.

CHARISMA IN ACTION: HILLARY CLINTON VS BARACK OBAMA

This section explores how the sublime and charismatic interrelate by considering the different aesthetic qualities Hillary Clinton and Barack Obama brought to the USAs Democratic Primary Election in 2008.

Since giving the keynote speech at the Democratic Convention in 2004, Barack Obama has been hailed in the media as charismatic, inspiring; almost Messianic. In contrast, his main opponent for the Democratic nomination in the 2008 election, Hillary Clinton, has been characterized as hard working, focused and supremely determined but too emotionally distant to be classed as charismatic. How do each of them create the impressions ascribed to them? Why might charisma have won the day in this particular Primary Election campaign? How might analysing charisma through the aesthetic of the 'sublime' shed additional light on their contest?

Understanding the Context: the Electoral Process in the USA

In the USA, Presidents are elected every four years and can only hold two terms in office. Presidential candidates are selected by the two major political parties, the Democrats and the Republicans, through what are called primary elections. As a result of these elections, one candidate is selected to represent that party in the General Election held in November every four years.

The Primary Elections are organized at a state level and the majority of these occur between January and June in the year of the General Election. Registered members of each party vote for their preferred candidate and, based on the numbers of people voting for each, voting delegates are awarded to candidates. At this stage in the Presidential Election, there are often a number of candidates vying to be their party's choice of Presidential candidate. In the spring of 2008, there were three main Democratic hopefuls, Hillary Clinton, senator from New York and former First Lady; Barack Obama, senator from Illinois; and John Edwards, senator from North Carolina.

In the early months of 2008, all the pundits put their money on Hillary Clinton winning the primaries and being the Democratic nomination to go forward to the General Election. However, in the first primary held in Iowa, Barack Obama staged a startling win. In fact, Clinton only came in third, after both Obama and Edwards. She was able to regroup and capture the next primary held in New Hampshire. However, Obama proceeded to win in South Carolina, Virginia, Maryland and the District of Columbia. Hillary struck back by taking her home state of New York and the key states of Ohio and Pennsylvania. After a prolonged and often bitter battle, Obama emerged as the candidate with the most votes from delegates, the greatest popular vote, and the largest number of 'super delegate' endorsements[3] and took the party's nomination during its Convention held in Denver, Colorado in August 2008. He then went on to win the General Election, defeating the Republican candidate John McCain.

Ostensibly, Obama should not have stood a chance against the political machinery of Clinton's campaign. Coming into the primary elections, she had access to far larger financial reserves, more political connections and a record which included six years of Senate experience during which she had worked on high-placed committees. Additionally, she enjoyed the high visibility she had gained as First Lady during Bill Clinton's years in office. Obama on the other hand, was a junior member of the Senate, had not proven himself on the world stage and is of mixed-race origin (his father was Kenyan, his mother of European descent from Kansas). Despite these obstacles, Obama's campaign prevailed.

Much of the media focused on the role 'personal style' played in the assessment of the two candidates (largely attributed to the view that there was very little discernable difference between their proposed policies). In particular, the media often characterized Obama as 'exciting and charismatic', where Clinton was more regularly depicted as 'hard working' and 'reliable'. On what were these assessments based and how might they have influenced the election?

Here, one key area in which both candidates regularly performed will be examined and analysed; that of speech giving. Of course there are many other arenas in which a political candidate's aesthetic performance might be judged. However, speeches are a particular platform from which they frame their reading of the context and express their agendas for dealing with it. In the analysis I will attend particularly to the texts of speeches, rather than considering the tone in which they were delivered or the body language employed when speaking. Although the experience of charisma is generated by much more than just the spoken word, the analysis of how each constructed their 'style' will begin with the narrative each attempted to convey. Even though the identical text could be read in a dull and boring manner and not catch listeners' attention, let alone their imagination, these narratives lay the foundation for what might be considered a charismatic encounter.

Two aspects of Clinton and Obama's narratives are studied: the way in which each candidate frames the context in which the election was taking place and the nature of the leader-follower relationship each candidate constructs.

Framing the Context

The speeches that both Clinton and Obama gave after the New Hampshire Primary Election on 9 January 2008 will be the focus of the first analysis. This was a critical point in the campaign. Clinton had come in third behind both Obama and Edwards in the previous Iowa caucus. Losing New Hampshire as well would have indicated her campaign was in very serious trouble. In fact, Clinton won the New Hampshire Primary by 39 per cent as compared to the 36 per cent of voters Obama attracted.

Clinton began her victory speech by announcing:

> In the last week I've listened to you, New Hampshire, and in the process I've found my own voice.

She then went on to say:

> I felt like we all spoke from our hearts, and I am so gratified that you responded. Now, together, let's give America the kind of comeback that New Hampshire has just given me.
>
> For all the ups and downs of this campaign, you helped remind everyone that politics isn't a game. This campaign is about people, about making a difference in your lives, about making sure that everyone in this country has the opportunity to live up to his or her God-given potential. That has been the work of my life.
>
> We are facing a moment of so many big challenges.
>
> We know we face challenges here at home, around the world, so many challenges for the people whose lives I've been privileged to be part of.
>
> I've met families in this state and all over our country who've lost their homes to foreclosures, men and women who work day and night but can't pay the bills and hope they don't get sick because they can't afford health insurance, young people who can't afford to go to college to pursue their dreams.
>
> Too many have been invisible for too long. Well, you are not invisible to me.[4]

Before commenting on this text, let us look at what Obama said in response to Clinton's win:

> There is something happening when men and women in Des Moines and Davenport, in Lebanon and Concord, come out in the snows of January to wait in lines that stretch block after block because they believe in what this country can be.
> There is something happening. There's something happening when Americans who are young in age and in spirit, who've never participated in politics before, turn out in numbers we have never seen because they know in their hearts that this time must be different.
> There's something happening when people vote not just for the party that they belong to, but the hopes that they hold in common.
> And whether we are rich or poor, black or white, Latino or Asian, whether we hail from Iowa or New Hampshire, Nevada or South Carolina, we are ready to take this country in a fundamentally new direction.
> That's what's happening in America right now; change is what's happening in America.
> You, all of you who are here tonight, all who put so much heart and soul and work into this campaign, you can be the new majority who can lead this nation out of a long political darkness.
> Democrats, Independents and Republicans who are tired of the division and distraction that has clouded Washington, who know that we can disagree without being disagreeable, who understand that, if we mobilize our voices to challenge the money and influence that stood in our way and challenge ourselves to reach for something better, there is no problem we cannot solve, there is no destiny that we cannot fulfill. Our new American majority can end the outrage of unaffordable, unavailable health care in our time. We can bring doctors and patients, workers and businesses, Democrats and Republicans together, and we can tell the drug and insurance industry that, while they get a seat at the table, they don't get to buy every chair, not this time, not now.
> Our new majority can end the tax breaks for corporations that ship our jobs overseas and put a middle-class tax cut in the pockets of working Americans who deserve it.
> We can stop sending our children to schools with corridors of shame and start putting them on a pathway to success.
> We can stop talking about how great teachers are and start rewarding them for their greatness by giving them more pay and more support. We can do this with our new majority.[5]

Both candidates note the difficulties facing the USA. Each uses this framing in a different way however. Clinton's language is 'up close and personal'. She speaks of the day-to-day difficulties people are having: losing their homes, not being able to afford medical care. The canvas that Obama paints is altogether much broader and further reaching. He pronounces that 'something significant is changing' and furthermore it can continue to change. His vision is one of unity and the end of the kind of political infighting which is not in the best interests of the people.

Obama portrays the degree of change required as fundamental and radical. He describes the era as a 'crossroads'. Clinton is just not as radical in her framing of the context. Times are hard for many people, she pronounces, but that difficulty is described as local, particular and relatively straightforward to 'sort out'. In other words, Obama presents a situation which is potentially 'overwhelming', of huge historic importance, whereas Clinton suggests 'there is much that is wrong' but it is all 'fixable'.

In Obama's other speeches, for instance in the 'A More Perfect Union' speech delivered in Philadelphia on 18 March 2008, he draws a vivid picture of the 'American journey'; interweaving images of pioneers leaving hostile lands to establish new lives for themselves in the 'promised land' of America, slaves contributing sweat, blood and their lives to the building of historic monuments and his own grandmother making racist remarks about black men. His depictions link the lives of ordinary Americans to mythological stories of human journeying. Additionally, he connects those icons and moments with today, suggesting that we too are living in historic times, times that others will look back on in awe and wonder. In doing so, he seems to place the follower in critical place of importance.

The very landscape which Obama evokes is panoramic, far reaching, and our place within it of historic importance. This is the stuff of the 'sublime' aesthetic. Additionally, the way in which he invites his supporters into his dream also resonates with Kantian thinking about how the experience of the 'sublime' is realized.

Engaging Followers

One of the most striking ways in which Obama and Clinton differ is in how they attempt to engage with followers. Obama's campaign message is almost completely devoted to the rhetoric of 'we'. Visitors to the Barack Obama website are instantly met by the quote, 'I'm asking you to believe ... not just in my ability to bring about real change in Washington ... I'm asking you to believe in yours'.[6]

Emphasis on his followers and their capabilities is a recurring theme throughout Obama's speeches. As early as his announcement of his candidacy in February 2007, he declared:

> We all made this journey for a reason. It's humbling but in my heart I know you didn't come here just for me, you came here because you believe in what this country can be.

> In the face of fear, you believe there can be peace. In the face of despair, you believe there can be hope. In the face of politics that's shut you out, that's told you to settle, that's divided us for too long, you believe we can be one people, reaching for what's possible, building the more perfect union.

In marked contrast, Clinton's speeches constantly refer to 'I'. The critical message operating through the primary contests was that she was the one with the most experience and as such she would be ready to be Commander-in-Chief from the first day of her Presidency. For instance, in a speech at Youngston, Ohio in February 2008 she asserted:

> What we need is a President who is ready on day one; ready to manage the economy, ready to be Commander-in-Chief in a dangerous world where there are always new threats and possibilities. I've visited over eighty countries, I've served on the Armed Services Committee, I've stood up to the Chinese government and said women's rights are human rights.

Often, when she mentions the American people, she focuses on the troubles they have had during the previous eight years, particularly in terms of being ignored by politicians in Washington. She promises to be a different kind of President, saying in her victory speech in New Hampshire:

> I intend to be that President, who puts your lives, your children first. I believe deeply in America. I believe deeply in what we can do together. There will be no more invisible Americans; we are in it for the American people, to deliver.

Although she uses the word 'we' here, she seems to mean, 'I'. Much of her campaign seems to have been built on her trying to convince the electorate that she, in fact, was the 'one' to lead the nation and that if she were elected, she would just get on and do so.

By framing the current situation America faces as a crisis and by then exhorting his supporters that they are the ones who can do something about it, Obama seems to neatly fulfil two key aspects of the 'sublime'. Clinton, on the other hand, characterizes the moment as one of deep troubles but these troubles are attributable to the refusal of those in Washington to recognize them and sort them out. She will be different, she declares, in that she both sees the troubles – 'I know what is happening in America' she asserts in her victory speech in New Hampshire – and she is willing to put the hard work in to make things change. In contrast, Obama's message suggests Americans themselves can contribute to changing history.

Physical Aesthetic

A final aspect of the aesthetic dimension of Clinton and Obama's performances to attend to is the way each presents themselves physically. Although Kant's theory of the 'sublime' does not strictly address this factor, the physical dimension is a key facet of a leader's aesthetic presentation. Ironically, although the embodied aspect of leadership is rarely considered, the fundamental way in which each of these two candidates is embodied (Obama as a man of mixed-race ethnicity and Clinton as a woman) is central to their identities within this election. Beyond Obama's race and Clinton's gender, there are other ways in which each uses their body which contributes to judgements made about them from an aesthetic perspective.

Tall and slim, Obama's early descriptions of himself pointed to his 'funny looks' and 'sticky-out ears'. He has likened his gawkiness to that of Abraham Lincoln and has repeatedly emphasized other connections between himself and this iconic President. Although his speeches incorporate high-flying narrative and historic images, his delivery is often measured and controlled. Benedict Nightingale, a writer for the UKs *The Times* newspaper, notes this when he writes:

> There's astonishing little of the actor about Barack Obama, and that is meant as a compliment. He doesn't soar or reach for rhetorical climaxes.
> He doesn't twist his audience's heartstrings even when he's talking of matters close to his heart. When he speaks of his wife or his 'precious daughters' there's no throb in his voice. And does this make him bland or dull? Quite the opposite.
> Somehow he has mastered the art of conveying feeling, strong feeling, without seeming emotionally manipulative. He stands there in his sober suit. His voice is firm, his body-language surprisingly still (Nightingale 2008, p. 5).

One of the tightropes Obama had to walk throughout the campaign was how to present himself in a way which would engage both black and white voters. There is a more typically 'African-American' style of delivery informed by the preaching tradition exemplified by the Reverend Martin Luther King and the Reverend Jesse Jackson. Obama's style may hint at these roots, without overtly depicting them. Achieving a balance which could attract both white and black voters was raised as an issue throughout his campaign. For instance, early reactions from black voters included those who reported to feel Obama was not 'black' enough to represent them.

In contrast Clinton faced her own challenges about how to present herself physically. The most striking example of the precariousness of her self-presentation was illustrated by an incident which occurred on the campaign trail in New Hampshire, subsequently known as 'Hillary's Tears'. After losing the Iowa Primary she was asked by a sympathetic woman supporter how it was that she kept going, despite the setback. When she responded, Clinton's voice cracked and her eyes ever so slightly welled-up. For a very brief moment, she seemed to waver emotionally. She very quickly regained her composure and carried on to answer other questions.

The media leapt on this brief lapse in Clinton's emotionally cool presentation. Of most interest in terms of this analysis is how this incident was subsequently interpreted by those who witnessed it. 'At last,' reported some, 'we are actually seeing the "real" Hillary Clinton – she actually has emotions underneath her steely calm' and this was interpreted favourably. Others berated her, 'If she cries over losing, how will she react when something really terrible happens'. There was even speculation about the extent to which this momentary lapse was actually 'staged' in order to win sympathy and support. (In fact she did go on to win the New Hampshire Primary, a win which has been credited to this incident.)

The resulting debate speaks to the difficulties faced by women taking up 'leader' roles in terms of how they might successfully embody those roles. Theorists such as Joyce Fletcher have pointed out that women leaders face the difficulty of being perceived as too 'feminine' and thus not able to withstand the difficult tasks associated with leading. Paradoxically, if they are perceived as being too 'tough' they can face the criticism of not being 'womanly' enough (Fletcher 2004). Furthermore, as the first serious female contender for the Presidential nomination of a major political party, Hillary Clinton had no previous role models to emulate. Although Barack Obama was the first mixed-race candidate, he could still align himself with other males who had previously held the job such as Abraham Lincoln or John F. Kennedy. Hillary Clinton had to forge her own aesthetic embodiment of a potential female President.

The difficulties associated with forging this aesthetic identity are apparent in the often harsh media commentary on Clinton's presentation. Daisy and Elena Grewel (2008) note this predicament when they write:

> Hillary Clinton won't be the last to face these problems. Angela Merkel of Germany and Segolene Royal of France have run similar gauntlets. Perhaps what distinguishes Clinton is her acute awareness of her predicament. To keep her image more feminine, she has changed hairstyles, suits – and even political opinions – in order to carefully maneuver around the gender-rooted obstacles in her way. Her critics have dissected each move, taking them as proof of her ruthless ambition.
>
> Whether we love her or hate her is not really the issue. Clinton's image in the

press has become like a distorted reflection. For some, she reflects the hopes that one day a woman will lead; for others she reflects a dangerous trend of women trying to usurp power from men. Regardless of whether she wins the Democratic nomination, her candidacy has already challenged us to clarify our definitions of what makes a good leader and to understand the pervasive role of gender stereotypes.[7]

In other words, there is almost always aesthetic ambivalence associated with women embodying the role of 'leader'. Interestingly, in her book about political leaders and charisma, *The Spell Binders* (1984), Ann Ruth Willner notes that throughout history, there have been very few female leaders who would be classified as 'charismatic' and those that have been often enjoy strong links to charismatic men.

Perhaps likening the charismatic to the sublime sheds new insight on why that might be the case. If the 'sublime' is experienced by a situation being perceived as overwhelming, it could be argued that women might not want to present a situation in such overpowering terms, for fear of being considered too 'soft' (by virtue of gender) to cope with it. A woman might more easily be seen to be competent at succeeding in a situation which is perceived as being difficult but 'fixable' through hard work and determination – much like the way in which Clinton construed the context of the 2008 Primary Election. Furthermore, women are also seen as 'soft' if they use too empowering a style. Perhaps almost to counter this prejudice, Clinton over-emphasized her own competence and ability to be Commander-in-Chief. Obama, on the other hand could engage the rhetoric of participation and 'we' because as a man this would not be perceived as self-deprecating.

Rather than pursuing this analysis from the gender perspective any further, in order to show how this analysis might be used more generally, the chapter will consider how another US President known for his charisma, John F. Kennedy, might be analysed through the lens of the aesthetic. By contrasting the aesthetic of Kennedy with that of these two Democratic politicians of the early twenty-first century, I will also explore the extent to which aesthetic is a product of a certain period of time.

KENNEDY AS CHARISMATIC LEADER

Like Obama, the 35th President of the USA, John F. Kennedy, was renowned for his powerful oratory skills and ability to deliver speeches of great vision and influence. Elected President in November 1960, he was the second son of a wealthy Irish-Catholic family from Boston. His father, Joseph Kennedy Senior, harboured political aspirations for his eldest son, Joe Jr, who was killed during a military operation in 1944. These aspirations were transferred to his next eldest son, John. John also served his country in the war effort and most notably was awarded the Navy and Marine Corps Medal for the 'extremely heroic conduct' he exercised in rescuing fellow servicemen from the water after their patrol boat had been sunk by a Japanese warship.

Kennedy campaigned against Richard Nixon in the General Election and won it on a campaign of newness and change. His predecessor as President was General Dwight Eisenhower, a hero of the Second World War. In his relative youthfulness and near aristocratic family connections, Kennedy embodied energy and glamour, a heady combination in the aftermath of the war years.

The world in the early 1960s was not enjoying a completely calm post-war period. A combination of factors, including the rise of the Soviet Union and the threat of nuclear war contributed to the perception of this as a time of uncertainty and threat. In schools, children rehearsed their response to nuclear attacks and many families constructed bomb shelters in their backyards. It could be argued that almost any period of history has its threats. However, having only recently deployed the nuclear bomb in Japan, the reality of this colossal menace to the very continuity of life on the planet was particularly present during these years.

Into this context arose Kennedy. His election in 1960, the closest in the contemporary history of USA Elections, was won against Richard Nixon who had served under Eisenhower as Vice-President. Like Obama, Kennedy embodied change in his very being; he was the first Roman Catholic to be elected as well as being the first President born in the twentieth century.

Kennedy is remembered for a number of notable speeches. Here I focus on two: his 'Moonshot' speech and his inaugural speech. These will be treated to the same analysis conducted on Obama and Clinton's speeches earlier; with special attention paid to the way in which Kennedy framed the context within which he was speaking and the type of relationship his rhetoric aimed to create with his followers. The 'Moonshot' speech is particularly significant in its illustration of the former. In this speech, given at Rice University, Houston, Texas in 1962, Kennedy challenged the nation:

> We meet in an hour of change and challenge, in a decade of hope and fear . . .
>
> We set sail on this new sea because there is new knowledge to be gained, and new rights to be won, and they must be won and used for the progress of all people. For space science, like nuclear science and all technology, has no conscience of its own. Whether it will become a force for good or ill depends on man, and only if the United States occupies a position of pre-eminence can we help decide whether this new ocean will be a sea of peace or a new terrifying theatre of war. I do not say that we should or will go unprotected against the

hostile misuse of space any more than we go unprotected against the hostile use of land or sea, but I do say that space can be explored and mastered without feeding the fires of war, without repeating the mistakes that man has made in extending his writ around this globe of ours.

There is no strife, no prejudice, no national conflict in outer space as yet. Its hazards are hostile to us all. Its conquest deserves the best of all mankind, and its opportunity for peaceful cooperation many never come again. But why, some say, the Moon? Why choose this as our goal? And they may well ask why climb the highest mountains? Why, 35 years ago, fly the Atlantic? Why does Rice play Texas?

We choose to go to the Moon. We choose to go to the Moon in this decade and do the other things, not because they are easy, but because they are hard, because that goal will serve to organize and measure the best of our energies and skills, because that challenge is one that we are willing to accept, one we are unwilling to postpone, and one which we intend to win, and the others, too.[8]

Could there be an aspiration with any greater mythological pull than the quest to put a man on the Moon? Being the first nation to land a man on the Moon would be a decisive move in winning the 'race for space', being waged between the USA and the Soviet Union. Although at the time President Kennedy stressed the importance of winning that contest in the needs of national security (in one noteworthy passage which would echo down the decades he refers to stopping other nations from placing 'weapons of mass destruction' in the heavens), in retrospect the symbolism of achieving such a goal seems to trump its means of securing national security.

The 'Moonshot' idea speaks to the 'sublime' in a palpable way. We gaze at this closest celestial neighbour each night, at once distant but somehow perpetually connected with us through the ocean tides, through notions of being 'Moonstruck'. There is perhaps not another celestial destination with as much pull, literally or mythologically, on the human imagination.

By setting a Moon landing as a goal for the USA, Kennedy told Americans that they were children of a different God from that of the Soviet Union. It was an outlandish goal divorced from the day-to-day realities of a messy military involvement in a jungle on the other side of the world or the Civil Rights battles brewing at home. Crazy as it was, it provided a common purpose under which the USAs disparate colours could unite. It framed the context as one of extraordinary possibility, a true turning point for all of human kind.

At a different level, the 'Moonshot' is an almost purely aesthetic aspiration. Placing a human being on the Moon is a dream that touches into man's deepest desire to understand the secrets of the cosmos. In that way it is perhaps reminiscent of Calvin's cry of significance into the night sky. It calls forth the sublime aesthetic experience in suggesting that such a feat could be achieved. This leads to the second aspect of the analysis – how did Kennedy engage with followers?

Like Obama, much of Kennedy's rhetoric exhorted his followers to appreciate their own power within the American political system. A key line from his inaugural speech on the 20 January 1960 challenged Americans to: 'Ask not what your country can do for you, ask what you can do for your country.'

In this speech Kennedy spoke rarely of 'I'. Instead, he exhorted the people of the USA to take up their power and create the country as they would have it. In this way, he induced the rhetoric of the 'we' in a way very similar to Barack Obama. In particular, he emphasized the responsibility of the new generation to take up the flame of liberty his election signalled, saying: 'The torch has been passed to a new generation of Americans.'

In analysing a number of Kennedy's key speeches, the extent to which they follow a formula of framing the context, as one of historic change, and then encouraging Americans that they can rise to the challenge of the times, is almost eerie.[9]

Physical Aesthetic

Finally, let us briefly consider Kennedy's physical aesthetic and the role it played in the perception of him as a charismatic leader. What is interesting from this perspective is the degree to which his true physical condition was masked throughout his campaign and Presidency. Kennedy went to some lengths to consistently portray himself as a fit and active man. He was often represented in the media playing football or sailing. Physical prowess could be seen as part of the larger Kennedy-dynasty aesthetic – the family portrayed itself as working-class Irish made good – and extreme toughness and masculinity was part of its mythology.

In truth, as a result of an injury acquired prior to his military service, Kennedy suffered from debilitating back pain during much of his time in office. Recently published accounts of his time as President note the degree to which the physical pain he suffered was kept from the general public. He did not want to be portrayed as 'weak' or 'sickly' in any way. He aimed to create a physical aesthetic consistent with that of a young, beautiful, healthy man, not troubled by infirmary or injury. His frequent use of pain killers enabled him to continue to portray this image.

The reason I refer to the apparent disconnection between Kennedy's actual physical health and the image he crafted is to highlight his awareness of the importance of his image. Although his challenges in producing an idealized version of himself were different from those faced by either Barack Obama or Hillary Clinton, he seemed keenly aware of the significance of his embodied presentation of the role for the way in which followers would relate to him. Although neither John F. Kennedy, Barack Obama or Hillary Clinton may have spoken about the importance of the 'aesthetic' of their enactment of the role, attention to this facet can be seen in the way in which Obama presents his ethnicity, Clinton presents her gender and Kennedy hid his disability.

REVISITING THE CHARISMATIC AS SUBLIME AESTHETIC

The chapter began by considering an aspect of charismatic leadership which has not been satisfactorily addressed either by Weber's theory of charismatic authority or subsequent theories of charismatic leadership; that is: 'What occurs in the space between leaders and followers when leaders are perceived to be charismatic?' The question was addressed by analysing charisma through the aesthetic category of the 'sublime', as theorized by Immanuel Kant.

In carrying out this analysis, two aspects of the charismatic encounter become apparent. Firstly, in order for the 'sublime' to occur, the perceiver must first encounter something – a person, a thing or a situation which they experience as overwhelming or threatening to their very existence. The 'sublime' is realized when in response to this overwhelming 'event' the person experiences their rationality stepping in and declaring, 'I *can* cope with this.' The person is thereby returned to their sense of power and mastery and enjoys a renewed sense of their capabilities as an agentic being. Similarly, the experience of charisma is clearly located within the perceptual world of the follower. In order for the experience of charisma to be aligned with the 'sublime' rather than the 'ugly' (or some other aesthetic category), it needs to impress the follower with a renewed sense of his or her own capability rather than serving to aggrandize or inflate the leader.

We have seen how the speeches of two US Presidents, Barack Obama and John F. Kennedy, paint just such a scenario. Both use sweeping narrative in which the present moment is situated as a 'turning point', an 'historic moment of crisis and change'. Furthermore, both pull for the strength, courage and ingenuity of the American people to rise effectively to the depicted challenge. In this way, their speeches fulfil these two key aspects of evocation of the 'sublime'.

The analysis here rests primarily on interpretations of speeches and the way in which framing a situation as critical might contribute to the possibility of a leader being perceived as charismatic. Certainly, it is not enough for leaders just to describe a context in a particular way for them to be hailed as charismatic. Followers must also accept the leader's version of the situation. This leads to another aspect which constitutes the 'in-between space' operating amidst leaders and followers; the way in which meaning is negotiated between the two. The book now turns to questions concerning the role of vision and sense-making in that process.

NOTES

1. Bass based his ideas on the work previously undertaken by James MacGregor Burns (1978) on distinguishing between 'transactional' leadership, in which there was a limited psychological relationship between leaders and followers and actions were undertaken on a purely transactional basis; and 'transformational' leadership, in which there was a high degree of connection between leaders and followers and through their relationship followers' views of themselves and their capabilities were transformed. See Burns, J.M. (1978), *Leadership*, New York: Harper and Row.
2. The destructive aspect of charisma is discussed by a number of authors, including Manfred Kets de Vries in works such as *Prisoners of Leadership* (1989), New York: Wiley, and more recently *Lessons on Leadership by Terror: Finding Shaka Zulu in the Attic* (2004), Cheltenham, UK and Northampton, MA, USA: Edward Elgar. Jane Howell (1988) has written about degenerative forms of charismatic leadership in her book chapter 'The two faces of charisma: socialised and personalized leadership in organizations', in Conger, J.A. and R.N. Kanungo (eds) (1988, pp. 213–36).
3. Super delegates are senior and influential members of the party whose votes count disproportionately higher than the general delegates from States.
4. *The New York Times*, http://www.nytimes.com/2008/01/08/us/politics/08text-clinton.html (accessed on 28 December 2009).
5. *The New York Times*, 'Barack Obama's New Hampshire Primary Speech', http://www.nytimes.com/2008/01/08/us/politics/08text-obama.html?_r=1 (accessed on 16 March 2009).
6. *Organizing for America*, 'Barack Obama', http://www.barackobama.com/index.php (accessed 15 November 2008).
7. Grewal, Daisy and Elena Grewal, 'Clinton Battles Bias Against Strong Women' *Truthout*, http://www.truthout.org/article/daisy-grewal-and-elena-grewal-clinton-battles-bias-against-strong-women (accessed 16 March 2009).
8. *The History Place*, 'John F. Kennedy "We choose to go to the Moon . . ."', http://www.historyplace.com/speeches/jfk-space.htm (accessed 16 March 2009).
9. Examination of the inaugural speeches of Richard Nixon and George W. Bush indicate a very different tone and focal point in their narrative, much more limited in their scope of framing the context and, in both of their speeches, there are many more references to how they see themselves fulfilling the role of President. For a fuller treatment of charisma and how it applies to US Presidents, see Willner, A.R. (1984), *The Spell Binders*, New Haven, CT: Yale University Press.

6. What is so important about the 'vision-thing'?

> The hermeneutic has to do with bridging the gap between the familiar world in which we stand, and the strange meaning that resists assimilation into the horizons of our world . . .
>
> David Linge
> Introduction to Hans-George Gadamer's *Philosophical Hermeneutics*
> (1976, p, xii)

'Vision' is an essential ingredient of most leadership theories. When leaders cannot articulate their 'vision' they can be harangued, as was US President George Bush Senior, for not having 'the vision thing'. What is so important about 'vision'? What differentiates successful 'visions' which are adopted by followers from unsuccessful ones which are ignored? This chapter suggests that a crucial aspect of a successful leadership vision is the extent to which it aligns meaning for those involved in a common activity.

One of the recurring themes running through this book is the notion of the socially constructed nature of leadership. Leadership occurs when people construct it to be occurring. Leaders are leaders because through either some formally recognized organizational symbol or through informal attribution by 'followers', they are deemed to be so. Such attribution can occur through a number of sources. For instance, in dangerous situations the person who is seen to be the strongest or quickest might be attributed with the leader role. In situations calling for particular expertise, the person who has that expertise might be expected to take up the leader role. However, another source of leadership attribution comes from the ability of an individual to frame and, in this way, create others' reality.

For instance, Nelson Mandela framed the unity of all South Africans despite their differences in ethnicity when he proclaimed in his inaugural speech:

> To my compatriots, I have no hesitation in saying that each one of us is as intimately attached to the soil of this beautiful country as are the famous jacaranda trees of Pretoria and the mimosa trees of the bushveld. Each time one of us touches the soil of this land, we feel a sense of personal renewal. The national mood changes as the seasons change.

We are moved by a sense of joy and exhilaration when the grass turns green
and the flowers bloom. That spiritual and physical oneness we all share with
this common homeland explains the depth of the pain we all carried in our
hearts as we saw our country tear itself apart in a terrible conflict, and as we
saw it spurned, outlawed and isolated by the peoples of the world, precisely
because it has become the universal base of the pernicious ideology and practice
of racism and racial oppression.[1]

In this passage Mandela articulates the sense of identity South Africans
feel for their homeland. Such framing provided a first-step towards developing a way of thinking which could realign the nation's political system.
Mandela's vision did not arrive 'from nowhere'. It was not something he
just 'dreamed up'. Instead, it sprang from an embodied awareness of the
deep divisions separating South Africans. It acknowledged those differences even as it highlighted commonly held sentiments amongst the disparate communities. In doing so, it held meaning for factions throughout
the country and served as a point from which, together, the future of the
nation could be forged.

Successful leadership visions are those which, like Mandela's, carry
significance for those who would engage with them. Ultimately, creating
such a vision is a process of meaning-making. There is a growing body
of literature which points to the centrality of meaning-making within the
leadership function.[2] But just what does meaning-making involve? Is it as
simple as the individual taking up the leader role proclaiming her or his
beliefs? What if followers do not agree with that version of reality? Surely,
followers themselves are always attributing meaning in their own ways?
How can a leader have any impact on the meaning that followers make?
Whether or not followers accept a leader's vision and then act on it determines whether or not leadership is seen to result. How does the translation
process between a leader's vision and subsequent action on the part of
followers occur?

This chapter takes a fine-grained look at that process. In particular it
problematizes the notion that leaders 'create' or even 'manage' meaning
for their followers through the attraction of tantalizing 'visions'. In doing
so, it challenges the assumption present in much of the sense-giving and
meaning-making literature that positions followers as relatively passive
receptacles for the leader's sense-making. Instead, the creation of meaning
is seen as a dialogic endeavour, emerging from processes of translation
and mediation between leaders, followers and the purpose towards which
their action is directed.

The philosophical school which focuses on the creation and exchange of
meaning is called hermeneutics. Although originally hermeneutics focused
primarily on how written texts, particularly religious ones, might be

interpreted across generations, its core ideas offer relevant constructions of human meaning-making processes. Before introducing hermeneutic ideas, let us start with a survey of what current leadership literature says about leaders as 'meaning-makers' or 'sense-givers'.

MEANING-MAKING AND LEADERSHIP

Linda Smircich and Gareth Morgan were among the earliest organizational theorists to consider the meaning-making function of leadership seriously. Their paper, 'Leadership: the management of meaning', published in 1982, highlighted the centrality of framing and defining situations as key functions of the leader's role. In fact, they suggested that within groups, people are recognized as being leaders because they are seen to: 'frame experience in a way that provides a viable basis for action by mobilizing meaning, articulating and defining what has previously remained implicit or unsaid, by inventing images and meanings that provide a focus for new attention, by consolidating, confronting or challenging prevailing wisdom' (1982, p. 258).

Meaning-making enables organizational members to work together towards a common interpretation of reality. Without such shared understanding organizational activity lacks coherence and common direction. In fact, Smircich and Morgan emphasize that such a shared understanding provides the very basis of organizational activity. Although clearly identifying meaning-making as crucial to leading, their article does not examine how such meaning-making occurs. Their account implies this activity is accomplished by leaders on an individual basis, although they do note that successful meaning-making occurs when leaders are 'able to define the situation in a way which organizational members accept as a basis for their action' (Smircich and Morgan 1982, p. 261).

The case study Smircich and Morgan present to illustrate their ideas vividly demonstrates the limitations of such an individualistic approach to meaning-making on the part of a formal leader. Their case tells the story of a Chief Executive Officer of an insurance firm who deems that a backlog of unattended claims must be dealt with by a particular date. In order to do this, he instigates 'Operation June 30th', an organization-wide effort to clear the backlog. He makes pronouncements that 'all hands must be on deck' and that everyone must 'put their shoulder to the wheel' in order to shift the growing pile of unaddressed claims.

Although the article indicates that, to some extent, the immediate problem of the backlog of work was rectified, the underlying reasons for the backlog were never questioned by the CEO. Smircich and Morgan reveal that interviews they carried out with staff indicated a high degree of cynicism among Board-level Directors as well as other organization members about the CEOs approach in this matter. Furthermore, although there were enough 'yes men' around the organization to respond to the emergency measures prescribed, the researchers reported that overall, a greater number of organizational members paid little heed to the leader's entreaties. Instead of serving as a unifying rallying call, 'Operation June 30th' was interpreted as yet further evidence that the CEO was not willing to address fundamental operational issues.

In their analysis of the situation, Smircich and Morgan suggest that even though the CEOs intervention was not completely successful, it did nonetheless serve as a meaning-making pronouncement, albeit one which generated negative interpretations. A more successful outcome might have arisen, the authors suggest, had the CEO attempted to deal with the equivocality which is always part of such an interaction, as well as trying to understand better the way in which his pronouncements might be interpreted by organizational members. However, is there more to successful creation of meaning between leaders and followers than provided by this explanation?

Moving forward, Joe Raelin's (2006) article 'Finding meaning in the organization' similarly focuses on the 'meaning-making' aspect of leading. Raelin offers a slightly different account of the meaning-making role of the leader. Rather than suggesting its success rests with the pronouncements of the individual leader's vision, he argues that a dialogic process is at work when meaning is effectively created between leaders and followers. Framing his argument around the concept of 'leadership vision', Raelin poses the question: 'Can a vision be heartily adopted if the ranks serve only as recipients of the vision? What if they don't believe in the vision?' (2006, p. 64).

Such a lack of buy-in seemed to be operative in the Smircich and Morgan case. Raelin contradicts more traditional 'visionary' leader accounts by suggesting that rather than creating a vision, leaders give voice to visions already present within their organizational contexts. He argues that rather than proclaiming his or her own individually determined 'dream' which might act as a touchstone around which organizational action can orient itself, a leader's vision must articulate something of the shared understandings inevitably embodied in existing organizational action. Following from this, in order to create such organizational meanings, leaders must first and foremost be sensitive to what is going on around them, as well as being fundamentally rooted in the core work of the organization.

The quality of engaged meaning-making which results from this kind of interaction between leaders and followers is central to Raelin's idea of the 'leaderful' organization.[3] Although Raelin's account offers a more complex rendering of the meaning-making process, there are still a number of important questions left unanswered. For instance, if the formal leader's role is to articulate the meanings of followers, is there room for their input into the sense-making process? In any group there will be multiple meanings attributed to incidents or utterances, how can a decision be taken about which is the most salient? What if the formal leader's vision really is so revolutionary that followers cannot 'follow' it? In order to explore these questions, I turn to the philosophical school of hermeneutics which addresses the way in which meaning is created and transmitted between human begins.

HERMENEUTICS: A BRIEF OVERVIEW

Hermeneutics is an ancient philosophical preoccupation concerned with how meaning is conveyed through language. In fact, Aristotle was one of the earliest philosophers to focus on how meaning is conveyed through written text. The first modern Western philosopher to be credited with conceptualizing hermeneutics is Friedrich Schleiermacher (1768–1834). For Schleiermacher hermeneutics is the 'art of understanding'. Interestingly he suggests that in any interchange of meaning, it should be assumed that 'misunderstanding results as a matter of course' (Schleiermacher 1838 [1998], p. 22).

The English philosopher William Dilthey (1833–1911) developed Schleiermacher's ideas, focusing particularly on how hermeneutics could inform the study of the human sciences. Central to Dilthey's project was the belief that because humans are sense-making creatures, any science which purports to study them must incorporate methodologies sensitive to these sense-making capabilities.[4]

Martin Heidegger (1889–1976) further elaborated on Dilthey's ideas in his major work *Being and Time* (1962), claiming 'understanding' as a key mode of the 'being' of human beings. He later rejected the use of the word hermeneutics, arguing that it still held the power of the tradition of metaphysics from which he wished to escape. Two ideas from Heidegger's account are introduced here because of the way in which they inform subsequent hermeneutic work: 'thrownness' and 'attunement'.

Thrownness

In *Being and Time* (1962), Heidegger argued that one of the key aspects of being human is that we are not located in the world through our own doing. Rather, we are 'thrown' into the particular place and historical time in which we find ourselves. We have no choice about the nation in which we were born, who our parents are, what kind of community we are born into or any other myriad of circumstances which define the possibilities which will be open for our development. Consequently at the most fundamental level, being alive and functioning in relation to others requires that we enter into a project of learning to understand the customs and norms of our time and locale. We learn a language which enables us to communicate with those around us. We learn that in the particular place in which we find ourselves, when people move their heads from side-to-side they mean 'no' (whereas people born into other communities will come to learn that sideways head movement means 'yes'). We learn what it is normal to wear, what it is normal to eat, the boundaries of what is considered acceptable and lawful behaviour.

In this way, understanding itself can be seen to be a 'thrown' project. We are 'thrown' into a particular culture, family, historical period which we must come to understand. From their particular position, an individual understands that certain possibilities exist for him or herself. For instance, as I have been born a woman, I have the choice to become a mother; a choice that is not available to my male partner. As I was born in the USA, I have had the opportunity to attend university and develop my career in a way that would not have been possible had I been born in a different country. If I were talking to a woman from Iran, the inherently different life possibilities open to each of us would colour our ability to make sense of one another's meanings. The starting point for establishing meaning between us would be grounded in our very different 'thrown' positions from which we experience our lives. Of course the difference is stark in the example of women from such diverse countries as the USA and Iran. However, the notion of 'thrownness' demonstrates that, to some extent, even those of the closest possible orientations, twins for instance, are still 'thrown' into slightly different worlds. Creating meaning between individuals inevitably begins from essentially different orientations.

Having an awareness of the extent to which we each operate from different 'thrown' perspectives is important for those attempting to create shared meanings within organizations. Doing so is complicated further by the fact that as well as each individual having their own 'thrown' reality, communities and organizations are also constituted by the particular socio-historic period and national culture in which they are 'thrown'. The meanings which are taken for granted by the senior US executives of a globally-based oil company will be a function of each of their individual circumstances; the fact that they work for a large company, the fact that it is American and the particular historic period in which the meanings are being constructed. Their perspectives will be rooted in fundamentally different concerns and world positions from those of their Nigerian employees. When such a company commits itself to 'responsible governance', the meaning of that declaration will be understood differently, depending on whether it is being interpreted by the CEO or a Nigerian worker mending a failing pipeline. Given the complexities involved, it is perhaps remarkable that meanings are ever aligned in ways that contribute to coherent organization or community action.

The notion of 'thrownness' also inverts the assumption that we 'make' history. Instead Heidegger argues that to a significant degree, history 'makes' us. This too has interesting implications for the notion of leadership, in that it questions the power of agency so associated with leading. Taking the notion of 'thrownness' seriously implies that leaders can emerge from circumstances rather than directing them. In fact, sometimes situations actually 'make' the leader. For instance, it was only in the aftermath of 11 September attacks on the World Trade Centre in New York that Rudy Guilliani was considered a serious contender for the Republican nomination for the US Presidency. The way in which he was perceived to spearhead the rescue efforts and unite residents of the shocked city demonstrated his capacity to lead in ways that had not been provoked by less traumatic events.

Attunement

A second idea offered by Heidegger is that of 'attunement' or 'mood'. This is a sort of 'precognitive' state which always colours one's ability to understand. There are certain aspects of 'mood' which are deeply held and very difficult to uncover but which affect every encounter we have with things and people in the world. In particular, Heidegger notes that we resist the notion of 'thrownness' with its attendant sense of lack of control. To mask this essential existential reality, Heidegger suggests that we try to ignore any hints which bring to the fore our lack of power to choose. In other words, at some level we may know ourselves to be 'thrown' but we do not want to think about it. Therefore, any perception which might indicate that we are out of control is denied. This fundamental starting point for being in the world influences our ability to understand others, particularly if others are telling us things we fundamentally do not want to hear.

This has interesting implications for those who think of 'leaders' as people who maintain a sense of control and 'knowing' no matter what the circumstances. Analysing the case study presented by Smircich and Morgan in the previous section through the lens of 'attunement' provides another interpretation of the CEOs actions. He proclaimed 'Operation June 30th' as the remedy for the problem of the backlog of insurance claims. This was a highly visible, agentic act. He, as leader, was proclaiming his vision of the organizational activity which would fix the problem. Those reporting to him knew the source of the problem lay elsewhere and would not be addressed through his prescribed action. However, they chose not to communicate this to the CEO. Their silence could be attributed to the reported belief on their part that their version of events would not align with the CEOs sense of power and possibility in 'sorting' the problem. Accordingly they felt their views would be ignored. By holding to the fiction of agency and being in control, the CEO fostered a 'mood' of passive deception in which the real underlying issues would not be addressed.

Heidegger offers three other aspects of attunement he calls 'fore-structures' which influence the extent to which understanding can be reached between people. These are:

1. 'Fore-having' (*Vorhabe*) – this is translated as 'what one has before having understanding', most notably: intentionality.

    Returning to the Smircich and Morgan 'Operation June 30th' case study, in order for meaning to be shared between the CEO and his followers, 'fore-having' suggests that they must share intentionality about their organizational purposes and how their actions might link into those purposes. If they are united around a notion of what constitutes the appropriate levels of customer care, the steps taken to deal with the backlog of claims might be handed differently from the way it would be engaged with if the intentionality is to 'get Head Office off our backs', or 'hit the targets so that we get our bonus'. Shared intentionality increases the possibility of coherent action on the part of organizational members.

2. 'Fore-sight' (*Vorsicht*) – this translates into 'the particular location from which one's intentionality is generated'.

    Every intentionality comes from a particular perspective. In the 'Operation June 30th' case, the CEO was driven by different motivations than those of other Directors. For instance, the researchers discovered that the Human Resources Director was not very bothered about the initiative because there was nothing in his sphere of activity which was affected by it. The Operations Director, on the other hand, worked in his own time during many Saturdays in order to be seen to be responding to the CEOs directive. Each person's 'fore-sight' concerning the matter influenced how they engaged with the initiative and the way in which they made sense of it.

3. 'Fore-conception' (*Vorgriff*) – which can be translated as 'what is previously grasped', in the sense of concepts or ways of thinking.

This includes the particular concepts used in the conversation between those engaged in the meaning-making event. In the 'Operation June 30th' case, in order for understanding to be reached, all those involved had to be working with similar conceptual constructions for words such as 'backlog', 'claim' or 'customer'. Although it may seem obvious that we have to share the meanings of particular words in order to understand one another, concepts can be slippery constructions. At what point in the case did a 'claim' become part of the 'backlog' and when would it have been 'work in progress'? Variability of terms can be a potent source of misunderstanding especially when measurements are put into place to concretize working practices.

These ideas offer a much more complex picture of the building blocks required for shared meaning-making to happen between individuals. Their applicability to understanding the meaning-making aspect of leadership will be further developed by considering the work of another phenomenologist, Hans-Georg Gadamer.

HANS-GEORG GADAMER

Hans-Georg Gadamer (1900–2002) is recognized as picking up the 'hermenuetical baton' from Heidegger and for developing Heidegger's ideas further in a book called *Truth and Method*. First published in Germany in 1960, *Truth and Method* purports to be a philosophical inquiry into 'understanding understanding'. As Gadamer explains, for him '[the work of hermeneutics] is not to develop a procedure for understanding, but to clarify the conditions in which understanding takes place' (1975 [2004], p. 295).

Three concepts are central to Gadamer's project and have particular relevance to the way meanings become aligned: his notion of 'prejudice', the 'hermeneutic circle' and 'fusion of horizons'. After introducing these ideas they will be used to analyse the role leadership plays in meaning-making through considering a case study involving the Eden Project, a sustainably built 'living theatre of plants' located in the UK.

The Role of Prejudice

Gadamer uses the word 'prejudice' in a very different way from its colloquial meaning. For him, 'prejudice' is an absolutely essential aspect of any act of understanding. To appreciate his sense of the word, we need to allow for a much more neutral rendering of it.[5] Gadamer asserts that all understanding is only possible because of and through our prejudices. He writes:

> Long before we understand ourselves through self-examination, we understand ourselves in a self-evident way in our family, society and state. The focus of subjectivity is a distorting mirror. The self-awareness of the individual is only a flickering in the closed circuits of historical life. That is why prejudices, more than judgements, constitute the historical reality of one's being (1975 [2004], p. 278).

Our very grasp of language is accomplished through previous understandings of words and concepts. In turn, every word is steeped in the particular history through which we first came to know it. In this way, Gadamer suggests that understanding should be thought of less as an individually-based act and more as 'participating in an event of tradition, a process of transmission in which past and present are constantly mediated' (ibid., p. 102).

Prejudice arises from the fact of our 'thrownness'. We come to understand the way things 'are' through the historical and cultural milieu in which we interact with them. Furthermore, our understandings build upon one another and are linked in complex and interdependent webs of meaning. For instance, when I hear on the radio that British Airways has made profits of 52 million pounds in the last year, I understand that to be bad news, only because I know that in the previous year the airline made profits in excess of 200 million pounds. If I were told that the family-run stationery store where I purchase paper made profits of 52 million pounds last year, I would regard that information rather differently. Furthermore, the notion of profit itself is situated within a capitalist economic system in which such information is deemed to be important.

Of course, Gadamer realizes that all 'prejudices' are not 'correct' and incorrect 'prejudices' can obfuscate any proximity to 'truth' in our interactions with the world. What, therefore, is the ground for the legitimacy of a 'prejudice'? Gadamer responds to this question by asserting that 'prejudices are legitimized when they are grounded in the things themselves' (1975 [2004], p. 101). Furthermore, crucial to doing so is to notice the way our 'prejudice' automatically positions us to see things in a certain way. For instance, if a person holds a 'prejudice' that women are not as capable of being political leaders as men, it is important for them to recognize the way this prejudice colours their views of political leaders. Rather than just denying 'prejudice', the committed hermeneut rigorously searches for ways in which this view colours his or her engagement with the world. For instance, they might begin to notice their tendency to expect more from female political leaders than they do from males or they may begin to look for similar shortcomings in male politicians that they criticize in females. The point is that hermeneutic engagement requires both acknowledging and testing 'prejudices' rigorously.

For those working within organizations, another key source of 'prejudice' is the organization's history. Gadamer points to the pervasive power of history as the ground from which 'prejudice' grows. Appreciating its pervasive role is critical in aligning organizational meanings. The story of a newly-appointed senior manager of a small specialist unit within a bank, who I coached, illustrates this point. The unit was comprised of people who had been recognized as underperforming for some years. The new, enthusiastic manager had been selected to lead the group and 'sort out' the underperformance issues. She had good ideas about how they could reorganize their work and begin to make a more substantial impact on the business. All of her efforts to enthuse her team and engage them in this new 'vision' for how they could be were met with cynicism and disinterest. She tried a number of different approaches to no avail. In an effort to understand their reaction she began to explore the group's history.

During the previous five years, the group had been placed in seven different parts of the organization, and directed by seven different managers. Over the most prolonged period of settled working (nine months), the group began to show some improvement but this declined immediately when, once again, they were relocated and placed under the authority of yet another manager. The senior manager, who is the focus of this story, replaced the previous manager after only three months. When she joined them she assured the group she would be with them for at least two years but history had told them differently. No matter what she did, the group performed to a minimal level. Six months into her leadership of them, they began to show glimmers of change. At this point, she was (inevitably!) moved onto another posting. The bank decided to disband the working unit and placed the individuals within separate departments of the organization.

This story illustrates the pervasive effect of history in the way meaning is made. Time after time, this group's experience of being managed was that just as they began to make progress under the direction of one 'leader', that person would change and they would have to work for someone new. This resulted in the group feeling continually disturbed and unable to settle into regular work patterns. No matter what was then said to them, the meaning they made of pronouncements from those more senior was that their words would be proven wrong, which in fact, they were. This example illustrates another concept key to Gadamer's work, that of the hermeneutic circle.

Rethinking leadership

The Hermeneutic Circle

Although the idea of the hermeneutic circle is central to Gadamer's work, Schleiermacher is credited with first articulating this notion. In his definition, the hermeneutic circle refers to the way in which the whole and the parts of language relate to one another. Schleiermacher writes: 'Complete knowledge is always in this apparent circle that each particular can only be understood via the general of which it is a part, and vice versa' (Schleiermacher, quoted from Schmidt 2006, p. 14).

It is through the interaction between individual words and the whole of a sentence to which they belong that we both understand the individual word and the entire sentence. Understanding is a reflexive process which occurs in the interaction between the individual and the whole of which it is a part.

To elaborate on this further; in order to understand a sentence as a whole, each word needs to be understood. Understanding the meaning of each individual word is only accomplished as a result of understanding the whole sentence. This is perhaps most evident when the same word can have several meanings. For instance in the sentence, 'Please close the window blind', 'blind' has a different meaning than it does in the sentence, 'As a result of car injury, Victor had gone blind'. More subtle nuances are also conveyed in the relationship between individual words and the sentences they constitute, such as in the case of the word, 'sustainable', in the following sentences: 'in order to be sustainable, the oil company needed to extract an extra million barrels of oil each day' and 'Friends of the Earth work to promote more sustainable ways of living for us all'.

Significantly, the hermeneutic circle indicates the way in which wholes and parts of language units are interdependent. Heidegger concluded that the hermeneutic circle was not necessarily 'a vicious circle' but one which needed to be attended carefully in order that meaning and understanding could be newly created each time we engage in language (Heidegger 1962, p. 194). This leads once more to the realization that meaning and understanding are never 'given' things. Instead, meaning is iterative and emergent. This has important implications for the process of meaning-making as a function of leadership. For instance it indicates that constructing meaning through dialogic processes might often be more appropriate than unilaterally uttering declarations. Central to such dialogic engagement is the practice of asking questions.

The Dialectic of Question and Answer

Throughout his text, Gadamer stresses the role of openness in the art of understanding. In order to understand another person or a text, one

must be as 'open' as possible to the difference which the other is expressing. One of the fundamental ways in which that difference is discovered is
through the process of questioning. All questions are not, however, equal.
Gadamer points out that there are some questions, which by their nature,
are directed not towards openness but towards the answer the questioner
wants to hear. He reminds us that, 'Every question points in the direction
of what is asked, and places what is asked about in a particular perspective' (Gadamer 1975, p. 361). Asking the 'right' question is not easy
but doing so distinguishes between authentic dialogue – which actively
pursues difference – and inauthentic dialogue – which constantly narrows
and restricts possible meanings.

Critical to 'good' questioning is openness to the difference the other has
to offer. Gadamer suggests that the orientation to the other which is most
likely to result in authentic dialogue is that of 'I/Thou'. 'Thou' denotes
that the other is seen as a distinctive and respect-worthy individual who
has something genuinely important and different to say. Holding such a
stance makes it more likely that the listener will be open to the claims of
the other. Gadamer points out this does not mean that whatever the other
has to say should be blindly accepted but that, 'I must accept some things
that are against me, even though no one forces me to do so' (Gadamer
1975, p. 361).

Questioning and listening to the answers one hears is a key way in
which one learns of one's own prejudices. When someone says something
that really does not make any sense to you, you are 'pulled-up short'.
Identifying the source of this feeling may reveal one of your own prejudices. Gadamer suggests that being 'pulled-up short' alerts us to the meanings which are not comparable with what we expect. He elaborates on
this, writing, 'without this kind of alertness to the discrepancies between
my expectations and what I hear the foremeanings that determine my
own understanding can go unnoticed' (1975 [2004], p. 271). Gadamer
argues that we cannot stick blindly to our own fore-meanings about a
thing if we truly want to understand the meaning of another. In this way:
'Hermeneutically trained consciousness must be sensitive to the texts [the
other's] alterity . . . The important thing is to be aware of one's own bias,
so that the text can present itself in all its otherness and thus assert its own
truth against one's own fore-meanings' (1975, pp. 271–2).

Of particular significance here from the perspective of leadership is that
often followers are conceptualized almost as 'things' to be influenced and
directed in a way determined by the leader. A hermeneutic rendering suggests that in order for meaning to be truly forged between people, both
must be open to the other. Such openness necessarily requires that leaders
take into account their followers' perspectives and meanings as well as for

followers to consider the perspectives of their leader. Meaning-making can then be a jointly negotiated activity. The 'follower' does not just incorporate the meanings of the leader as indicated by much of the leadership literature. Instead, the dialogic process enables co-created meaning to emerge from authentic engagement between leaders and followers. Meaning created in such a way would serve as a robust touchstone from which aligned organizational action could take place.

Gadamer proposes a special term for the process by which co-created meaning emerges, 'fusion of horizons'.

'Fusion of Horizons'

One of the key ways in which Gadamer's concept of understanding differs from more traditional accounts is that in his view, understanding is achieved, not through 'reconstruction' but through a much more dynamic process. Instead of understanding having occurred when person 'A' tells person 'B' something which 'B' can parrot back to 'A', Gadamer proposes that true understanding is achieved between 'A' and 'B' when a new meaning is created between them. He suggests that in this way, person 'A' cannot know what the outcome of trying to convey something to person 'B' will be before their conversation begins. Instead, understanding occurs when together they fuse their viewpoints in such a way that new meanings are produced. In this way, from Gadamer's hermeneutic perspective, understanding is not reconstruction but 'mediation' (Linge 1976, p. *xvi*).

Mediation is itself a sense-making activity. The role of the translator, according to Gadamer, is to 'say something differently in order that the original meaning can be apprehended by another' (Linge 1976, p. *xx*). In order to facilitate this process, the translator must understand enough of both languages involved to be able to convey the significance of meanings across linguistic worlds. In doing so, the translator inevitably subtly changes both meanings. It is only through this nuanced exchange of meanings, however, that understanding can be reached between those involved.

There is an additional element which plays a pivotal role in whether or not 'fusion of horizons' occurs. Gadamer writes, 'The hermeneutic conversation between interpreter and the text involves equality and active reciprocity – both parties are concerned "about something"' (Gadamer quoted from Linge 1976, p. *xx*). This 'something' is the larger purpose towards which understanding is directed. This fundamental purpose acts to frame meaning-making conversations. Following from this instead of proclaiming a 'vision' which is subsequently issued down a hierarchical line, perhaps the leadership requirement here is to 'hold the purpose' so that meaning can be co-created between those participating in a creative dialogue.

Just as openness is required in order to fully engage with the other's difference, Gadamer stresses that those engaged in a meaning-making event must also be open to the message of the purpose of the event. He emphasizes this throughout his writings, suggesting, 'The hermeneutic conversation begins when the interpreter genuinely opens himself to the text by listening to it and allowing it to assert its viewpoint' (Linge 1976, p. *xxi*). Although here he is referring to the process of an interpreter trying to understand 'text' – I suggest that the purpose to which uttered words are in service might similarly have their own 'viewpoint'. This is perhaps the power of mission statements, in that they can hold important organizational purposes which exert their own influence on meaning-making activity within social systems.

Creating space in which such conversations can occur becomes a requirement of the means by which 'fusion of horizons' can occur. Protecting the possibility for such spaces becomes a key leadership activity for enabling the alignment of meaning within organizations. Although providing and protecting such spaces may seem a rather passive activity and less visible than agentic 'proclaiming'; without it, visions can be nothing more than collections of words, as witnessed by the 'Operation June 30th' case study.

Let us explore how these ideas might inform the practice of leading by examining the story of an organization in which the translation of vision to a reality based on shared meanings explicitly lies at the heart of its existence, the Eden Project.

ALIGNING MEANING AND PRACTICE: THE CASE OF THE EDEN PROJECT

The Eden Project is a 'living theatre of plants and people', as well as a 'refuge for the world's endangered species' (Smit 2001, p. i). The attraction is located in the Southwest of England in the rather remote, primarily rural county of Cornwall. Eden is most famous for its two massive greenhouses and extensive gardens. The greenhouses house hundreds of plants from around the world in specially regulated 'biomes', or temperature controlled environments, which enable plants from different Mediterranean or humid climates to grow within them. The tropical biome even boasts a 25 foot-tall waterfall and huge banana trees. The spectacular nature of Eden has to be understood within the context of its location in England, noted for its wet and chilly climate. Many of the plants growing within the biomes would not be seen by the British public except when on foreign holidays. What makes the project even more remarkable is that the site upon which it is built was previously land used for china-clay extraction. The Eden Project has literally transformed what was a great welt on the landscape into a place of beauty and abundance.

Eden is the brainchild of Tim Smit, an ebullient and forthright Dutchman who has made his home in the UK and had previously completely regenerated a huge ramshackle historic garden also in Cornwall, know as the Lost Gardens of Heligan.[6] Work on Eden began in 1995 and the attraction opened to the public in the spring of 2001. More than a million visitors a year make the trek down the country roads to this out-of-the-way bit of England to enjoy the marvel which is Eden.

In his vision for the site, Smit pronounced that

> Eden would be dedicated to inspiring people to reflect on the vital role of plants and come to understand the need for a balance between, on the one hand, husbandry –growing them for our use – and stewardship – taking care of them on behalf of all living things (Smit 2001, p.162).

But how could this vision be achieved in practice? How would this goal shape the decisions that would be made about building materials, ways of working and suppliers and contractors that were engaged? This case study is based on research I conducted during 2006 into how leaders successfully mobilize their organizations towards more ecologically sustainable ways of operating. As part of the research I attended meetings and conferences at Eden as well as interviewing key people who had been involved in constructing the site.[7] In this account I will primarily draw from conversations I had with the Head of Sustainable Construction at Eden at the time, Caron Thompson, and the Project Manager for Phase Four of the site's construction, Andy Cook.

It quickly became apparent that 'aligning meaning' was a key preoccupation of those tasked with formally leading aspects of the project. Phase Four of the construction site involved the creation of an educational centre which would be recognized as an 'exemplar of sustainability'. Caron and Andy, as well as others I interviewed, repeatedly talked about the need to translate across different professional and organizational discourses in order to help people understand how their jobs contributed to this overall goal. Most noticeably, all of those interviewed spoke of the way in which such understanding had to be worked out together among the groups of people involved. Caron and Andy saw their role in this process as asking the questions which would prompt individuals to determine for themselves how they could best contribute to the overall project.

One of the difficulties which continually arose was how actions could be 'fixed' within an aspiration which was so vaguely articulated. 'What did it *mean* to be an exemplar of sustainability?' This was a recurring question, not just for Caron and Andy but for most of those involved in the project. More importantly, how should such a goal ground organizational action? Three themes arose from the study which link with the hermeneutic themes introduced previously:

- How meaning could be aligned around contested concepts, such as 'sustainability';
- How stakeholders could reach a common (enough) understanding of the overall purpose in order to make decisions which would lead to appropriate action; and
- How decisions could be made among disparate stakeholder groups with different perceptions of priorities and ways of achieving outcomes.

Aligning Meaning and Key Concepts

Under close examination, the meaning of almost any word or concept can become vague and inexact. Even very straightforward concepts have a variety of meanings and could be understood in different ways, given the circumstances (is a chair always something that provides the possibility of seated rest, or is it sometimes a representation of a senior-level of authority, for instance?). Additionally, any utterance will be interpreted within the wider context of which it is a part. The words suddenly shouted by a team's manager will have different significance depending on whether shouting is part of that manager's normal behaviour or if they rarely raise their voice. Understanding how to act will depend on the sense made of the particular incident and the way it fits into a broader context.

How much more difficult it is to align meaning around concepts which are admittedly already contested, such as 'sustainability'. Our understanding of 'ecological sustainability' within the organizational context is emergent. Currently, there is a lack of clarity about how ecologically-based principles can successfully be translated into organizational practices.[8] Certainly concepts such as 'reduced carbon footprint' and 'waste reduction' are providing some foundations for what can be done organizationally. However, the complexities involved in implementing ecological principles within organizational practices are coming to light as increasing numbers of organizations begin to respond to environmental imperatives. There are few established templates for how this might be done and in many ways the Eden Project was at the vanguard of these attempts in the UK.

In such a context, meaning-making has to begin somewhere! Caron Thompson talked about the importance of beginning itself. Only by taking some action could understanding of how to be an exemplar of sustainability begin to emerge. For example, she said:

> We started with some broad principles. We were not going to use PVC in any of the buildings. We aimed to produce zero waste. We would use local contractors. What being an exemplar of sustainability meant emerged as we 'did it', as we talked about what it might mean, as we tried to align decisions to this aim.

Significant here is the extent to which meaning emerged through taking action which was broadly aligned with the vision of becoming an exemplar of sustainability. Given that there was no ready-made handbook about how to do it, those involved had to begin and reflect on the learning which resulted from their actions. The process of acting and reflecting produced the kind of learning which emerges through engagement with the hermeneutic circle. After doing something, those engaged needed to step back from that action and re-evaluate it in terms of the 'whole' towards which they were directed. As they took another action, they created another piece of the puzzle which contributed to their sense-making process. As the 'whole' of what it meant to be an exemplar of sustainability could not be known upfront (apart from as a guiding 'principle' towards which organizational intentions could be directed), its lived meaning could only be discovered through the taking of action that could then be evaluated in light of the broad vision towards which they were directed. A key task for leaders engaged in such a process is to provide the space and opportunities for people to jointly construct meaning, rather than determining the meaning on their own and conveying it to others.

Andy Cook talked about how he began to see his job in line with this idea:

> It became clear that no one person had the answer to how to be an exemplar of sustainability. We had to talk together to figure out what it might mean. It was kind of like a puzzle, everyone had a piece of it. I began to see my job as just getting the right people in the room together with the right knowledge so that we could figure it out together.

Still, there had to be some kind of 'glue' which motivated people to continue to engage with one another. At Eden, the 'glue' is almost palpable in the general feeling of excitement and enthusiasm for the project itself which was apparent on the many occasions I visited, both as a researcher and as a member of the general public on holiday. From the start, people were excited about the project and were proud to be involved in it. As Andy explained:

I've been involved with building lots of different buildings, but the thing that is different about what we've done at Eden is that whenever I pass it, I get this feeling of pride. 'I was part of that', I think – it really makes a difference. There was a lot of goodwill around the place.

This sense of 'goodwill' exemplifies Heidegger's idea of 'attunement'. There was a general 'mood' of 'can do' inherent in the project which influenced how people engaged with one another. The pride and enthusiasm generated by being part of it provoked willingness to work together and resolve the differences that arose between them. Merely 'getting everyone in the room together' would not necessarily result in constructive conversations however, no matter how great the goodwill between people. Particular capabilities were required to help bridge the language worlds of the different professionals and stakeholders necessary in creating the reality of Eden. What are those capabilities?

How to Engage People in the Meaning Alignment

How did formal organizational leaders such as Caron and Andy succeed in evoking engagement from others? In Gadamer's terms, how did they go about 'fusing horizons' with others so that new meanings could emerge which would direct further action?

Both Caron and Andy recognized the 'translation' function of their roles as highly significant. It had become such a 'taken for granted' aspect of their role that they no longer recognized it as a special capability. When pressed to articulate how she made it happen, Caron responded:

You do have to do your homework. So when I was going to meet a sound engineer, I got a few books about acoustics, so I would be able to speak their language. You have to show that you are willing to come to their side of things. You also have to show that you have something to offer them, as well as information you want to get back from them.

Caron spoke of the extra steps required to actively create novel ways of enabling people to see the world from perspectives other than their own. One of the aspects of the Eden Project she especially championed was inclusivity. In fulfilling the 'social justice' dimension of sustainability,[9] she was concerned that Eden should be accessible to the largest segment of the population as possible, including those with physical disabilities. Caron hoped that the buildings would have the 'feel' of inclusivity, rather than merely fulfilling minimum statutory requirements. Key to achieving this was engaging the architects involved in designing the site.

Keen to have the architects understand the constraints of sight-impaired people for example, she invited them to walk around the site for a day wearing specially-made 'reduced-sight' goggles. As a result, the architects recommended the use of more high contrast paint, floor surfaces which had distinctive 'feels' as well as banisters constructed of more touch-friendly materials, such as wood. Significantly, Caron did not have to tell them what to do; in fact, she would not have known the range of possibilities for creating spaces which were more inclusive in their design. Having organized the experience in which they had a better sense of the difficulties associated with this kind of being in the world, they were able to work from their specialist knowledge and design more appropriately for it.

Andy, a construction engineer by trade, demonstrated his ability to make the effort to speak someone else's language the first time we met. Prior to our meeting I had sent him an article about leadership in which Plato had been quoted. A few minutes after shaking my hand, he quoted a bit of Plato to me, something I had not quite expected of a construction engineer! Reflecting on that small gesture on his part, I noticed how it conveyed to me his willingness to 'speak my language' and to spend time preparing in order to meet me on my terms. This was not just an isolated occurrence, as a number of Andy's colleagues also referred to the way in which he often made the extra effort to understand the world from their perspectives.

These two examples indicate the work required in translating. Creating understanding involves more than just listening carefully and recounting what is said to another group of people. In order for understanding to occur, the translator must comprehend enough about what is being said to be able to discern its significance and be able to articulate that significance in a way that can be comprehended in the perceptual and linguistic worlds of others. Doing so requires preparation on the part of the person mediating understanding; they must do the work that enables them to construct conceptual bridges between those whose understanding they wish to facilitate.

Caron spoke about the importance of preparing in order to have 'something to contribute to the conversation'. For her it was important that she was not just seen as the 'go-between' mediating professional discourses. She prepared in advance in order to have a view about potential outcomes. This commitment on her part could relate to Gadamer's assertion that for understanding to be created, those involved must see the task as a reciprocal activity. All of those involved must recognize what the other has to offer and be willing to offer something him or herself. This suggests a much more active role on the part of the translator than many accounts might indicate.

This raises another aspect of how leaders work to align meaning; the manner in which they involve others. Gadamer stresses the importance of 'openness', as demonstrated by the kinds of questions people ask. Perhaps of equal importance to the questions asked is the manner in which they are posed. People soon know if their opinions are being sought merely as a cosmetic exercise. The importance of coherence in word and action was raised by those interviewed in terms of 'walking the talk'. An episode which clearly demonstrates the need for actions and words to cohere occurred at Eden when the material which was being substituted for PVC ran out. Andy explained:

> We were in a bit of a tough spot, because we were coming up close to a deadline, and we needed to complete this part of the build. The thing is, the part of the build where we would have been using the PVC – to be honest, no one would have known it was there. We probably could have got away with it. But I knew that once we said, 'Yeah, go ahead with it' – well that would be it really. So we stuck to our guns. Held out for the replacement PVC material. It cost us, but it was the right thing to do. It was the right thing to do because the construction guys would have seen what we had done, and the whole power of what we meant about 'being an exemplar of sustainability' – well it wouldn't mean anything.

The importance of coherence between words and actions in order to align meaning is demonstrated by another touchstone story around Eden, about the day that the waste was 'contaminated'. Someone had put the wrong kind of waste in the recycling bins. This meant that instead of being able to be recycled, the waste would need to go to landfill instead. Eden had pledged itself to zero waste, so this was a substantial infringement of a very public and clear policy position. Caron Thompson told the story:

> When the site foreman found out about the contamination, he was really angry. He marched down to the site, and began turning over the rubbish bins. It was the lunchbreak and all the construction guys were sitting around, but in a minute or two they were up on their feet, re-sorting the rubbish. The problem of contamination never happened again!

In telling the story, part of Caron's amazement was that the construction workers actually *did* get up from their lunch and begin to re-sort the rubbish. 'They could have just sat there', she said. She interpreted their actions as a signal that at some level they had bought into what the project was about. Being careless was a kind of 'testing the waters' but their re-sorting the rubbish indicated they were on board with the project's philosophy.

Caron told another story which signalled to her that the quality of engagement from people at all levels who were involved in building

Eden, was different from that she had experienced in other construction projects:

> There was this builder who came up to me one day and he was curious about what all this 'sustainability' stuff was about. He was particularly intrigued by the recycling we were doing. A few days later, I had a phone call that the builder wanted to see me. I was a bit surprised, as I knew he wasn't on site that day. I went downstairs, and he was holding this sort of bird house. He said, 'This is what you mean, isn't it? – My son and I, we always hunt round building sites for discarded bits of wood and things, and then we try to make something beautiful out of them'.

It was through this conversation, she said, that she realized the message Eden was trying to get across was being communicated to all of those who were engaged in the project.

A final area to consider here is how this kind of meaning-making process impacts on decision-making. When there are multiple perspectives involved in key decisions, how can consensus be reached? How does meaning alignment work in such situations?

Meaning Alignment and Decision-making

Another story from Eden illustrates the challenges involved in aligning meaning around a contested concept such as 'sustainability'. As mentioned earlier, Phase Four of the project involved constructing a building which would serve as an education centre for the site. The building itself had multiple purposes; it was to be a showcase for sustainable building and design, it had to be able to accommodate a range of educational offerings and it had to be beautiful or, in Caron Thompson's words, to incorporate the 'Wow!' factor. The design template which informed the building's construction was that of a tree. The outer cladding of the structure is fashioned to resemble a tree trunk and the internal ceiling struts are arranged in swirling 'branches' laid out in the naturally occurring Fibonacci series.[10]

A point of contention arose around the decision about the choice of building material for the roof. The architects' choice was copper. Although it would be a brilliant bronze colour during its early years, after a while through the process of oxidation it would turn green, resembling a vast canopy of leaves and thereby completing the 'tree' effect. Aesthetically, there was little doubt that copper would create a stunning effect. However, the building was also intended to be aligned with Eden's mission of being an 'exemplar of sustainability'. How sustainable was incorporating a material which would necessarily be extracted from the earth and shipped to the UK from a far distance?

Various options for sourcing the copper for the roof were debated. Should they source the material from recycled copper? Would it be better to give the business to a copper mine which was upholding sustainable practices and thus use new copper? In fact, should a completely different material be used instead? Apparently, this was one decision which raised much heated discussion within the team of people charged with making it, as well as generating a good deal of external debate and comment in the wider community.[11]

The decision was taken to construct the roof from copper and to source it from a socially and environmentally-oriented mine operated by Rio Tinto in Utah in the USA. In doing so, they intended to send a signal to other mining companies that the business was being given to a company which took care in its mining practices, redeveloped mined land and did as little harm as possible in the extraction process.

This decision remains a contested one. However, those involved in making it reported that after much discussion and debate the decision was based on a consensus among them all. In fact, coming to a consensus was seen as critical if they were all going to be able to remain united behind this controversial stance. Caron explained:

> We all made our contribution to the discussion. It's not a cut and dried answer at all. But in this case, this is what we decided to go with, and having made that decision, it was important that we stood arm in arm with it. We had to be united in facing the comeback we then generated.

Certainly, the decision they reached can still be debated (as it is within the local community and media). However, significant to note here is the way in which the decision was reached. This decision was only accomplished through the alignment of meanings between those engaged in reaching it. In order for this alignment to occur, there had to be a deep understanding of one another's perspectives or 'prejudices' to use Gadamer's term, as well as a sense of attunement in the very way in which they conducted their dialogue.

Lessons from Eden

Like many other organizations, in order to survive Eden must balance its financial viability with its aspirations to be environmentally responsible. This tension is especially felt in the very fact that its continued existence depends on attracting large numbers of visitors to a rather remote and unspoilt part of England. Indeed, there are those who argue that if those behind the Eden Project were truly concerned with ecological sustainability, it would not even exist, given that its presence creates increased car traffic on very small roads and additional strain on natural resources arising from tourists' demands.

There is no 'right or wrong' way of achieving such a balance and it is questionable as to whether or not a perfect solution even exists. However, creating shared meanings capable of informing how such a balance might be achieved results only from ongoing discussion and dialogue. In order to realize this goal, the *meanings* that people attribute to different decisions have to be explicitly expressed and discussed, rather than just their structural or financial consequences. It is only through more deeply inquiring conversations in which individuals have the opportunity to expand not only on their view but also on how that view is informed, that a true 'fusion of horizons' can emerge. Such a mode of engagement potentially brings about new meanings for all of those involved.

When asked what made the Eden Project different from other construction projects on which he had worked, Andy Cook was quick in his response: 'I've never been involved in a project where you just had to keep talking and talking and talking so much'. 'Fusion of horizons' can only be achieved through talk. This talk needs to have certain qualities; those engaging in it must own their own prejudices and viewpoints and be willing for them to be altered. They must recognize each other as having something valuable to contribute (and they must prepare for conversations so that they *do* have something valuable to contribute). Most critically, they must maintain a real curiosity and openness to the possibility of completely new meanings and understandings emerging from their engagement with others.

The role of the 'leader' in such a process does not require the ability to clearly pronounce the way forward. Instead, providing a safe space in which inquiring conversations can occur is vital. That is not to say that 'vision' is no longer necessary. The case of the Eden Project provides clues about the nature of that vision, however.

WHAT CONSTITUTES A SUCCESSFUL VISION?

This chapter began with the question, 'What is so important about the 'vision-thing?' It has subsequently developed the concept of 'vision' as a starting point for aligning meaning among organizational members as a basis for coherent action. Without such shared meaning, leadership visions can be hollow pronouncements. Accomplishing shared meaning is a dynamic activity itself which occurs amongst those who engage with it and consequently co-create it. As such, visions which have any chance of co-ordinating organizational action only do so through the hermeneutic process of meaning-making.

Meaning-making and its alignment is facilitated by ongoing dialogue and discussion in which those involved disclose their intentionalities, perspectives and emotional responses around the situation in question. In order for these conversations to occur, the various viewpoints and voices need to be invited to engage with one another. There is a requirement for safeguarded space and time in which such conversations can happen. Often there is a need for someone to help translate meanings across different professional discourses or value-based agendas. A hermeneutic rendering suggests that once the overarching purpose is identified and articulated; gathering the individuals, providing the space and facilitating translating across discourses are key tasks for those taking up the leader role. Such engagement enables the requisite meaning-making to occur which can be mobilized to transform 'visions' into realities.

This suggests a very different purpose for a leader's 'vision' from that suggested by the picture of the sole individual pointing into a far distant horizon willingly pursued by placid followers. In that rendering the attention is focused on the 'vision' and its power to inspire and motivate others. Creating such a vision is a rarefied and cerebral process. Attending to the space between 'visions' and 'meaning-making' instead suggests a far messier type of engagement. The leader may well sight the far-off realm but mobilizing towards it requires stepping back into the maelstrom of followers' realities. It involves discussion, debate, compromise, experimentation, uncertainty, ambiguity, giving up long-held beliefs and taking on new ones on the part of all of those involved, including the 'leader'.

Perhaps most importantly, hermeneutics – the philosophy concerned with understanding understanding – tells us that creating understanding is an active and potentially flawed process. It is more likely to result in misunderstanding than in understanding. Rather than 'trying to get it right', framing the process as one of active experimentation and inquiry might result in surprising and potentially helpful insights born of truly shared meaning-making adventures.

There is perhaps no circumstance which better demonstrates the difficulties associated with creating shared meanings than that of leading change. Leaders are particularly called to 'manage meaning' during times of formally driven, organizational change efforts. The next chapter reconsiders the question, 'How do leaders lead change? Its starting point is to challenge the very way in which the notion of 'change' itself is conceptualized.

NOTES

1. Quoted from http://www.famousquotes.me.uk/speeches/Nelson-Mandela (accessed 3 June 2009).
2. See for instance, Drath, W.H. and C.J. Palus (1994), *Making Common Sense: Leadership*

as *Meaning Making in Communities of Practice*, Greensboro, NC: Center for Creative Leadership Press.

3. See Raelin, J. (2003), *Creating Leaderful Organizations*, San Francisco: Berrett-Koehler Publishers.
4. Although Dilthey was primarily concerned with developing an appreciation for the role sense-making plays in social sciences, his ideas might be equally important to the practice of leadership, especially if leadership is conceptualized primarily in terms of its sense-making and meaning-making roles.
5. It is interesting to note that the word 'prejudice' did not acquire negative connotations until the Enlightenment, when the possibility of objectivity arose and rigour in research came to be equated with eliminating any form of subjectivity.
6. See the Lost Gardens of Heligan at http://www.heligan.com/flash_index.html (accessed 5 June 2009)
7. This research was conducted with the aid of Future Foundations, a non-governmental agency dedicated to developing ecologically sustainable construction practices within the Southwest region of the United Kingdom. I would like to acknowledge the help of Lesley Seymour, Director of Development for Future Foundations, who assisted me in the research and enabled me to gain access to the Eden Project as well as other sustainably-built projects in the region.
8. This is not to deny that key information about what constitutes ecological practices does not exist. Organizations such as The Natural Step have very clearly outlined the basic parameters of ecologically sustainable practices. The argument that I am making here is that currently there are very few organizations which have successfully translated this available knowledge into everyday organizational practices.
9. 'Sustainability' is increasingly theorized as being constituted by three dimensions: financial, ecological and social, combined in the term 'the triple bottom line' coined by John Elkington in 1994. For a more detailed account, see Elkington, J. (1998), *Cannibals with Forks: The Triple Bottom Line for 21st Century Business,* Oxford: Capstone.
10. For photographs of the Core Building see Eden Project, 'The Core', http://www.eden-project.com/visiting-eden/whats-here/the-core/index.php (accessed 5 June 2009).
11. For more detail about the copper used in the Core Building's Roof, see Eden Project, 'From Rock to Roof', http://www.edenproject.com/documents/rock-to-roof.pdf (accessed 15 June 2009).

7. How do leaders lead change?

Co-authored with Martin Wood[1] and John Pillay[2]

Fundamentally, everything stands still – the thawing wind, however, preaches to the *contrary*!

Friedrich Nietzsche
Thus Spoke Zarathustra
(1884 [1995], p. 201)

For many leadership theorists, leadership and change are almost synonymous. The whole point of leadership, some authors suggest, is to influence individuals, organizations or communities to move from the 'status quo' into something different. This is often in an attempt to more closely align the organization with the changing environment in which it is situated. Many organizational change theories accord the leader great powers of persuasion, motivation and agency in 'making' change happen.

A much more complex view of how leadership functions has been introduced throughout this book. Rather than being something that occurs through the agency of one individual; followers, context and the purpose to which effort is directed, all contribute to its occurrence. How might this more complex view inform our understanding of the role of leadership within change processes? What are the assumptions about change itself that underpin how we think it happens? What *is* change and how do we recognize when it has occurred?

In order to explore this territory, this chapter draws from a branch of philosophy known as 'process thinking'. Process thought problemitizes the idea of change itself. Rather than considering 'stasis' as the natural state of existence, it suggests that reality is continually in a state of flux, with innovations constantly arising and retreating. Process philosophy turns on its head the notion that in organizations things stand still and leaders must 'push them along' in order to generate 'change'. Instead, change is seen to occur inevitably as individuals go about their daily routines making small adjustments in response to local conditions. Given this conceptualization, how might 'leadership' affect changing processes? How might change, which is already occurring, be directed towards organizational goals? Is there any way in which leadership can encourage change to happen more quickly given a 'process' view of change? These are some of the questions this chapter addresses.

The chapter is organized in the following manner. Firstly we[3] briefly examine more traditional leadership change theories and consider their limitations. Ideas from the philosophical school known as 'process thought' are then introduced. Process philosophy is fundamentally concerned with the nature of reality as constantly changing and therefore has much to offer in terms of a radical reconceptualization of how change itself occurs. These ideas are then used to analyse an example of a corporate turnaround process in order to explore the extent to which they offer new insight into what happens during formally-introduced organizational change efforts.

HOW LEADERS CREATE CHANGE – UNDERLYING ASSUMPTIONS

That leaders 'make change happen' is a belief core to many assumptions about how organizational change works. When organizations experience difficult periods, one of the primary levers used to stimulate a shift is replacing the CEO. In the UK, one of the most vivid illustrations of this belief occurs within the Premier League Football Association. Increasingly, over recent years in an effort to find a winning formula, teams replace their managers when they experience a string of losses. Replacing the person in charge often seems to be the only lever such clubs imagine that might generate any change in their footballing fortunes. Occasionally, this strategy seems to work but the results are more mixed, indicating that a change in manager is not the only determinate of a club's success.[4]

However, when the success of an organizational transformation effort corresponds with a change of CEO, that CEO is often credited with the upturn in company fortunes. Witness the high profile of individuals such as Jack Welch, Chairman and CEO of General Electric from 1981–2001, who is largely credited with the increase in the organization's market value from US$14 billion to US$410 billion during his time leading the organization. Such claims have historically come under critical scrutiny. For instance as early as 1977, Jeffrey Pfeffer questioned whether the attribution of causation to individual social actors actually meets the necessary requirements for a causal explanation. He further wondered whether it is possible that aspirational attitudes and characteristic types of behaviour result from the over-simplification of a vast pool of environmental data into a few key people (Pfeffer 1977).

Following from this observation, in high profile turnaround cases observers might be overestimating the role of individual leaders to explain and account for organizational activities, performance and outcomes. Henry Mintzberg has made this point several times and invokes it once more when he questions *Fortune* magazine's superficial assertion that 'within four years, Lou Gerstner added more than US$40 billion to IBMs shareholder value'. Mintzberg asks the not unreasonable question, '*All by himself?*' (2004, p. 22, original emphasis).

The view that leaders make such a dramatic impact on creating organizational change has its roots in more fundamental assumptions about the nature of change itself. In particular, as Westerners steeped in Enlightenment ideas of 'cause' and 'effect', we are sensitized both to assume and look for those causal precedents to outcomes. This fundamental principle underpins many ideas about leading change that we take for granted.

For instance, many of the theories of change which inform our thinking are 'synoptic' in nature. In other words, they rely on 'snapshot summaries' of where an organization 'is' at different points in time. We imagine that change has occurred in an organization when it is recognizably different at 'Point B' than it was at 'Point A'. Kurt Lewin's 'Unfreeze, Change, Refreeze' model (1951) is indicative of this kind of thinking. In this model, in order to change the organization, person or situation, certain ways of being must 'unfreeze' to allow them to alter during the 'change' phase. These changes then 'stabilize' at 'Point C'. Although this is a rather simplistic model, its basic idea of 'steady state, change state, regain steady state' underpins much of the theorization about how organizational (as well as other) change occurs.

From a process perspective this simple model poses difficulties. If everything is already in flux, how can a point of 'unfreezing' be identified? Is there something about the scope and degree of change which would make it recognizable as the 'change' phase? What should we be paying attention to during that phase? How would you know that you have reached 'Point C'? Are there aspects of 'Point A' which you may want to retain in the new state and, if so, how might you go about achieving that state? Can the process in fact be 'managed'? How do contextual factors which arise throughout the process affect it?

Looking more closely at the role of leaders in making change happen, we will turn to the work of the former Harvard Business School Professor, John Kotter, who has written extensively about the role of leaders in change efforts. In his model, the leader is charged with undertaking eight steps in order to enable change:

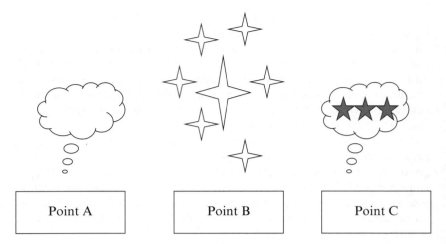

Figure 7.1   Lewin's unfreeze, change, re-freeze model

- Establish a sense of urgency;
- Create a guiding coalition;
- Create a vision – develop a picture of the future which is easy to communicate;
- Communicate the vision;
- Empower others to act on the vision;
- Create short-term wins;
- Consolidate improvement and produce more change; and
- Institutionalize new practices (Kotter 1996).

The model enjoys a good deal of face validity and certainly the books and articles which elaborate on each step have enjoyed wide popularity. However, underpinning Kotter's ideas are rather unquestioned assumptions about the nature of both change and leadership. Significantly, his ideas belie a synoptic view of change based in the belief that there is a recognizable 'here and now' from which a change effort begins and an identifiable 'endpoint' towards which the change is directed. Holding such a view of change, the role of leadership is to produce a vision of that 'endpoint' and to mobilize energy towards it. This is accomplished through the use of 'top-down' authority, in which the leader and his or her 'coalition' exert pressure in certain ways to achieve the vision they create. Chapter 6 has already questioned the extent to which visions are so readily imported into followers' consciousness.

Steven Appelbaum et al. (2008) take a more academic approach to analysing the literature concerning how leaders guide change. They identify three key models of change which underpin theorization about 'transformational change'; that is change that results in a 'strategic reorientation' of the organization (2008, p. 16). These are 'punctuated equilibrium theory' which conceptualizes change as occurring in incremental and radical shifts (Tushman and Romanelli 1985); Dunphy and Stace's (1993) model of ascending categories of change (fine tuning, incremental adjustment, modular transformation and corporate transformation); and a 'contingency change model' which differentiates between structural/technical changes and behavioural/social changes (Waldersee and Griffiths 2003). Appelbaum et al. proceed to examine six empirical studies which specifically address issues of leadership style and the outcomes it generates dependent on the focus of the change initiative. Although they purport to take a fine-grained approach to identify the causal relations between leaders' actions and organizational outcomes, we would argue that their research methods do not allow a rich enough picture to be constructed to fully satisfy this claim.

Like Beer and Nohria (2000) before them, Appelbaum and his colleagues (2008) note the difficulty in really understanding 'successful' organizational change processes and cite the relative lack of success of the majority of formally authorized initiatives. For instance they quote a figure of between 55 per cent and 75 per cent of change initiatives that do not achieve the majority of what they set out to achieve. They suggest that targets and measurements used to evaluate the effects of change are often manipulated in order to indicate the desired effects. Finally, although their study indicates a slight advantage in adopting a 'transformational leadership style' in order to engage the kind of follower support needed for successful change initiatives, the link is inconclusive. Appelbaum et al. suggest the need for 'further empirical research in the related fields of change success and organizational change leadership' (2008, p. 24) in order to gain further insight into the interplay of change and leadership style. Rather than pursuing that agenda, we wonder whether there is a different way of conceptualizing change itself which can shed new light on how formal organizational change occurs and the role of leadership within that process?

ENTER PROCESS PHILOSOPHY

Process philosophy, or process thought, is a distinctive sector of the philosophical tradition. Its roots can be found as far back as the Greek philosopher Heraclitus (c.500 BC), whose thinking stressed the transience of physical substances and the importance of processes and qualities. In contrast with much contemporary philosophical – and management – thinking, which searches for substantial and enduring properties, process thinkers characterize the 'substance' of reality in terms of perpetual change, movement and transformation. From this viewpoint, processes of *becoming* are regarded ahead of the distinct *being* of things or substances. For process thinkers, change is the norm and that taken-for-granted state of 'stasis' at the beginning of any change process is elusive and imaginary.

Nicholas Rescher in his book *Process Metaphysics* (1996), offers a broadly-based introduction to process thinking when he writes:

> What is characteristically definitive of process philosophy as a distinct section of the philosophic tradition is not simply the commonplace recognition of natural processes as the active initiation of what exists in nature, but an insistence on seeing process as constituting an essential aspect of everything that exists – a commitment to the fundamentally processual nature of the real (1996, p. 8).

The process-inspired worldview is most closely identified with the British mathematician and philosopher Alfred North Whitehead (1861–1947), whose treatise *Process and Reality*, first published in 1929, elaborates the 'process' view. Other twentieth century philosophers such as William James (1842–1910), Henri Bergson (1859–1941) as well as Giles Deleuze (1925-1995), make distinctive contributions to process thought. For instance, much of Bergson's work focuses on 'time', William James pays particular attention to the pragmatic aspects of living in a process perceiving world and Deleuze offers insight into aspects of 'transformation' and 'difference'.

Like phenomenology, process philosophy embraces a range of approaches and concerns. In order to make sense of this vast and complex field, here we introduce three themes which run through much of the writing about process thought. Once these have been introduced, we will look at their implications for leadership and explore them more fully through a case study of a turnaround situation in a UK-based financial services firm.

Emphasis on Interconnections

Process thinking rests on the general theory of relatedness and continuity in social affairs. According to this way of thinking, life and society cannot be split into distinct and identifiable parts but rather must be conceived as an undivided, active process that is always shifting. Throughout their writings both Whitehead and Bergson suggest that life and nature are not distinct things or substances but instead are sensations, feelings and ideas seized from original process. Both philosophers assert that evolution is continuous. Living *is* changing, it is inventing. Nature's essence, its *élan vital*, is the creative advance into novelty.

Departing from Whitehead, Bergson argues the corresponding process of isolating, immobilizing or securing actual occasions from the limitless flow of 'virtual' possibilities is an 'imitation', which, although useful for capturing life, is 'a counterfeit of real movement' (Bergson 1912, p. 44). Synoptic models of change, such as Lewin's are good examples of this in that they draw attention to the difference in a being or organization between 'Point A' and 'Point C' but they do not adequately capture the movement between these points, in other words, the change itself.

Bergson is primarily a philosopher of temporality which he considers eludes our intellectual spatialization of things. He argues that we conceive immobility to be as real as movement and then mistake one for the other – an error which Whitehead called 'the fallacy of misplaced concreteness' (1967, p. 51). Nonetheless, time is always proceeding, it never completes: it is something lived and not merely thought. This is not to deny that time cannot be conceptualized. Clearly it can. Bergson's point is simply that our conception of time as a series of positions – one then the other – and so on is a matter of abstractive thinking and *not* a property of concrete experience (living time). Simply located positions are surface effects we employ to give substantiality to our experience but under whose 'givenness' the fluxing nature of reality is neglected.

In order to grasp this principle, Bergson argues, we must reverse our mental habits to see that mobility is the only actual reality. We must loosen ourselves from the intellectual force underlying the 'already made' and step more directly into the perpetual flow of the 'being made' (1983, p. 237).

These ideas are fundamentally informed by the concept of 'historicity, the second 'process theme' introduced here.

The Role of Historicity in Process Thought

Echoing Gadamer's ideas of prejudice and its impact on how we come to understand, process philosophy stresses that what we experience in the here and now is essentially derived from the past. It is inescapably embedded in the historicity of past events and in turn, it shapes future events. For instance, the way security is now handled in airports throughout the world emerged in the aftermath of the terrorist attacks on the USA on 11 September 2001. Without that occurrence, only being allowed to eat with plastic knives and forks while on an aircraft would make little sense. We have since seen how security measures themselves continually respond to new revelations of approaches terrorists might take to destroy mid-flight aircraft.

Whitehead articulates the impact of the past on the present when he writes that the 'passage of nature' or, in his words, its 'creative advance' is a fundamental condition of experience (Whitehead 1978). In this continuous advance or universal becoming, every occasion of experience is the outcome of its predecessors. Occasions of experience or 'actual entities' have a certain duration in which they arise, reach satisfaction and perish. They do not simply disappear without a trace. However, they always leave behind consequences that have the potential for entering into other passing moments of experience. Relating this idea to organizational change, it can be seen that arrival at a new 'Point C' will be the result of a multitude of factors both internal and external to the organization. That 'Point C' will subsequently influence potential futures. The possibility of identifying exact causal relationships from this perspective can be seen to be highly problematic.

There is an important distinction to be made between how process thinkers believe reality to 'be' (that is in constant flux and change) and how it is possible for human beings to relate to that constant flux, particularly in terms of how we can perceive it. The problem of perception from within a process worldview is the next theme explored.

Perceiving from a Process Perspective

Following from Whitehead, our knowledge about the world does not reside in a set of abstract and simply located entities – such as 'managers', 'leaders', or even 'organizations' – acting independently of one another. This simple location, though handy, definite and manageable, is an error of mistaking abstract concepts for substantial processes, that is 'the fallacy of misplaced concreteness' (Whitehead 1967, p. 51) once again. This abstraction from the immediate flow of experience tends to fix distinct and identifiable parts as timeless instants while omitting how they arrived there as well as what they are emerging towards.

The process view argues that the immediacy of each actual occasion is relational and 'arises as the bringing together into one real context diverse perceptions, diverse feelings, diverse purposes, and other diverse activities' (Whitehead 1927, p. 9). In other words, we might say that our immediate perception and subsequent meaning conceptualization are blended into one. The concreteness of experience, therefore, is constituted (paradoxically) in its passage. The first two lines of a popular Christian hymn, 'Abide with me; Fast falls the eventide' (Whitehead 1978, p. 209) characterize this possibility. Here, the perceptual permanence of 'abide' and 'me' in the first line is matched by the perpetual passage of 'fast' and 'falls' in the second line. Bringing these ideas together creates a new synthesis (passage *and* permanence; perishing *and* everlastingness).

Bearing this paradox in mind, Bergson enumerates two opposing tendencies for apprehending reality. The first is the logic of the *intellect,* with which we are most familiar. Through our intellectual perception we experience the world as an already determined series of solids. This view forces on us a static conception of the real which, if taken too far, cannot embrace the continuity of flow itself. The second is the method of *intuition*, whereby we plunge into the very life of something and identify ourselves with it by a kind of 'indwelling'. Here reality is expressed as 'fluid concepts', quite different from the static abstractions of traditional logic. On its own the intellect's 'spatial' abstraction of things is too deterministic. However, the flow of the actual world without a corresponding logic is too indiscernible, too 'inaudible'. Life is realized by infusing the intellect with intuition and not simply by reducing one to the other. It is a kind of intermediate position, an interval or existence placed halfway between both (Bergson 1983).

From an organizational theory perspective, Haridimos Tsoukas and Robert Chia allude to these two different ways of knowing organizations when they write about the need for concepts which enable meanings to be shared and contribute to joint action, but also the need for perceptions, which enable knowing from the 'inside'. In making this assertion, they draw on William James and write:

> Sensible reality is too concrete to be entirely manageable. We need to abstract it to harness its fluidity and concreteness on our conceptual systems to act systematically on it. It is not therefore only the case of change being immanent in organizations, but also the case of change being channelled, guided, led – in short of being organizational change (Tsoukas and Chia 2002, p. 577).

To summarize, according to process thinkers such as Whitehead and Bergson, our perceptual experience is a whole that cannot be separated into distinct zones – people/world or mental/physical – without involving the interplay *between* physical sensations and mental valuations. For example, think of what happens when you notice a vague feeling of emptiness in your abdominal cavity. As you attend to it, you might notice how it seems to rise into your chest and change to a slight tingling. At this point you must make a judgement; are you having a heart attack or are you only experiencing heartburn from eating a spicy meal the evening before?

As this example shows, what is significant in this never ending flow is the 'sense' we make of the perpetual coming into being and dissolution at a given point in time. However, sense is constructed not just in a given moment but as a result of the way in which the present relates to both past and future moments. In the above example the tingling sensation felt in the abdomen could have been linked to dinner eaten the night before. Had such a spicy meal not been eaten, another way of interpreting the discomfort experienced would have been identified. Perhaps the tingling could be attributed to nervousness associated with a job interview occurring the following day. This shows how sense is made of the moment-to-moment indwelling of physical and perceptual perceptions both in relation to previous moments but also through intuitions from the future.

Likewise, in an organizational meeting when the person leading the discussion suddenly slams his or her fist on the table and exclaims, 'this isn't good enough!' in a rather loud voice; this intervention is interpreted in relation to the individual's history of making such violent declarations. If this is an unusual behaviour, it may have more impact than if the individual regularly indulges in such outbursts. Those attending the meeting will make sense of this reaction by comparing it to the person's 'normal' behaviour, considering how it relates to the situation in which it is occurring (have profits significantly fallen?) or an anticipated future (is the organization about to be taken over in a hostile bid?). Perception of the 'here and now', therefore always involves the integration of both the up-close and particular moment, as well as a larger awareness of the maelstrom from which that perception momentarily emerges.

How do these three themes: interconnectedness and becoming, the role of historicity and the nature of perception, relate to notions of 'change'? Perhaps the idea of 'the event' will be helpful here.

Change as an 'Event'

If everything is constantly changing, how do we explain events which seem to stand out and signal that an important difference has occurred? Certainly the 11 September attacks on the World Trade Centre in 2001, the Tsunami in the Indian Ocean in December 2004 or the closure of Lehman Brothers in September 2008 were changes of a scale beyond the 'continual flux' suggested by process thought. How do such significant happenings relate to notions of continual becoming and historicity?

Through the lens of process philosophy, such occurrences are seen to have their genesis in an entire series of aligned processes. For instance, the collapse of Lehman Brothers will have been based in a series of decisions the investment house had made for years prior to the day it declared bankruptcy. Those decisions would have themselves been made within a context of worldwide de-regulation of banking processes and unforetold growth in unsecured credit. Historical events, such as the near collapse of another formidable investment house, Bear Stern, six months prior to Lehman Brother's demise will have contributed to the decision by the US government and other financial institutions not to come to the rescue. All of these factors and many more will have contributed to the 'event' of the organization's closure on 16 September 2008.

In process philosophy terms, Deleuze talks about an 'event', or *l'evenement* as a process of integration that produces an intensity of experience or unity of feeling 'that makes something – something rather than nothing – emerge' in the here and now (Deleuze 1994). The organizational theorists, Stephen Linstead and Torkild Thanem (2007), liken the event to the intensified sites of over-crossing where the beams of several lasers intersect. As an example of this, in his book, *House of Cards: A Tale of Hubris and Wretched Excess on Wall Street* (2009), William Cohan indicates how worried Wall Street analysts had been about the possibility of a domino-like collapse in world financial markets six months before things began to slide out of control. He suggests that there had been signals of the problems as early as 2005. However, the myriad of factors coalesced in the autumn of 2008, and in the 'concrete experience' of Lehman Brothers' demise, closely followed by that of Morgan Stanley, the reality of the chaos within financial markets could not be ignored.

The collapse of Lehman Brothers illustrates Deleuze's point that events are neither things that simply occur, such as an organized social occasion, nor things that simply reveal familiar definitions. An event does not mean that 'a man has been run over', 'a storm is coming' or 'a friend is arriving'. Instead, it points to the cracks that run through and disrupt lives and things, rearranging familiar identities, characteristics and relations along the way (Deleuze 1993, p. 76). In this way, the event refers to a *discontinuity*, a break, split or fracture. It is an unexpected, anomalous phenomenon. It sticks out from the mundane and the regular. It is something that takes us by surprise, something that seemingly comes out of nowhere. The actual sensation of an event is accompanied by a change in the relation between familiar standpoints, elements or groups. The attacks on the World Trade Centre certainly served to rearrange the relationship between the USA and the Muslim world (if not the rest of the international community). In early 2009, the rearrangements as a consequence of the collapse of Lehman Brothers have yet to be fully revealed and appreciated.

LEADERSHIP AS AN 'EVENT'

Process philosophy offers the possibility of conceptualizing leadership itself as an 'event'. This is very resonant with the model of leadership underpinning this text, in which leadership is seen as a 'moment' which is realized in the interpenetration of a person taking up the 'leader' role, those who would follow him or her, the purpose towards which their action is directed and the particular context in which they are located. When these strands join together in an intensive way, the experience of the leadership 'event' or 'moment' emerges. An illustration of such a moment could occur during the undertaking of a common leadership activity, that of chairing a meeting.

In the example of chairing a meeting, leadership is often very much identified with the person chairing. However, there are many different strands which contribute to the moment in which leading occurs. For instance, the room in which the meeting takes place will have been booked by someone, who might have had to take a lead in securing it (especially in organizations in which meeting space is at a premium). Someone will have had to organize an agenda and they may or may not have been the person designated to chair the meeting. The meeting will have been organized in order to progress certain aspects of the organization's business and those purposes may have been decided by others who will not be at the meeting (as in the case when a division of an organization meets to produce an implementation plan for a strategy that has been decided elsewhere in the organization). The organization will be operating within a certain context which will also play its role. For instance banks in which such meetings have been held in the early months of 2009 will have been affected by the world financial situation.

The moment when the Chair formally opens the meeting may be when 'leadership' is experienced most 'intensely' but it could not have occurred without the confluence of all of these strands. Even during the meeting, the enactment of 'leading' can move around as different organizational members take up positions and make interventions which are experienced as more or less 'leaderful'. In this way, the person identified as the 'leader' at any one point acts like a 'lightening conductor' for grounding significant interactions and collectively-informed perceptions.

The notion of an 'event' provides a novel way of conceptualizing the experience of leadership. It throws into sharp relief the limitations of theories which focus on the particular characteristics and traits of the person who would take up the formal 'leader' role. An individual may be blessed with an abundance of 'self-confidence', 'vision' or 'communication ability', but if they are not able to take up the role in a way which enables them to attend to the specific moment and respond to its requirements, these capabilities can be wasted. It also opens up the 'space' of leadership, suggesting that at any given time any individual, whether they hold a formal 'leader' role or not, can contribute to and exercise a major impact on the collectively produced leaderful moment. This might be particularly important in relation to the role of leadership vis-à-vis organizational change processes.

LEADING CHANGE FROM A 'PROCESS' PERSPECTIVE

As we have seen, process philosophy argues that change, rather than stability, more accurately describes the nature of reality. A number of organizational theorists, including Haridimos Tsoukas, Robert Chia, and Martin Wood[5] have already made significant forays into the implications of applying ideas from process philosophy into conceptualizing organizations and how they change. In fact Tsoukas and Chia (2002) suggest that we should think of organizational 'becoming', rather than organizational change, in an attempt to signal the ongoing nature of organizational flux.

If this is true, and change is always already occurring within organizations, why is it that so much attention is given to the notion of 'organizational change'? Tsoukas and Chia (2002) suggest that there is a distinction to be made between 'change in organizations', which they point out is always occurring, and 'organizational change'. In their terms, organizational change occurs when localized changes are institutionalized more broadly within the organization and become incorporated into everyday routines. A key enabler of this, they suggest, occurs through managers in powerful positions exercising their 'declarative powers' and bringing organizational attention to practices they want repeated. Perhaps exercising 'declarative powers' is a key role for leaders wanting to facilitate organizational change from a process perspective. There are other things they must do, however, before they begin declaring.

Attending to Patterns

Reality from a process perspective can be a very confusing experience. How does one make sense of life as a constantly altering kaleidoscope of colours, sounds, bodily feelings, growing and diminishing intensities? If we take that kind of awareness into our experience of organizations, we can soon become overwhelmed. 'Sensible reality is', as William James points out, 'too concrete to be entirely manageable' (1909 [1996], p. 247). In order to harness it in any way, we must abstract it. One of the key ways in which we use abstraction is by attending to patterns.

An important role for leadership, amidst the swirl of concrete experience, is to recognize patterns and then to bring them to others' attention. Here we are purposely using the word 'leadership' to indicate that people throughout the organization can be aware of different emerging trends. In fact those located in more junior hierarchical positions may enjoy particularly important insight to small shifts in the organizational context. For instance, those placed in customer facing roles might be sensitive to patterns of customer reactions than those situated in loftier organizational positions, who may not be in a position to notice. Telephonists and receptionists are often the first to observe different levels of customer or stakeholder interactions, as well as the issues that prompt them to make contact.

For example, the potential popularity of text messaging was a trend that senior executives at Nokia did not initially spot. It was only through the leadership of younger managers in the organization who themselves began to use this form of communication that the company began to capitalize on the potential of this technology. In fact text messaging has now become the 'most highly used form of interpersonal communication throughout the world' (Grey 2008) and organizations use it for purposes as varied as delivering payslips to announcing redundancies. People throughout an organization can exercise leadership by identifying emerging patterns and articulating what they see in a way that can be translated into organizational action.

Using 'Declarative Power' to Institutionalize Localized Changes

As hinted above, there is a step that needs to be taken between the point of spotting an emergent pattern and responding to it with appropriate organizational action. This is accomplished through exercising 'declarative power'. Individuals at different levels in the organization have access to different levels of power associated with their position and thus will have different levels of authority attached to what they might say. Generally, the CEO of an organization enjoys greater levels of authority and the declarative power to go along with that authority. This perhaps begins to account for why so much emphasis is placed on the role of CEOs in enabling change.

A good example of a CEO using his declarative powers to guide immanent change in an organization is the case of Stuart Rose, the Chief Executive of Marks & Spencers retail stores in the UK. At the beginning of 2005 Rose hit the news headlines with his proclamation of 'Plan A', a radical strategy for reducing Marks & Spencer's environmental impact.

Among the targets Rose outlined were commitments to reduce the organization's carbon footprint by 50 per cent, to generate zero waste and to source its raw materials through fairtrade agreements.[6]

Although Rose's announcement seemed sudden for those who had not been watching Marks & Spencers closely; on deeper examination, it is clear that the organization had steadily been moving towards such a commitment. Certainly Rose was one of the first CEOs to make such a public statement about his firm's commitment to operating in a way which would lower the firm's impact on the environment. However, there had been many employees within Marks & Spencers who had been leading 'green initiatives' within the company for many years prior to his announcement.

In fact, it was through one of their promptings that Rose attended a showing of the Al Gore film, 'An Inconvenient Truth', which graphically depicts the imminent effects of climate change unless large-scale action is taken very quickly. Rose's viewing of the film (along with a number of his senior managers) provided a springboard for his 'declaring' environmental sustainability as a key priority for the organization. This pronouncement probably would not have led to effective action had there not been grassroots activity towards this end already taking place within the company.

Rose has 'led' this change to the extent that he has declared achieving a higher level of environmental sensitivity as a key priority for the organization, thus amplifying local changes already occurring within it. He has backed up this spoken commitment by holding his senior managers accountable for achieving their 'Plan A' targets in the same way that they are accountable for reaching their financial targets. In summary then, rather than leading through 'creating a vision' and 'communicating it', Rose has noticed and formalized activities that were already happening in the company, he has demonstrated the priority of this change by holding people accountable for targets and he has made public statements about the company's stance.

What if an organizational member notices something occurring in the environment which they believe might be very important for the organization to pay attention to but no one will listen? What might be a 'leaderful act' in such circumstances?

Creating Disruption

Imagine being a middle manager of a large organization. You notice something in the external environment that could negatively affect your firm's ability to continue to be successful. For instance, you might have worked for Kodak as a film processor just as digital photographic equipment began to enter the market. You notice how this new technology enables camera users to be much more in control of the photos they process. Whereas traditional technology meant that an entire film had to be processed in order for the client to get two or three good pictures, digital photography allowed people to choose photos before they processed them into prints. Even more worryingly, this technology enabled photographs to be stored on computers rather than being printed.

You bring your concerns to the senior management of the company and they are dismissed. They argue that the technology is expensive, that people like photographic prints and that certainly this technology will not have the impact you are proposing. What can you do?

From a process philosophy perspective, one of the key levers for generating accelerated change is to create disruption in the system. This can involve exacerbating existing scenarios so that they become critical – in order that they become 'intensified' and reveal discontinuities and cracks in the system. Creating such disruption is recognized as a viable 'change' strategy by many organizational change theorists. Robert Quinn, for instance, in his book, *Change the World: How Ordinary People can Achieve Extraordinary Results* (2000), highlights 'creating disruption' as a critical tactic for bringing people's attention to important patterns and shifts. Process philosophy suggests that the reason this can work is because disruption creates an intensified experience which interrupts people from seeing the situation in their habitual ways. Creating disruption can be done for both well-intended and degenerative purposes. Certainly creating disruption for the sake of unsettling and manipulating people can be not only unpleasant but unethical. However, when used to alert people to shifts in the context which may be dangerous or challenging, such disruption can actually be beneficial.

Examples of such beneficial disruptions are well-known among those fighting for social justice, for instance. Rosa Parks' refusal to give her bus seat to a white man in the 1950s was such a form of creative disruption which served to spark the simmering Civil Rights Movement for African-Americans in the USA. Wangari Muta Maathai's planting of trees in Nigeria could be seen as creative disruptive action. It not only brings our attention to the relationship between trees and ecological health but has caught the attention of Nigerian leaders to the extent that she has been jailed for her actions on several occasions.[7] As Muta Maathai's story demonstrates, there are risks associated with such interventions, both for those instigating them and for the change process itself. This is because, as process philosophy tells us, the direction of change when a myriad of factors come together cannot be predicted.

Let us explore the insights process philosophy offers our understanding of organizational change by using it to analyse one of the most dramatic formal organizational change processes; that of corporate turnaround.

THE CASE OF JV CORPORATION

The research for the following case study was undertaken by John Pillay, one of the co-authors of this chapter. Working as an organizational consultant specializing in effecting corporate turnaround, John interviewed a range of people who had been employed by JV Corporation throughout the three years in which the turnover was undertaken in order to better understand their perceptions of the change. Included in the people interviewed were the company's CEO, most of the executive directors, the change programme directors and senior operational managers.[8] Here the data Pillay collected is analysed through the lens of the ideas from process philosophy introduced earlier.

Background to the Case

JV Corporation (name withheld) was formed in 2000 as a Business Processing Outsourcing (BPO) joint venture between two UK-based banks and an IT service provider. A third bank also joined the consortium as a shareholder roughly one year after the creation of the company. The organization had at that stage several thousand employees and was based across multiple sites in the UK. The majority of its staff were employed in back office processing operations, much of which entailed semi-skilled labour and manual handling tasks.

The early years of the organization's history were very difficult for shareholders, management and staff alike. A formally instituted change programme was created at the inception of the joint venture to consolidate processes and technologies onto a single operational platform. In 2003, approximately 500 staff were employed to drive this programme which involved site closures, technology change and process re-engineering. By the end of 2004, the programme was in significant trouble and had little tangible success to record. At this stage the company was also making heavy losses. At the end of 2004, the company was deeply in debt and it was believed that the owner shareholders were seriously considering withdrawing from the joint venture.

The failure of the change programme seemed to be a major source of concern for the organization and its shareholders. The Change Director described the situation from his perspective:

Basically the whole thing was an absolute mess . . . to give you an example, I think that at one point in the whole of the world [the majority shareholder] had something like 8 or 9 'red' rated projects . . . so these were ones that would go up to [the CEO] to reference. And of those 8 or 9 I think that I had 6 of them. And so that just goes to highlight the level of concern that there was around the whole place.

There were many stories about failed projects, some of which had serious consequences for the organization. An operations manager explained the impact of failed change from his perspective:

[There were] massive changes you know. Tens of millions of pounds of investment infrastructure, of software support, all that sort of stuff . . . And I sat in various meetings including very senior, the most senior people in our organization . . . saying 'we shouldn't be doing this. And if we do it we cannot know the cost of failure here. It could be tens of millions.' And the collective group ignored my comments and went full steam ahead. It cost us millions and millions and that was simply because we jumped too far too fast and didn't have the strength and depth to (a) appreciate the size of the problem or listen and (b) invest a bit up front to fix it.

In many ways it seemed as though the failings of the change programme symbolized many of the issues present in the JV Corporation prior to the turnaround. What is most interesting from a process thinking point of view is that from these interviews, it is clear that the factors impacting on JV Corporation's failure were well-known throughout the company. The fissures and discontinuities were clearly evident for those who cared to attend to them.

As is so often the case, an apparent catalyst for significant change was the appointment of a new CEO. In the time which is subsequently labelled as 'the turnaround', during 2005 and 2006, a number of other key changes in personnel and ways of operating were made. A new management team was put into place, the business was refinanced, the organization reduced its headcount by approximately 40 per cent, the change programme was stabilized and the company started to turn a profit for the first time. At the time of writing the JV Corporation is on track to pay back its debts and contract renewal is regarded as almost a formality with its major shareholders. The post-turnaround organization has stable operations and there is a healthy portfolio of new business.

The following sections analyse themes arising from the interviews Pillay conducted in terms of the three 'process thinking' aspects seen to be particularly relevant to the role of leading within formal organizational change initiatives. Let us start by considering how the JV Corporation story illustrates the importance of attending to patterns.

Attending to the Patterns

As alluded to earlier, a recurring theme offered by those interviewed was that many of the problems in the organization were well known, but were not discussed directly between the management team and shareholders. A senior leader described his role in breaking through this 'undiscussable' barrier:

> It was a case of the Emperor's new clothes. People were in denial about what was going on. So I did some analysis saying 'if the trajectory we are going on at the moment continues and we don't bring some element of order, then what does the end picture look like?' So it was about building the picture of the stark reality. Bringing [it] to light, so that no-one could deny what the burning platform would look like. Getting to a position where, you know, there is conscious incompetence rather than unconscious incompetence.

This quote illustrates both the importance of individuals located throughout the organization spotting patterns and utilizing 'disruption' as a key way of encouraging people to pay attention to them. He highlighted to the others 'what the burning platform would look like'.

Exercising authority in declaring 'what the burning platform would look like' was also critical. For instance, reflecting on his early months with the company, the newly appointed CEO reported:

> And the first thing I did in the early months was try to work out what the key problems were. On a daily basis I would sit down with the head of operations, the head of major programmes that looked after its clients, the head of key functions and we would say how much progress have we made to resolve today's issues, how much progress have we made to fixing the past, what resource do we need, what priority do we need to give. So it was absolute focus from the top of the organization.

The CEO then went on to explain that this news was not well received by the majority shareholder:

> The parent company went apoplectic when I told them what I thought the level of the shortfall was, which was worse than they thought . . . And we wasted so much time . . . senior management prepared for three days a week for two, two-hour bollockings from [the majority shareholder]. But you know we had to work up the financials to work up a proposal, a way forward, we had to make up some stories.

This quote illustrates the difficulties associated with articulating patterns if they reveal unpalatable 'truths'. This is perhaps one of the most significant reasons that emerging patterns are ignored – they reveal realities that the organization will find challenging and even frightening. In many ways it is much easier just to ignore such trends. In the case of JV Corporation, the CEO was willing to voice these unpleasant truths. It was only then that the organization could respond effectively to the situation. This demonstrates the vital role of exercising declarative powers when taking up the leader role in change processes.

Using Declarative Powers

Seeing the patterns does not on its own influence change; making those patterns apparent to others is critical. Bearing in mind the more collective view of leadership offered here, it is important to note that it was not just the CEO who can use declarative powers to bring attention to those institutional practices which need to be adapted. Sometimes those positioned in lower parts of an organization's hierarchy must exercise their own declarative powers to bring attention to dangers, or opportunities, they perceive. Many of those interviewed commented on how they had personally tried to engage and influence the new CEO, for example: 'We'd go out in groups and obviously have a big conversation . . . he would allow us to get our messages across to somebody we knew would do something about it'.

The fact that the CEO did something with the information people were telling him is also crucial. In JV Corporation there were numerous stories about how the new CEO 'took on' the key issues discussed; thereby encouraging further candidness. An interviewee expressed this in the following way: 'Me and a few others were saying, you know there were three or four things that we mentioned to him over a curry, and they have been done . . . In the end we were singing folk songs about him'.

The CEO deliberately set up sessions where staff could talk with him about the patterns they saw and what needed to be done. These sessions included dinners, drinks and even overnight meetings 'with nightshift staff' where the CEO and groups of trusted managers talked informally about what they noticed going on in the company. Given the number of interviewees that cited these discussions and the effect that they had, it was clearly felt that the CEO valued their opinions and was acting on them. One manager who had been part of these sessions noted:

> [the CEOs] different, you know, a real bulldog and he had that respect . . . It just gave you confidence as well. When he sat down, when he sat down with you, it just inspired confidence. I think it goes to show you what a strong leader will give to an organization.

One of the initiatives introduced by the CEO and his executive team which most clearly allowed them to exercise 'declarative powers' was a rolling cycle of staff roadshows, which continue to this day. The CEO explained this philosophy:

> Get in front of the people. You have to, even if it is a really difficult message and people hate you for it. And you know, I'm considered to be a fascist by some people in some locations despite what we achieved in others they consider me a bit of a saviour. You've got to just get out there and tell them the truth, give them some hope about where you are going. And if there is no hope, still tell them the truth.

Such a forum provides a formal mechanism through which a leader might exercise declarative powers. On a day-to-day basis, however, messages are conveyed by what a leader 'does'. Within the JV Corporation, creating disruption proved to be an important enabler for the turnaround.

Creating Disruption

Perhaps the idea most clearly supported by the JV Corporation case is the role disruption plays in creating the 'event' of change. A multitude of disruptions were actively implemented within the company, the most ironic of which was the radical reconfiguration of the formal change programme itself. In a major signal to staff and shareholders, the new CEO suspended the programme and undertook a re-evaluation of priorities. In the words of one programme manager, there was the view 'we need to lock down here, and stop the haemorrhaging and consider what we really can do and can't do'. Many aspects of the change programme had been written into agreements with shareholders and clients, so suspending it was regarded as a significant challenge to the status quo.

The Risk Director recalled the personal drive of the CEO in resetting the change programme:

> We felt that we were obliged to [carry on with] the change [programme]. But he just got in a room with a bunch of people for weeks on end and we went through every single bit of change and where we were at and what the implications were. And one by one he put them into one of three buckets: stuff that we were never going to do, because it didn't make sense to do it, because it was too difficult, or because it was you know, ill-thought out. Things we definitely had to do to keep the business alive and there was a smaller bucket of changes we could make . . . he was extremely brave.

One of the most significant disruptions created was the resetting of the senior programme management team. Many saw this as a critical milestone in the JV Corporation's turnaround. This was not the first time the change management team had been reorganized but on this occasion the shift was perceived to be significant. In the words of the incoming Change Director: 'people were saying "I've had enough of this now"'. It seemed as though previous attempts had lacked the same degree of conviction. A number of interviewees remembered the disappointment that had followed an earlier attempt to reset the change programme a few years earlier and how its failure had badly affected morale.

Commenting on the purpose of resetting the change programme, the CEO noted 'I realized that change was destroying my ability to deliver a good service'. He went on to emphasize that a new attitude to change needed to be created: 'We stopped change being allowed to land and fail . . . we stopped a lot of change, but change that had to go through we tested much more rigorously to ensure that when it landed it worked and it didn't destabilize the operation'.

Another key disruption was caused through the substantial reduction in the workforce. Reducing headcount is another commonly used organizational change tactic. However, the CEO explained that the rationale for reducing numbers in this case was not so much to reduce costs as to 'free up the organization's mindset'. He explained: 'You can change people, and you can get a lot more out of them, but I do think that you need to change an element of the DNA. The old adage "fire people with enthusiasm or fire people with enthusiasm". You know, you have got to do both'.

In addition to reducing the size of the organization, reporting structures changed in line with the diminished role for the majority shareholder. Business units, support areas and premises were restructured as a part of these changes. In the view of the operations director, layers of management and processes which had existed before got in the way of delivering accountabilities, thus stifling the capacity of the organization to deliver its core services: 'They had an unbelievably complex efficiency measurement process that clever people had built . . . I had masses of data . . . I decided to chuck all that away because it was all totally meaningless . . . So we threw it all away'.

In the pre-turnaround organization there had been high dependence on heavy documentation and reporting systems. Another disruption occurred as these tracking mechanisms were overhauled and replaced in all the main parts of the organization. A programme director described how he changed reporting systems for his project management teams: 'I quite consciously decided that I would forget methods and processes, and I would focus on getting some outcomes out. So I deliberately ignored the organization and its methods and I put in place management processes; my own, that allowed me to drive people to focus on outcomes'.

A final form of organizational disruption worth noting here is change to the management routines instigated throughout the organization. Perhaps most significantly, the CEO described the new management philosophy as based on 'close' management: 'We actually micro-managed. I think that what you need from a change programme perspective is to implement a process which has very close management, very regular management'.

The requirements for close scrutiny of the change and operational parts of the JV Corporation business gave rise to new management routines and an abandonment of old systems. One of these became known as the 'Exec review'. The CEO described it in the following way:

> Our rules are simple, every week every project has to provide an update on what it is up to, where it has fallen short, what it is planning to do in the immediate future and where it needs help. And the basic rules are absolute integrity. No surprises . . . the thing I don't accept is, being told you knew you had a problem weeks ago and you haven't told me about it. Dead heroes are no use to me.

This quote brings the analysis full-circle back to the importance of perceiving patterns, especially if they indicate potential problems for the organization. Whereas those in authority can sometimes 'shoot the messenger' who brings attention to discomforting trends, the CEO in this instance encouraged just the opposite behaviour. 'Tell me about the problems before they arise', he requested. From a process thinking viewpoint, a key role for leadership is to encourage those who recognize potentially dangerous patterns to speak up, rather than remain silent.

Analysing the JV Corporation case through the frame of process thinking reveals some of the paradoxes inherent in leading change which are often ignored by more traditional change literature. Rather than spearheading new initiatives, leading calls firstly for being attentive to small; and not so small shifts in both the external and the internal contexts. Using the authority vested in one's formal position is important, not so much for pushing the organization in a certain direction but for amplifying and enabling positive shifts which might already be occurring. Knowing when to create disruption and how to do so in a way that will not destabilize essential organizational elements is also vital. The final section of the chapter explores these ideas in greater depth.

LEADING CHANGE FROM A PROCESS-ORIENTED PERSPECTIVE

What new insights does process philosophy bring to the question, 'How do leaders lead change?'

Leading, which enables desired change to occur within organizations is still important from the process viewpoint but perhaps in a different way from that suggested by more traditional accounts. Whereas those accounts tend to rely heavily on synoptic assumptions about the nature of change, emphasizing the role of an individual leader's vision and ability to mobilize people towards that vision, a process-oriented view, suggests a leader's efforts might be better spent attending to trends and patterns already emerging from a given context. For instance, managers in the JV Corporation knew that much of what was being touted in the formal change process was, as one manager put it, 'a case of the emperor's new clothes'. In the localized contexts in which daily work was occurring, managers had long recognized the patterns indicative of failure of the formal change programme.

It seems that until the new CEO arrived, no one either listened to their perspectives or provided an opportunity for them to share their perspectives. Importantly, this was one of the key actions taken by the new CEO; just listening to people recount their versions of the reality of the change process. In this way, rather than formulating a radical vision, he attended to what was already present. Having reached an understanding of the organizational landscape, he then exercised the declarative power invested in the CEO role to announce and support shifts necessary for those localized contexts to work more effectively. Those commenting on his actions noted the courage it took to instigate critical shifts, such as diminishing the role of the majority shareholder in the executive team, halting the formal change programme and making people accountable for a few key performance indicators. A process orientation then does not dismiss the need for leaders in enabling such a formally-driven organizational change process to occur; but, what that leader is called to do is slightly different.

In particular, the need for someone to take the lead in enabling collective sense-making processes to occur is highlighted. In a world of constant flux and change, individuals need to know what to pay attention to in order to accomplish the pragmatic necessities of living and working. For instance, if I am so overwhelmed by the myriad of data which infuses my senses every instant of my life, I will not be able to discern that instead of stopping to listen to the song of a skylark, I should keep walking to avoid a collision with an oncoming tractor. Leaders can play an important role in helping organizational members to frame the 'concreteness' of their working lives in a way that enables them to pursue organizational purposes. Such is the power of measurements and targets. To be truly effective however, targets need to be grounded in shared understandings of the way in which they contribute to organizational aims.

Of course, in the model of leadership presented throughout this book, such sense-making does not occur solely through the insights of the 'leader' at the top of the organizational hierarchy declaring them as true for the rest of the organization. The point is that wherever 'leadership' is exercised during the formal organizational change processes, an important aspect of 'leading' is using one's authority, whether it is positional, expert or referent, to 'declare' a version of reality which can then be engaged with by other organizational members. Chapter 6 has argued that such sense-making is dialogic rather than monologic and, in this chapter, the example of the JV Corporation further supports this. Organizational members referred on numerous occasions to the fact that the CEO listened to their views and in acting on them demonstrated the two-way nature of the sense-making process. Leading in contexts of change often requires taking the first step in initiating such a dialogue.

It is important not to neglect the role power plays in deciding how collective versions of reality are achieved. Generally, heads of organizations or communities are invested with the positional authority to declare the version of reality to which organizational members are encouraged to subscribe. If the head is inept at spotting significant patterns or often mistakes what is inconsequential for what is essential, organizational dysfunction can result. Furthermore, if the head does not draw from the resource of individuals who might be more astute at identifying these patterns, the organization could be heading for trouble. How might others involved in such a situation contribute to the organization's leadership in such a way that a more positive scenario might emerge?

This chapter has suggested the importance of 'disruption' as an enabler of organizational change. As disruption causes attention to be drawn to the discontinuities, the irregularities and anomalies between a prescribed course of action and emerging reality, it can be a powerful means by which a collective's energy can be mobilized. Although creating such disruption can be one means by which organizational members might exercise leadership, such action also requires the exercise of discernment and wisdom if it is to lead to generative ends. How one might take up that role wisely is a question due some consideration and is the focus of the next chapter. In doing so, it will revisit notions from phenomenology and hermeneutics introduced previously in the book.

NOTES

1. Dr Martin Wood is Senior Lecturer in Organization Studies at the York Management School, York University, UK.
2. John Pillay is a DBA student at Cranfield School of Management, Cranfield University, UK and a Change Program Director at ANZ Bank, Melbourne, Australia.

3. As this chapter is co-authored by three people, the pronoun 'we' will be used throughout, as opposed to the 'I' used in previous chapters.
4. See Keith Grint's book *The Arts of Leadership* (2001), Oxford University Press, for an analysis of the correlation between football teams, their managers and their success.
5. See their articles such as: Tsoukas, H. and R. Chia (2002), 'On Organizational becoming rethinking organizational change', *Organization Science*, 13 (5), 567-582, and Wood, M. (2005), 'The Fallacy of misplaced leadership', *Journal of Management Studies*, 42 (6), 1101-1121.
6. For more information about Marks & Spencer's 'Plan A' see: http://plana.marksand spencer.com/ (accessed 8 June 2009).
7. See the story of Wangari Muta Maathai (2008) in her autobiography: *UnBowed: My Autobiography*, by Wangari Muta Maathai, London: Arrow Books.
8. The study was undertaken as part of the Doctorate in Business Administration programme at Cranfield School of Management, Cranfield University. It was supervised by Dr Ashley Braganza of Brunel Business School. For a fuller account of the case, see the conference paper: Pillay, J. and A. Braganza (2008), 'The architectonics of transformational change: towards a dialogic theory of corporate turnaround', Proceedings of the 2008 British Academy of Management Conference, Harrogate.

8. How can individuals take up the leader role wisely?

> To be a really good and noble guardian of the State requires [one to] unite in himself philosophy and spirit and swiftness and strength.
>
> Plato
> *The Republic, Book II*
> (380 BCE [1992], p. 229)

The contemporary philosopher Alisdair MacIntyre begins his seminal book, *After Virtue* (1985), by describing a scenario in which a catastrophe has befallen the human race and continuity between the past and the present has been severed. Only scraps of the previous history and culture remain and without a connecting narrative, no one is sure of their significance. Some things are recognized as being symbolic but no one can interpret them. People have vague memories of different modes of thinking but without a direct link to the past they are unable to glean any insight from them or apply them to the present context. MacIntyre suggests that such a situation is analogous to that experienced by many of us when attempting to incorporate ethical thinking and behaviour into our lives. We know there is something of importance called 'ethics' but we do not quite understand its legacy nor why certain principles influence our thinking so much.

MacIntyre goes on to observe the incommensurability of different ethical approaches when applied to particular situations. For example, he revisits the question of whether or not abortion is ethically correct. Approaching the question from one set of ethical principles, the rights of the child as a creature deserving moral consideration dictate that abortion is not ethical. However, from a standpoint that recognizes the mother and her desires as primary, abortion is seen as not only ethical but as an important means by which women's rights are preserved.

How to make decisions between competing claims for ethical correctness is a conundrum many of those taking up the leader role face on a daily basis. This is particularly true in our increasingly interconnected world in which contrasting moral values compete with one another in the decision-making realm. What is the ethically correct choice on entering a country in which the way things are done is through bribery, when one's ethical stance (or one's firm's ethical policy) prohibits the giving of gifts or money for these purposes?

How might the head of an organization committed to using locally manufactured components resolve the effects of that decision on poorer economies which depend on their sales for people's livelihoods? Which system of ethics should prevail in such decision-making arenas? The ability to make ethical decisions amongst competing versions of 'what is right' calls for more than the application of abstract ethical principles. It requires wisdom.

Drawing on the work of Horst Rittell and Melvin Webber (1973), the British leadership scholar, Keith Grint (2005a), distinguishes between three types of problems which regularly face those in authority. The first he terms 'critical' and are generated by crises in which decisions need to be taken quickly, without recourse to deliberation. In such circumstances 'command' power is used by those in authority to clarify what needs to be done immediately. The second type of problem, 'tame' problems are those faced by managers and involve the identification and implementation of a particular system to deal with issues that have previously been encountered. The authority of leadership, however, is needed when dealing with the third type of problem, what he labels 'wicked' problems. Those are new dilemmas which have not arisen before and for which there are no 'right' answers. Grint argues that leadership authority in these types of situations is by far the most difficult to enact because it involves asking 'the right questions rather than provid[ing] the right answers because the answers may not be self evident and will require collaborative processes in order to make progress' (Grint 2005a, p. 1473).

Discovering the right questions, gathering the information such questions generate and then navigating a way forward by applying ethical principles with discernment constitute wise leadership. How can these capacities be developed? What can individuals do if they aspire to taking up the leader role not just ethically but with wisdom as well? Finally, if leadership is conceptualized as a collective process rather than one solely located within individual actors, are there ways in which wisdom can be collectively embodied and enacted? In other words, can 'leadership', as well as 'leaders', act wisely?

This chapter addresses these questions. It begins by surveying some of the ideas which inform current thinking about the intersection of leadership and ethics, highlighting some of the issues which remain problematic within the field. It goes on to consider how those taking up the leader role might hone their capacity to do so with wisdom, by revisiting ideas from phenomenology, hermeneutics and aesthetics. In particular, practices associated with each of these schools of philosophy are offered as methods for developing ethical insight. The chapter ends by exploring the possibility of wise collective leadership practices through discussing ideas of virtue and 'phronesis' or practical wisdom.

ETHICAL LEADERSHIP, WISE LEADERSHIP

What is the relationship between ethical action, wisdom and leadership? Let us start by considering the term 'ethical'. The words 'ethical' and 'moral' are often used interchangeably and, in fact, differences between them are contested within philosophical literature.[1] The leadership scholar, James MacGregor Burns, advocates drawing a distinction between three different 'leadership values': ethical virtues, ethical values and moral values. 'Ethical virtues' he describes as 'old fashioned character tests', attributes to which a person should aspire such as kindness, generosity and sobriety. In other words ethical virtues are 'rules of personal conduct' (Burns 2004, pp. *ix–x*). Ethical values are more aligned with valued forms of behaviour, such as trustworthiness, reliability, reciprocity and as such are variable from culture to culture. Moral values he defines as more collectively determined tenets associated with fraternity and include qualities such as justice, community and equality (p. x).

Burns' recognition of those things 'moral' as having a communal basis is echoed in other writers' distinctions between the ethical and the moral, with 'ethics' being associated with individually-based reflection on questions of 'right or wrong' and morality often more closely associated with the normative societal codes for living with one another. Both definitions are grounded in the question of how one should conduct oneself in the world vis-à-vis other people. Whereas it is relatively simple to agree that we should not deny one another life by acts of murder, the tension comes in making ethical decisions which affect our own well-being as well as those around us. Rather than pursuing the argument about the differences between the 'moral' and the 'ethical' further, in this text I would like to focus on the purpose behind both, which concerns how we might best conduct ourselves in relation to one another.

Being able to traverse this territory and arrive at satisfactory answers is particularly important for individuals taking up the leader role. The philosopher and leadership scholar Joanne Ciulla emphasizes this point when she writes:

> Leadership is not a person or a position. It is a complex moral relationship between people based in trust, obligation, commitment, and a shared vision of the good. . . . Ethics live at the heart of all human relationships and hence at the heart of the relationship between leaders and followers (2004, p. xv).

As Ciulla's quote suggests, ethics could be seen to be at the very heart of leading. This is largely because of the part influence plays within the relationship between leaders and followers. Defining leadership as a relationship in which the leader influences followers without recourse to coercion,

James MacGregor Burns counters the question of whether or not Hitler was a leader by arguing that since he used severe methods of coercion in order to maintain his authority, he is better classified as a tyrant than a leader. By relying on threat, rather than persuasion and influence, one gives up any pretence of 'leading', he argues (Burns 2004, pp. xi–xii).

Of course, the distinction between influence and threat can often be thinly defined (and perhaps even more thinly experienced). Even well-intentioned influence can give off a whiff of manipulation. Treading the 'ethical' side of the influence/coercion line is often not a clear-cut choice. In acknowledging the difficulties associated with navigating this territory, two issues inherent to the leadership relationship which require ethical consideration become clear. Firstly, ethics is fundamentally about a relationship between people. Human relationships imply ethical considerations. As mentioned previously, this is because humans are considered to be (in most civilizations) beings worthy of 'moral consideration'; that is they need to be considered from a moral perspective.

Different philosophical systems suggest that this consideration should be exercised in different ways. For instance, from a Kantian perspective, it is never morally permissible to use human beings as 'means to ends', no matter how virtuous the ends. Utilitarian perspectives might differ on this point, suggesting instead that using human beings as 'means to ends' in ways that provide the most happiness or the least pain for other humans could be morally justifiable. The point here is not to determine which is correct but to bring attention to the fact that in most human communities it is assumed that humans need to be considered from a moral perspective.[2] As here leadership is conceptualized as a phenomenon enacted amongst groups of people, it follows that all of those involved in leadership should be considered from a moral perspective.

The second reason that ethics are at the heart of leadership relates to the first and concerns the power relations inherent in its enactment. Most definitions suggest that leadership includes an influencing process. Whether influence is accomplished through hierarchical relations and the ability to bestow rewards or whether it is accomplished through referent power in which followers are influenced by the sheer attractiveness of a leader's personality, power is still involved. If power is to be exercised appropriately and wisely, the ethics of using that power must be acknowledged. It is important to bring the nature of that power to an articulated and conscious level in order that it can be enacted wisely.

The trouble is that what is ethically correct in a given situation is not always easily determined. Certain acts may be effective or appropriate in some situations but not in others. Even a seemingly obvious ethical principle, such as 'do not kill other human beings', is contestable in times of war or in the face of mortal threat. (Although there are ethical systems which insist that even in those circumstances it is right to refrain from killing.) It is hard to identify a maxim which would hold true in any situation and at any historical period of time. Ethical practice is contextually, historically and culturally determined.

The context-specific nature of ethics becomes clear for organizations operating across cultural and national boundaries. In nations where child labour is the only means by which families can earn enough to live, is it morally correct for Western companies to enforce their own laws concerning the employment of children? Is there such a large distinction between the overt bribery which is part of getting business done in some countries and gift-giving practices between suppliers and buyers which is the norm in others? How is the ethically correct action determined in such instances?

The majority of organizational and community leaders with whom I come into contact want to make the best decision when they encounter such quandaries. Many executives lose sleep over difficult decisions about who to fire during downturns in the economy or how to implement policies which might hurt people in the short-term but could enable longer-term benefits. These are highly contested judgement calls. One senior manager of a UK-based financial services organization which is consistently regarded as one of the best in terms of its ethical reputation reflected on how he thinks about business ethics in the following quote:

> If there is a law about it, or a code of ethics or code of practice about it, then it's not really an ethical issue. Then it is just a case of, if it says you don't do this, you don't do this. What we think of as ethical issues are those in which there is no clear-cut policy or law to which one can refer. It's then that the manager involved has to exercise ethical judgement.

I am suggesting here that making such ethical judgements requires the application of wisdom.

Wisdom involves making judgements between possible different ethical options. Going back to the opening section of this chapter, exercising wisdom requires an understanding of the informing principles behind different ethical positions and taking a meta-view as to which is most apt in a given situation. For Aristotle (1976), wisdom and virtue are very closely linked and require the ability to discern and enact a balance between extreme positions. For instance, the virtue of courage occupies the balancing point between cowardice and recklessness. Wisdom is required in exercising such judgement.

More than merely indicating that such a balancing point exists, how might philosophy contribute to leaders' ability to embody wisdom in their decisions and actions? Questions about the ethical dimension of leadership or management have been one domain in which philosophers have made significant contributions already.[3] This chapter does not take the more usual route of rehearsing different philosophical positions which could inform ethical debate (for example, deontological, utilitarian, consequentialist.) Instead it introduces philosophical practices which might enable individuals to develop the capacity for dealing wisely with the ethical dilemmas they face when taking up the leader role. To do this, I turn once again to phenomenology, hermeneutics and aesthetics.

PHENOMENOLOGICAL PRACTICES AND ETHICAL DELIBERATION

Although phenomenology encompasses a broad range of different philosophical ideas as indicated in Chapter 2, there are several consistent themes present in the writings of those aligned with this tradition. In particular, phenomenologists understand human apprehension to be an embodied activity dependent on how we are physically related to other phenomena. Appreciation of this is recognized through phenomenology's attention to 'aspects', 'sides' and 'identity' and the recognition that our perceptual apparatus limits us from ever experiencing the 'other' in its entirety at any one point in time. In other words, phenomenology acknowledges our limitations as perceptual beings.

This recognition of human limitation seems to be an important starting point for ethical engagement from a phenomenological point of view. At its very basis, phenomenology recognizes that as human beings we are not omnipotent and can never know everything about a given situation. Such an understanding perhaps warrants caution as a first principle for taking up ethical stances.

However, it is not enough to be cautious, those enacting the leader role are charged with taking action as well. Does phenomenology offer us any process which might enable our ability to engage with dilemmas ethically and with wisdom? Perhaps the phenomenological practice of 'dwelling' offers a potential way forward.

'Dwelling'[4]

Philosophically the term 'dwelling' is most clearly linked to the work of Martin Heidegger (1889–1976). Heidegger was a pupil of Husserl and is recognized as developing the older philosopher's ideas in radical ways, particularly through his book *Being and Time* published in 1962. The essay 'Building dwelling thinking' (1971) in which his idea of 'dwelling' was developed, was written in the aftermath of the Second World War when Germany was suffering from an acute housing shortage. Thus the problem of 'dwelling' was one of both literal and metaphorical resonance for his audience at the time.

For Heidegger 'dwelling' is a central mode of human existence. Heidegger was a great etymologist and in his essays he often refers to the history of words to disclose deeper nuances of their meanings. In this case he links the word 'dwelling', in German *bauen*, to the German verb *bin*, that is, 'to be', thereby linking *bauen* with an essential aspect of being. To be, Heidegger asserts, is to dwell.

At its heart, dwelling is a reciprocal way of being in the world. As we dwell, we make an impact on the world and it also makes an impact on us. For instance, when I garden, which is in many ways a quintessential 'dwelling' activity, my actions affect the soil. I dig the earth and place apple trees and roses into it and in doing so I modify the landscape. Even as I garden, however, the earth also makes an impact on me. Digging the soil makes my muscles ache, the moistness from the ground invades my nostrils and infuses my awareness with the musty scent of decay, the songs of birds and drone of insects tickle my inner ear. I am altered, as I alter the ground around me.

In a similar way, when I dwell in the role of leader, I affect others around me. When I intervene in a situation, it subtly shifts and the way in which it changes also exercises its influence on me. For instance, perhaps as the leader of an organization I might decide to restructure reporting lines in such a way that a number of people are no longer required. Letting them go impacts on the organization both overtly, in that other people have to undertake their work differently, and symbolically, as those remaining make sense of the restructuring activity. Their new work patterns and reactions contribute to emerging organizational practices and identity which, in turn, impact on the way in which I am able to take up the leader role.

Throughout this book leadership has been conceptualized as essentially a participative endeavour and one in which the relational element creates something anew. The constant exchange at the centre of leadership relations could be seen to be indicative of dwelling. There are three further concepts which might bring further insight into how dwelling occurs and could aid ethical deliberation. The first is 'staying with'.

Staying with

There is a particular quality of dwelling noted by Heidegger which is still present in the way we colloquially use the word. In common language, dwelling often refers to a leisurely or lingering way of engaging with the world. For Heidegger dwelling connotes 'staying with' someone or something, in a particular mode of attentiveness. When we dwell with something or someone, we 'stay with' them in such a way that we give them the necessary time to reveal themselves to us. This kind of 'staying with' requires the capacity to not impose one's own beliefs onto the other. Instead, it is indicative of a kind of open acceptance without immediate judgement of the situation, thing or person.

Being open in a way that enables things to reveal themselves is an idea central to much of Heidegger's philosophy. He was very much aware of the way in which things hide even as they appear to us. This echoes more general phenomenological notions of identity and the idea that there is always more to know about everything. Through the notion of dwelling, Heidegger suggests that a first step in knowing something or someone's identity more fully is to 'stay with them' with a deep quality of attentiveness. This open attentiveness enables them to reveal more of themselves.

I remember experiencing this revelatory way of being with things through 'pond watching' with a childhood friend, Craig. We would cycle to an island off the coast of Maine and peer into rock pools and just wait. What always amazed me about this process was that I often thought I had seen everything there was to see in the water by the time I had gazed into it for five minutes. Through his patience, Craig taught me that the more I waited and kept looking, the more I would see. On first gazing into the pool I might notice stones, a few swimming creatures or the way the light played on the water's surface. Ten minutes later, I was able to see whole worlds of minute creatures, crawling, swimming, careening just under water or sometimes slightly above it. What often looked like bleak grey and brown stones revealed gold and silver undersides. The more I looked, the more I saw. I think there is something in the willingness to watch patiently for whatever appears which approaches Heidegger's idea of 'staying with'.

Reflecting on my pond gazing a bit more, I realize that as a result of watching closely, I experienced a deep sense of appreciation for the worlds which revealed themselves under my gaze. The tiny crabs and pond skaters going about their lives seemed worthy of respect as fellow living creatures, completely whole and self-sufficient in their watery world. My presence subtly affected them, casting shadows where none had been or occasionally by providing them with a morsel of bread from my lunch. Watching them also affected me, both physically and psychically. Such an encounter is indicative of the reciprocity at the heart of dwelling.

The willingness to 'stay with' a difficult ethical dilemma is perhaps the first step to finding a way to engage ethically with it. The kinds of dilemmas which warrant this degree of attention are complex ones, not the routine problems which fill managers' days. When faced with such conundrums, practicing staying with it might enable the situation to reveal its myriad of dimensions, thereby opening up the range of possible resolutions.

Comportment

The second aspect of dwelling vital to its enactment according to Heidegger is 'comportment'. 'Comportment' is the qualitative mode in which we carry ourselves into the world. It is our characteristic way of physically and emotionally engaging with 'the other'. For instance, some people habitually demonstrate a kind of comportment which invites openness and consequently allows others to reveal more of themselves. Alternatively, individuals may comport themselves in such a way that limits contact with others and does not invite engagement and connection. The way in which one comports him or herself has consequences in terms of how much 'the other' reveals and therefore how much of a situation is able to be known.

The North American environmental philosophers, Jim Cheney and Antony Weston (1999), highlight the importance of comportment to ethical engagement in their concept of 'etiquette'. This is not etiquette in terms of proper table manners or what to bring hosts when visiting others' homes but concerns the orientation with which we engage with one another. Cheney suggests comportment which embodies an 'epistemic commitment to respect' (Cheney 2002, p. 5) is fundamental to right relations with other people, as well as other more-than human entities with which we live our lives. This is a way of relating to others which embodies a deep level of respect, based on more than the principle of 'moral considerability'. Importantly, such an orientation allows the 'other' to 'be' significantly different without having to subsume that difference into the perceiver's own identity.

Relating this idea to leadership, it can be argued that the way in which those taking up the leader role comport themselves in relation to others will significantly determine how much of a situation is revealed to them. We saw in Chapter 6 how managers involved in Smircich and Morgan's 'Operation June 30th' case study refused to tell their CEO about the failure of his strategy because they assumed 'he would not want to hear their views' (Smircich and Morgan 1982). This unwillingness would have been conveyed not through the things he said but through the manner in which he comported himself. Likewise, those who regularly dismiss bringers of unappealing news may find themselves isolated from key dimensions of complex ethical situations.

Participation

A third aspect of dwelling with implications for ethical engagement is participation. Although participation has been previously mentioned, it is worth elaborating on the significance of dwelling-oriented participation. This kind of participation is active and engaged and truly involves 'getting one's hands dirty'. A leadership development programme conducted for senior medical surgeons and administrative staff illustrates this point. During part of the workshop, people had to switch roles. For a time one of the porters took up the senior surgeon's role (without actually operating on patients!) and the surgeon wheeled patients around the hospital. At the end of the day, the surgeon reported his astonishment that the porter stayed in the job. 'I couldn't do what you do!' was his observation. 'How do you keep people calm, negotiate all the other people in the hospital, and hardly get any recognition from anyone else?' he asked. This contrived but actual participation gave both parties insights to the other's world that would have been impossible otherwise. From such an experience, a more grounded ethical relationship can emerge.

Importantly, dwelling requires not only openness to the 'other' but also openness to one's own self. One's own reactions and responses to situations should not be ignored in deference to the viewpoint and perspective of the other but instead should be held in balance with that of the other. Being open to another's ideas and responses while simultaneously holding a sense of one's own values presents a formidable challenge. Its difficulty is exacerbated for those acting as leaders because of the power inherent in the leader role.

Arriving at wise ethical judgements through the practices of staying with, comportment and participation is not simply achieved. Developing 'dwelling' capabilities relies on exposure to actual engagement with such conundrums. Often very complex dilemmas can only be approached incrementally and then the skill of being able to 'stay with' and participate in the consequences of one's intervention becomes key.

What do these ideas mean in practice? The following section describes how ethical dilemmas are resolved within a UK-based financial services firm which enjoys an industry-wide reputation for its ethical orientation.

FBZ SERVICES

FBZ Services (a pseudonym) is regularly rated as one of the top financial institutions in the UK for employee satisfaction. In an industry sector known for questionable ethical practices, it maintains a reputation for high ethical standards. This case is based on a series of interviews I conducted with senior managers in a regional head office of the firm. The conversations focused on the perceived role senior managers played in promoting and maintaining the strong culture of ethical behaviour for which the organization is known.

Perhaps of significance is the fact that FBZ services is a mutual, rather than a publicly listed company and this status regulates how the firm operates. All of the employees are shareholders in the business, as are all of the organization's customers. Organizational history plays an important role here; the very basis upon which this organization was established was as a reaction against big banks. Members, including customers and employees, have always exercised influence in how the operation is run. This may contribute to the very inclusive 'feel' of the organization. Even in its cultural artefacts, inclusivity is highlighted. For instance on entering the regional office I was struck by the colourful array of photographs hanging on the wall, not of the 'great and good' of FBZ services but of the recently held summer staff party. The sense of inclusivity was further amplified by the non-hierarchical feel of the place. Only the most senior managers had their own offices, everyone else worked in an open-plan area. The middle manager who had organized my visit retrieved coffee for me rather than his secretary.

When asked about the role senior managers played in establishing the culture of ethics for which the firm was known, those interviewed readily identified actions taken. For instance the chief executive officer had recently produced a video entitled, 'How We Do Business Around Here'. In the video, values around truthfulness, transparency and accountability were stressed. Everyone in the firm had watched the video and those I spoke with reported that it had been received with goodwill rather than cynicism. A key guideline the CEO stressed in the video was that when faced with situations in which there was no clear-cut ethical rule or code of practice, people should, 'put themselves in the shoes of the people involved'. In other words, people should use their own subjectivity as a guide.

Those interviewed cited a number of instances in which this advice had been taken seriously. They recounted the story of an insurance claim from customers who had maintained a life insurance policy with the firm for more than 20 years. For a brief period while they renegotiated the terms of the policy and were not strictly covered, the couple went abroad on holiday. Their broker understood that as soon as they returned their intention was to sign the new policy.

While away, the husband tragically died. Legally they were not covered by a policy and therefore FBZ services was not required to honour any claim for life insurance. The senior manager involved described what happened next:

> It was a tough situation. Legally, we were not bound [to pay]. But ethically, this was a couple who had been with FBZ for the previous 20 years, always on

time paying their bills, and with the strong expectation on everyone's part that they would be continuing to pay the company, that this was just a minor period of non-cover due to their holiday plans. Actually, it wasn't a difficult decision to make in the end. We put ourselves in their shoes. Here is this woman; she has just lost her husband while they were on holiday. If she were my mother, or my aunt, what would I want her insurance company to do? We paid out the claim.

This story demonstrates enactment of the kinds of behaviours indicative of dwelling. The key action here is 'putting oneself in the other's shoes' that is getting as close as possible to the situation. Many principle-based approaches suggest an almost diametrically opposed approach would be more appropriate, that of 'stepping back' and taking an 'objective stance'. Dwelling suggests a different kind of engagement, one which encourages 'getting up close' rather than drawing back. This does not mean that one should collapse into solely subjective responses. The senior manager involved also had to assess what was best for the organization as well. In those terms, he had to prioritize the different ways in which action might be beneficial to the firm. Certainly, not paying the claim might enhance the firm's financial position but it would also negatively affect its reputation. In deciding a way forward, the FBZ manager took into account a range of consequential factors, including his emotional response, rather than basing his decision solely on financial considerations.

There is a second story which demonstrates the way in which the espoused behaviours of the CEO were enacted by staff throughout the organization's hierarchy. A new head of marketing was appointed who initiated changes which were not perceived to be aligned with the ethical stance of the firm. As one senior manager reported:

When Mike [a pseudonym] came in he had big ideas about how to get more marketing impact while increasing profits. He introduced a new sales device, which meant that people who only recently joined the organization were offered a higher rate of interest than people who had been part of the organization on a long-term basis. A lot of people thought this went against our stance about taking care of our shareholders. There was quite a lot of rumbling in the organization about this, but when this did not catch senior managers' ears, sales people began to take the situation into their own hands.

It transpired that in the evening when off-duty, staff began phoning old clients and advising them to withdraw their funds and reapply for accounts, thereby enjoying the benefits of new customers. After a while more senior managers began to notice what was happening. The senior manager telling the story said the situation was like 'ground level subversion'. In his terms, 'those on the ground level did not believe this policy was in line with the ethical stance of the company, so they took it into their own hands to do something about it'.

This is an interesting example for a number of reasons. Firstly, it demonstrates that employees had clearly digested the ethical intent of the firm to the extent that when a contravening policy was introduced they took engaged action to subvert it. In this way, they took up the role of 'leaders' in ways that more senior managers did not. Secondly, the FBZ employees' actions demonstrate how 'dwelling' which informs ethical action might occur in practice. One way of analysing the story is to suggest that employees put themselves into the shoes of their long-term customers and imagined how they would feel. They 'stayed with' that imagined reaction. From that position, they took action which would realign the organization's espoused values and its practices. When senior managers discovered what had been happening, Mike was fired and the incentives awarded to new customers were terminated.

Another philosophical practice which might offer a way of developing the capacity to engage well with ethical dilemmas is inherent within hermeneutic approaches. In Chapter 6 the book already explored the way in which a hermeneutic rendering sheds light on the meaning-making process which occurs between leaders and followers. The following section considers how this philosophical approach might contribute to an individual's ability to take up the leader role with wisdom.

HERMENEUTIC CONVERSATIONS AS WAYS TO WISDOM

Earlier in the book key aspects of hermeneutics such as prejudice, attunement, the hermeneutic circle and fusion of horizons were introduced. Central to hermeneutic thought is the notion that meaning is co-constructed and occurs through an emerging process of dialogue between meaning-seeking individuals. It was further suggested that all meanings are not 'equal' in terms of their capacity to account for aspects of reality. Some 'meanings' have greater explanatory merit than others. This claim hints at the importance of the processes through which meanings are created in terms of their resulting validity. Meanings achieved through the coercive domination of one individual may not enjoy the same level of explanatory merit as those achieved through open processes allowing for the expression of multiple perspectives. This implies that in some way, effective meaning-making relies on ethical engagement between those involved in understanding a given situation.

As well as suggesting this fundamental prerequisite for valuable meaning-making activity, the hermeneutic process itself is accomplished through practices which contribute to ethical engagement. In particular, I will look more closely at the activities of inquiry and engaging with the hermeneutic circle.

Inquiry

The beginning of this chapter referred to the work of Keith Grint which suggests that rather than finding the right answers, the job of leaders is to identify the right questions (Grint 2005a). Hermeneutic practice involves doing just that; discovering the right question to ask of a given situation or circumstance. But what constitutes a 'right' question? How would we know one when we heard it? Finding the right question is not always easily achieved, largely because our questions habitually arise from our existing frames. Sometimes the things about which we most need to ask are those that we most readily take for granted. How can we learn to ask questions about the things we believe we do not need to question?

One starting point for finding such questions is with feelings of vague unease or discomfort that can arise from the very edges of our awareness in certain situations. Learning to attend to unformed feelings of disquiet and the questions they prompted was a central theme in doctoral work undertaken by Patta Scott-Villiers, a senior conflict resolution facilitator working with major aid agencies in Africa.[5] A large part of her research focused on the role hermeneutic inquiry can play in the process of conflict resolution. Here part of her story is recounted in order to illustrate the power of paying attention to the earliest intimations of questions, especially when they disturb preconceptions and assumptions.

Scott-Villiers worked as a senior manager with a major international charity in Sudan during the civil war in the 1990s. She tells of how she came to understand that the role she and her fellow aid workers were playing in alleviating starvation was not quite what it seemed. Her story begins at the point when tens of thousands of people who had been refugees in Ethiopia poured back into southern Sudan where she and her colleagues had established a camp to assist them on their way home. After a few weeks, news came that the areas from which the people had come were safe, and everyone expected that the displaced people would soon start to leave the camp. But they did not. She also noticed how the children were not getting healthier. Despite the high nutrient diet which they were being fed, they still looked up at her from hollow eyes and delicate frames. Scott-Villiers began to wonder what was really going on.

It began to dawn on her that something very distressing was occurring. Through opening her perceptual awareness to what lay before her eyes, out of reach of her assumptions, she began to realize that the food and medicine were not reaching the children. It began to dawn on her that the boxes of supplies were being ghosted away to feed soldiers. The starving and haggard people were being used as a front, a means of attracting Western resources.

Many years after this event, she began to explore her perceptions of this situation from a hermeneutic perspective. She began to notice how her assumptions about her role coloured what she chose to see. She began to appreciate how her orientation as a Westerner informed her understanding of her role: she was making necessary aid, food, medicine and shelter, available to impoverished people. However, this was not the only way of interpreting her place in the larger landscape. Scott-Villiers was jolted into a new appreciation of her role in this situation. Whereas originally she had framed her efforts as helpful and benevolent, she began to recognize their naïve quality. She began to fully recognize the consequences of Western largesse for the poor in Africa.

This realization encouraged her to begin a journey into understanding her own way of understanding, a hermeneutic journey. A key part of that journey has been learning to ask questions. Maybe even more importantly she has learned to attend carefully to the disconnections, the subtle points of disquiet, often at the edge of her consciousness which alert her to the fact that all is not what it seems in a given situation. This is the time to begin asking questions, she asserts as a key finding in her research.

Sometimes it is not very easy to know what needs to be asked, however. How can we begin to ask questions when we are not even certain how to articulate them? Rather than being a question with any definitive answer, this question itself has a moral and perhaps mythical dimension. Being willing to engage in the quest for the question is the first step to finding it. Throughout time, mythological stories have highlighted the importance of identifying 'good' questions. The word 'question' itself has as its foundation the word 'quest' – a journey into the unknown. These mythic tales also reveal another critical aspect of 'questing', however, and that is the courage to pose the question once it is identified.

The story of Parsifal is such a tale. In this tale which has its roots in Anglo-Saxon mythology, Parsifal is a young knight who leaves home to undertake his quest. On his journey, he encounters a kingdom which is a shrivelled husk of its former self. He learns that the ruler of the kingdom has been suffering from a malady for many years and that as he has degenerated, so too has his kingdom. Parsifal is invited to spend the night and join the King's court for dinner. The meal is a rather grim affair, without music or dancing and not even a jester to liven up the proceedings. Although Parsifal is fully aware of the court's distress and the sadness of the King, he acts as if nothing is amiss. It is only after leaving the kingdom and travelling for many years in which he slays a number of dragons and performs other knightly feats that Parsifal once again returns to the kingdom. This time, however, he poses the question that has been troubling him throughout his trials. When they have a moment together, Parsifal asks the King, 'Your Highness, what is the matter?' The question itself is a revelation. New life flies into the kingdom, shrivelled roots begin to restore themselves and the old King smiles and is rejuvenated. Merely asking the question provides the key to restoring vitality and life to the kingdom. It is as if the power of the question is to restore the connection between people's experience of reality and what they are willing to 'declare' about that reality. When people deny that something is wrong, a certain deadness sets in as demonstrated not only by the Parsifal tale but by Scott-Villiers' story of the Sudanese relief camp as well.

Both of these stories highlight not only the difficulties associated with finding the right question but also the challenge of summoning the courage to give it voice. Finding the right question often starts with a willingness to ask the wrong question or, at least, to acknowledge there is something unknown about the situation. Expressing 'not knowing' can be difficult for those leading, who may equate leading with knowing. There is a paradox here, encapsulated by the suggestion, 'Enacting leadership is about knowing what to do, when you don't know what to do' (Logan 2009, personal communication). One action a person can take when they do not know what to do is to ask a question. Such inquiry is crucial to ethical engagement. However, questioning alone is not sufficient. Taking up the leader role wisely also requires engagement with the hermeneutic circle.

Engagement with the Hermeneutic Circle as Ethical Practice

Let us return to the perception that 'something is not quite right' which leads to the asking of a question. What is it that prompts the initial dissonance from which the question arises? Part of the dissonance can be attributed to the way specific information or perceptions relate to the 'whole' of a situation. In Patta's story, the specific circumstances she was noting, that 'the people were not going back to their homelands' and that 'the children were not gaining weight', jarred against her assumptions that 'it was safe for the people to return to their lands' and 'the children were being fed nourishing diets'. For a while she ignored this contradiction. Eventually, however, the facts were too overwhelming to dismiss. She had to see what was going on, even though it did not match her assumption about what should be happening.

Attending to the hermeneutic circle alerts us when the parts and the whole do not cohere. Perhaps actively looking for such disconnections is a starting point for enacting leadership wisely. It is interesting to reflect on this idea in the light of the crisis which swept the world's financial markets in 2009. How many of the leaders of that industry were actively looking for indicative signs that all was not well long before the demise of Lehman Brothers in September 2008? Perhaps the onus for doing so should have rested even more firmly with 'watchdogs' of the industry. Yet in his story about the role regulators have played in the crisis, Terry Macalister, a reporter for the UKs *Guardian* newspaper, writes:

> The Chairman of the City watchdog, the Financial Services Authority admitted yesterday that regulators had failed to fully recognize the risky manner in which the banking system had developed over the past few years. Lord Turner, who became FSA Chief in September, told BBC1s Andrew Marr that regulators around the world 'had failed to see that by 2004 the banking system was moving in a direction that created a "large systemic risk".
>
> With hindsight, the FSA, like other authorities throughout the world, was focused too much on individual institutions, and the processes and procedures within them, and not adequately focused on the totality of the systemic risks across the whole system, and whether there were entire business models, entire ways of operating, that were risky (Macalister 2009, p. 7).

Bringing a hermeneutic orientation to a situation demands actively reflecting on the relationship between 'parts' and 'wholes'. This kind of thinking appreciates the systemic nature of contexts and in doing so seeks to assess the ethical implications of the ways in which a system's parts interrelate, as well as the integrity of individual system parts. Such awareness of and willingness to explore interrelationships between 'parts' and 'wholes' is critical in leading wisely. As demonstrated by the banking crisis, the failure to appreciate the 'whole' as well as the 'parts' has resulted in a downturn of unprecedented proportions affecting millions of families and businesses throughout the world. Even though it may be proven that leaders of the financial institutions involved never acted unethically, the resulting crisis could be attributed to a lack of wisdom operating within the sector (as well as within the larger social structure of which financial services is a part). One way that lack of wisdom has been manifested as indicated by the quote above, is through the failure of leaders within the sector to connect 'parts' with 'wholes'.

Is there another philosophical practice which could have alerted us to the impending fall? What might have been perceived had we chosen to notice what was occurring in the banking sector from an aesthetic perspective?

AESTHETICS AND ETHICS

The connection between the 'good' and the 'beautiful' has long been theorized. The beautiful, say philosophers such as Plotinus, Plato and Aristotle, provides us with a physical manifestation of the good. Rather than revisiting the debate about what constitutes beauty and therefore the good, here the question is posed: is there an aesthetic practice which can contribute to the enactment of wisdom? My suggestion is that such a practice does exist within the aesthetic domain; it involves honing the exercise of judgement.

How does one exercise 'good' judgement? Kant's entire treatise, *Critique of Judgement* published in 1790 ([2005)], addresses just this question from the perspective of how aesthetic taste might be developed. Here I am suggesting that Kant's ideas about how one learns to discern the 'beautiful' might be applied to questions of how one discerns the 'ethical'. Let us begin by considering his theory of how one can reach judgements about what constitutes the beautiful.

Perhaps the most important point about Kant's formulation of the beautiful, as mentioned in Chapter 5, is that contrary to the colloquial saying that 'beauty lies in the eye of the beholder', for Kant that which is beautiful is recognized as such on its own merits. Rather than the beautiful being in the eye of the beholder, it is our responsibility as perceivers to hone our judgement to be able to discern that which is beautiful. For Kant, the 'beautiful' exists independently of individual human subjectivity. Instead it is a judgement made on the basis of 'universal human subjectivity' and is given to those things which embody 'symmetry, harmony and balance' in their form. Furthermore, according to Kant, 'the beautiful presupposes and maintains the mind in restful contemplation' (1790 [2005], p. 63).

Being able to recognize the beautiful involves developing and refining one's taste. Kant elaborates on how this is done through explication of four different 'moments':

- Firstly, the perceiver must be oriented to that which is perceived in a 'disinterested' way. Pleasure is evoked when contemplating the beautiful because it is beautiful, not because it brings us pleasure. (For instance, we may gain pleasure from eating fudge brownies but that does not mean they are beautiful.)
- Secondly, judgements about the beautiful are universally determined. For something to be beautiful, anyone who has refined their sense of taste will judge it to be beautiful. That which is beautiful embodies qualities such as symmetry, harmony and proportion.

- Thirdly, judgements about the beautiful are 'necessary' when a thing embodies certain proportions and exudes harmony and symmetry, it is necessarily judged to be beautiful.
- Finally, in order to judge the beautiful, the perceiver must regard it without intentionality, or in Kant's terms, 'without purposiveness'. The beautiful is beautiful because it is beautiful, not because it has utility. A rose is beautiful because of its symmetry and the sense of contentment contemplation it evokes in us, not because it can be sold for a certain amount of money (Kant 1790 [2005]).

Of course Kant is not the only philosopher to theorize about the beautiful and many of the claims he makes have been contested by philosophers after him. However, there are two aspects of his philosophy which offer useful contributions to the question of how individuals might take up the leader role wisely. The first concerns being able to discern the 'pleasurable' from the 'beautiful'.

Kant clearly distinguishes between these two aesthetic categories. For him, being disinterested means we are able to take pleasure from something because it is beautiful; we do not find something beautiful because it brings us pleasure. In this way beauty is a much stricter task-mistress than pleasure is. Both beauty and pleasure tend to attract us but it is beauty's inherent symmetry, harmony and ability to instil peacefulness which enables it to lead us to the good.

The second aspect of Kant's theory of aesthetic judgement follows from the first; that is beauty's 'lack of purposiveness'. That which is beautiful has no purpose other than to 'be' beautiful. In Kant's account, the judgement of something's 'beauty' should be made quite separately from a judgement about its utility. In making this distinction, Kant reasserts the importance of the question, 'Is it beautiful?' as superior to the question, 'Will it work?' when making aesthetic judgements.

How might these ideas be applied in practice? What kinds of aesthetic judgements, for instance, could be made about the world's financial markets prior to the crisis of 2008–09? The words ill-proportioned and overextended might be more appropriate than harmonious and symmetrical. For example at the beginning of 2009, the budget deficit of the USA topped US$11 trillion. Individual debt in the UK represented 60 per cent of GDP, meaning that on average, each individual in the UKs population owed more than they would earn in the next 15 years. In the world overall, 25 per cent of the world's population commandeered 80 per cent of the world's debt, with the gap between the rich and the poor increasing even in countries associated with communist egalitarianism such as Russia and China (IMF 2009).[6] At the beginning of 2008, the system may have seemed to have been working, but could it be characterized as 'beautiful' from a Kantian perspective?

Moving to a more contemporary rendering of how we reach aesthetic judgements, in her book *Science as Salvation: A Modern Myth and its Meaning* (1992), the British philosopher Mary Midgley elaborates on the notion of the 'yuck factor'. She defines this as the visceral response one has to certain proposals or situations. For instance, with advances in modern medicine enabling ever greater interventions into human life, we may encounter a proposed scenario to which our response is 'yuck'. We may feel that to transplant a heart is all right but to transplant a brain evokes the response of 'yuck'. Transplanting people's brains does not 'feel right'.

Midgley suggests that we should attend to such responses in our ethical deliberations. Of course, what one generation or culture finds distasteful may feel acceptable to another. However, the point remains that the 'yuck' response provides important information regarding one's aesthetic judgement of a questionable situation. It is our physical and emotional response of distaste which informs us that we are reaching an edge. Like the disquiet at the edge of consciousness when a 'part' does not quite fit with a 'whole', it alerts us to look again and review a situation's myriad dimensions rather than attend to those most outwardly apparent. Those attending carefully to the continuing imbalances in the world's financial markets may well find a response of 'yuck' rising from their awareness, for example.

So far this chapter has introduced practices: dwelling, hermeneutic conversations and aesthetic judgement which might provide the foundations of leading with wisdom. Is it just a matter of practicing these until acting wisely almost becomes inevitable? The Greeks, and in particular Aristotle, thought more than individual endeavour was required in the development of wisdom. Their notion of 'phronesis' or practical wisdom could only be developed through interaction with wise others. Given that throughout this book leadership has been theorized as an emergent phenomenon arising from social interactions, it seems entirely appropriate to end the chapter by considering the communal practices that might enable the development of wise leaders and, in fact, the possibility of wise leadership.

ARISTOTLE'S NOTION OF 'PHRONESIS'

Aristotle's *Nicomachean Ethics* (1976) offers an approach to ethics which focuses on the development of 'virtue'. For Aristotle, being able to act ethically was largely a function of one's character. Rather than supplying a template of ethical principles, individuals would be able to discern what constituted ethical behaviour once they had achieved the ability to act with virtue. Virtue itself is not an absolute but is a point of balance between opposing characteristics. For instance, courage is a virtue which operates midway between foolhardiness and cowardliness. In order to enact courage, one must find the mean between these two ways of being.

For the practice of leadership, what is key about Aristotle's ideas is how he believed such virtue could be learned. Rather than being something that could be achieved through reading and isolated contemplation, virtue could only be learned through engagement with a virtuous community. One had to live with and watch other virtuous others in order to develop virtue in oneself. In this way, central to Aristotle's view about the enactment of practical wisdom or phronesis as he called it, is participation in a virtuous community.

The notion that ethical behaviour results from engagement with ethical others has been adopted by a number of organizational theorists looking at the impact of organizational culture on ethical behaviours. For instance, the Rutgers Business School teacher, Edwin Hartman, suggests 'The right upbringing, in a good community, and long practice are necessary, though not sufficient to make us value and choose the right things. One way to choose to be a certain kind of person is to be in a certain kind of community' (Hartman 2006, p. 71). He goes on to suggest ways in which business schools might foster the kind of professional communities conducive to ethical development. A key recommendation he makes to business students wishing to enact virtue is to take care in choosing their profession because in doing so they are choosing a particular community and its inherent ethics. In particular he encourages students to choose jobs based on 'values that can sustain happiness' (ibid., p. 79).

Speaking with the community in which we work and live is an essential part of developing practical wisdom. Throughout Greek philosophy the importance of dialectic as a means of deciding right action is emphasized. Engaging in dialectic requires the capacity to contain what appear to be contradictory statements without collapsing them into one another. In this way, the ability to work with paradox and the tensions that it generates is at the heart of the dialectical process. This capacity is perhaps best understood in our contemporary times as the ability to create and live with 'both/and' conceptualizations, rather than collapse into 'either/or' dichotomies.

Engaging with dialectic potentially results in innovative outcomes which could not have been predicted by those engaged in the conversation at its start. In this way, dialectic can be a means to achieve the 'fusion of horizons' introduced in Chapter 6 as a goal of hermeneutic engagement.

Participating in conversations which aim to hold contradictions and inte-
grate them into new solutions, rather than dismissing or subsuming them
is a practice which could contribute to wise collective leadership. What
new insights might emerge if those leading their organizations regularly
gathered to deliberate together questions such as 'What is the wise way
forward here?' or 'What could we do to create a beautiful solution?'

Aristotle points out that in order to answer questions such as these, one
must firstly 'perceive' correctly (Aristotle, 1976). Perceiving correctly is
a function of recognizing what is morally salient in any given situation.
Investment bankers who engaged in 'creative practices' may have perceived what they were doing as providing 'exemplary customer service';
certainly a virtue worth pursuing. However, when those practices also
introduced large scale risks and in some cases were actually illegal, virtue
demands that prudence and legality be recognized as having a higher
degree of moral salience than 'exemplary customer service'.

Earlier, phenomenological ideas introduced in Chapter 2 demonstrated
that perception itself depends on many factors including the side of
the situation which is seen or the angle from which it is viewed. The
limitations of one person's perceptual frame also imply the drawbacks
of making ethical decisions on one's own. Aristotle's notion of phronesis
re-emphasizes the critical nature of conversing with wise others and living
with virtuous others in community in order to develop the capacity to act
ethically.

Ultimately, the aim of practical wisdom is continually to get better at
answering the question, 'What should I do?' However, there is a difference
between knowing what one should do and being able to act on it. Enacting
one's decisions about what to do often requires courage.

THE ENACTMENT OF WISDOM AND THE REQUIREMENT FOR COURAGE

The chapter has largely focused on the decision-making aspect of wisdom,
seemingly assuming that once the virtuous path is identified; following it
is an easy matter. Of course this is not true! Enacting what one knows to
be virtuous often requires courage. Courage is required to face the risks
associated with taking correct action. For instance, standing up to a corporate culture in which creative, but questionable practices, are the norm
at the expense of legal requirements, risks consequences ranging from
losing one's job to being marginalized or sidelined. Giving voice to one's
perceptions of wrong-doing requires courage especially when the cost of
speaking out is not known beforehand.

Almost paradoxically, such situations can provide the impetus for individuals who might not regard themselves as leaders to take up the 'leader' role. There are examples of individuals operating at any level in an organization's hierarchy who choose to act when they perceive something not to be 'right'. Like the middle managers in FBZ Services described earlier, they take steps to realign the organization's practices with its espoused ethical purposes. In the case of FBZ Services, those who lead the 'ground level subversion' were not reprimanded. In fact, it was the Senior Manager who had introduced the perceived unethical action who was fired (which itself reveals something significant about the nature of the community and the ethics it practiced). However, those employees did not know that would be the outcome. It would have taken courage to make the first phone call and begin to subvert a new organizational initiative.

This example indicates the way in which acting ethically and leading are often inextricably intertwined. Pointing out questionable practices, actively inviting discussion and disagreement that arise when multiple perspectives are involved in decision-making, looking for the unintended consequences of systems interacting are all actions which often require taking the leader role, however briefly. Such capabilities, I am suggesting, can be developed through practicing the capacity to dwell, engaging in hermeneutic reflection and conversation and exercising aesthetic judgement. These are not enough however. Aristotle tells us that participating in a community of wise others is also essential to developing the kind of character from which true virtue can be enacted.

The possibility of taking up the leader role with wisdom then becomes highly dependent on the collectively-based 'leadership' dynamic in which the individual leader is nested and its inherent ethical commitments. Wise 'leaders' are dependent on 'wise leadership', that is the aspiration to acting with wisdom on the part of all of those engaged in mobilizing action towards particular purposes.

This insight brings us full-circle to reconsider the very nature of leadership itself. We will revisit that question in the final chapter, which asks: 'What has it meant to rethink leadership?'

NOTES

1. For instance, see: Donaldson, T. and P. Werhane (1999), *Ethical Issues in Business: A Philosophical Approach* (6th edn), Upper Saddle River, NJ: Prentice Hall.
2. It is also true that the definition of 'human being' has changed through the ages. For instance during much of human history women have not been considered 'fully human' and denying a level of humanity to Africans allowed the slave trade to grow in Western Europe, North and Central America during the eighteenth century. Even today there are

debates about the extent to which disabled people or the mentally ill are due the moral consideration assumed for other humans.

3. For instance, see: Ciulla, J. (2004), *Ethics, the Heart of Leadership* (2nd edn), Westport, CT: Praeger, or Chapter 7 of Rost, J.C. (1993), *Leadership for the Twenty-First Century*, Westport, CT: Praeger.

4. I elaborate on the possible role of 'dwelling' in ethical leadership practice in the article Ladkin, D. (2006), 'When Deontology and Utilitarianism are not enough: how Heidegger's notion of "dwelling" might help organizational leaders resolve ethical issues', *Journal of Business Ethics*, **65** (2), 87–98.

5. See: Scott-Villiers, P. (2009), 'A question of understanding: Hermeneutics and the play of history, distance and dialogue in development practice in East Africa', School of Management, University of Bath, UK.

6. Data taken from the International Monetary Fund report accessed at: http://www.imf.org/external/data.htm (accessed 13 June 2009).

9. What has it meant to rethink leadership?

> To teach how to live with uncertainty, yet without being paralyzed by hesitation, is perhaps the chief thing that philosophy can do.
>
> Bertrand Russell
> *History of Western Philosophy*
> (1946 [1996], p. 2

At a recent leadership development event I was running one of the participants, a former officer in the military, approached me during the coffee break. 'It's all very well you trying to teach us something about leadership', he said, 'but at the end of the day, being a leader is a matter of breeding'.

Although expressed in relatively extreme terms, his is not an uncommon view and one I regularly encounter (though expressed differently!) when speaking with participants on such programmes. 'You either have what it takes or you don't', is a recurring theme. Such views belie the notion that leaders are somehow unique individuals born of certain lineages or blessed with special capabilities. What assumptions are behind such a point of view? More importantly perhaps, what purpose does such a view serve? Does the analysis of leadership offered here call it into question? This final chapter addresses these questions by reconsidering the implications of rethinking leadership through the lens of Continental philosophy.

Firstly, let's revisit one of the key assumptions at the heart of the aforementioned military Officer's pronouncement, the conflation of 'leaders' and 'leadership'.

WHY IS DISTINGUISHING 'LEADERS' FROM 'LEADERSHIP' SO IMPORTANT?

The 'The leadership "moment" model' (below) which has underpinned much of the framing of this book was introduced in Chapter 2.

The diagram represents the idea that leadership emerges from a collective process created through the confluence of a particular situation or context, people involved in that process who take up roles as 'leader'

Figure 9.1   The leadership 'moment'

or 'followers' and a purpose to which their collective action is directed. In it, each aspect plays an important role in the leadership experience. This model arises from an understanding of leadership as a 'moment', explained by phenomenology as the kind of entity which cannot be separated from the context from which it arises. In fact, its very appearance is totally dependent upon that context.

This formulation helps to resolve one of the ongoing debates within the larger leadership studies literature. This is the tension between more reductionist accounts informed by a positivistic paradigm which assume leadership to be an objectively determined phenomenon constituted largely by the actions of an individual leader and those more grounded in a socially constructed ontology in which leadership is not about individuals at all but about social processes and attributions. Extreme social constructionist accounts even deny the possibility of leadership as an explanatory social phenomenon at all, witnessed by Gemmil and Oakley's claim that: '[charismatic] leadership is an illusory social phenomenon, representing a black hole in social space that serves as a container for the alienating consequences of the social myth resulting from intellectual and emotional deskilling of organizational members' (1997, p. 278).

Considering leadership as a 'moment' resolves this split by integrating the actions of individual leaders into the construction of leadership. As one aspect of a continually evolving phenomenon, sometimes the role that an individual leader plays comes to the fore. At other times, the context or the purpose to which activity is directed might 'take the lead' in creating leadership.

For example, I recently interviewed entrepreneurs involved in an initiative to create and introduce a hydrogen-powered car to the European market. As well as inventing an ecologically sustainable product, the group of scientists and engineers who have come together to launch it are trying to enact a different kind of governance structure in the way they work together. Their entire system of financing, as well as the way in which the car will be marketed and used by consumers must reflect their overarching aim of sustainability. For instance, rather than selling the cars, they will be leased to customers and returned to the company when the customer no longer wishes to drive it.

Although the idea has been initiated by one person, the way in which he interacts with the rest of those involved in the project is not experienced as particularly 'leaderly'. Instead, their collective action is organized around the purpose they have set themselves. When asked about how he experienced leadership operating within the group, one respondent reflected,

> We want the organization to be truly sustainable, both in the way that we work and in the end product we produce. That's the 'leader'. The purpose has to be bigger than any of the individual egos involved. I'd say the real leader of our work is the purpose. Every decision we make, every way that we organize ourselves is determined by how it affects the ecological sustainability of the wider community.

In this way, the 'purpose' aspect of the leadership moment is the driving force behind the way in which the collective organize their activities and work together.

At other times, the context may play a more prominent role in how leadership comes about. This is particularly true in times of crisis. We have already considered in Chapter 3 what Hurricane Katrina could tell us about leadership through its absence. An alternative way of analysing that event is by noticing the role context played or should have played in a response to that catastrophe. The storm and its aftermath created an event which, it could be argued, should have been the primary focus of the leadership system. Rather than attending to individual responsibilities and lines of command, the specific 'here and now' situation should have been the predominant factor around which a leadership response was organized. Instead, retrospective analysis has shown that one by one designated 'leaders', from Ralph Nagin, the Mayor of New Orleans, through to Michael Brown, Head of FEMA and even George W. Bush, did not adequately respond by only attending to their particular bounds of responsibility. The context needed to be addressed as a 'whole' and perceived as such by those involved in order to best construct a leadership, rather than leader response. As a colleague so aptly put it when reflecting on the situation, 'there were too many leaders, and not enough leadership'. (Bathurst 2009, personal communication).

Understanding leadership as a 'moment' implies that all of those involved in its enactment need to attend to its systemic and dynamic nature, not just the 'leader'. The leadership moment implies that we are all responsible for effective leadership. In order to find our place within it we need to ask questions such as: 'Which part of the leadership dynamic needs to be attended to at this moment?', or, 'Where might I best position myself in order to most effectively contribute to its effectiveness?' This implies that even if I hold the 'head' position within an organizational hierarchy; in order to enable leadership to emerge at a given point in time I might need to follow, rather than to lead. Even world leaders, such as Barack Obama or Dmitry Medvedev, have to discern when they need to step back and allow others to take the lead. But what does 'taking the lead' entail? Does Continental philosophy provide clues to this which are distinctive from more psychological or sociological accounts?

WHAT DOES 'TAKING UP THE LEADER ROLE' ENTAIL?

In some ways, taking up the leader role from the perspectives offered here might not appear to be so different from that depicted in more tradition-ally fashioned accounts. However, through problemetizing the purposes towards which leader activity is directed differently, a new understanding of what leaders need to do to bring them to fruition emerges. The book has explored two key purposes commonly recognized as central to taking up the leader role, 'creating vision' and 'leading change'.

Chapter 6 offered the idea that creating a vision which makes sense and can be translated into reality involves a process of co-constructed meaning-making between leaders and followers. In this way, visions cannot just be 'bestowed upon' passive followers if they are to be translated into lived realizations. Hermeneutics suggests that instead, the active engagement of both parties needs to be involved and through their interaction new mean-ings are jointly discovered.

For example, Tim Smit, the creator of the Eden Project in the UK was the first to imagine that the china claypits on which the attraction is built could be transformed into a site of abundant vegetation. However, in order to convert his dream into reality, he needed to communicate it to others in ways they could understand. Additionally, bridging the gulf between his vision and the language worlds of the architects, designers, civil engineers and construction managers who would actually build it was critical. The leader's role in such an endeavour requires the capacity to facilitate understand-ing between different ways of conceptualizing reality and providing and

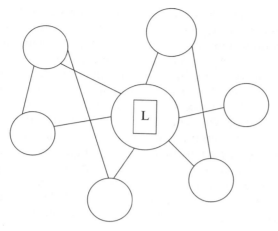

Figure 9.2   Leading as 'hub of meaning-making

safeguarding spaces in which dialogue can happen between them. Rather than bestowing meaning from the top of an organization's hierarchy, the leader's role in meaning making might be better conceptualized as positioned at the centre of a hub of interacting relationships. Facilitating conversations between people at the end of different 'spokes' becomes a key task. Figure 9.2 above tries to capture this notion pictorially.

Similarly, by considering 'change' through the lens of process philosophy, being able to identify emerging patterns and discern vital information from 'noise' was highlighted as a key capability for those leading in organizational systems already in a process of 'continual becoming'. Recognizing patterns is not enough; once again the importance of leaders 'declaring' their perceptions in ways which enable followers to focus their attention is also crucial. Here, the power associated with formal organizational roles becomes vital in enabling those declarations to be heard and acted upon. Perhaps business leaders such as Lou Gerstner and Jack Welch, who are credited with successfully navigating IBM and GE through transformations, were particularly skilled at recognizing patterns and enabling those in their organizations to respond to them effectively. However, there are enough examples of change being initiated from lower managerial ranks to suggest that positional power is not the only way in which institutionalized organizational change occurs. Process philosophy implies that identifying and amplifying changes which are already inevitably occurring within organizational systems can be the genesis for such shifts and these are activities which can begin anywhere in an organization's hierarchy.

In summary, rather than proposing that leaders need to 'provide the vision' of a new and different future in pursuit of organizational change, process philosophy indicates that reading the emerging patterns and being sensitive to already occurring changes is central to institutionalizing preferred ways of operating. Rather than 'providing the answers', hermeneutics suggests that 'asking the right questions' becomes crucial in the meaning-making process which enables organizational members to understand how their work contributes to the organization's or community's purpose. Taking up the role of leading according to this analysis is much less heroic (although it still requires courage) than more traditional renderings. It demands perceptual acuity, sensitivity and the ability to connect with others in emerging contexts. Lest we fall into the trap of paying most attention to the role leaders play within leadership, let us turn to another element of the leadership dynamic; the role of 'followers'.

WHAT DOES TAKING UP THE 'FOLLOWER' ROLE ENTAIL?

For those without the formal authority afforded to 'head' roles, being able to perceive the particular moments in which one's expertise, knowledge or perspective is precisely what is needed in order for leadership to occur is crucial. This may be by taking up the lead role more explicitly or it might be done from the position of an engaged and influential follower position. How can the ideas introduced here enrich our understanding of the critical role followers play within the leadership moment?

Merleau-Ponty's notion of 'flesh' provides a novel rendering of the follower role. The reciprocity at the nub of perception infers that leaders only know themselves through the gaze of their followers and, likewise, followers know themselves through their leader. This means that leader, as well as follower, identities are co-constructed through their intersubjective perception of one another. Within such a systemic construction, each party exercises significant yet subtle influence over the other.

How this operates is most dramatically apparent in times of mutiny or coups, in which followers usurp a leader's authority and assume the leader role themselves. It occurs more subtly in the gradual waning of power which occurs as leaders lose the appeal of their followers and are able to exercise less influence over them. It happens whenever followers choose to follow their own viewpoints and ways forward rather than be influenced by a leader, in the form of passive dissent or passive aggression.

A healthy enactment of the influence followers exercise on leaders is held in the term 'constructive dissent', which the UK leadership scholar, Keith

Grint (2005b), highlights as a key follower activity which contributes to effective leadership. Constructive dissent involves followers questioning leaders' decisions or perhaps providing them with additional information or an alternative viewpoint which might enable the leader to view the situation at hand differently. As an explicit way of exercising followership, constructive dissent can be a powerful means of supporting the possibility of wise leadership emerging from a particular context.

The vital role followers play in creating the 'flesh' of leadership is often more nuanced than overt acts of constructive dissent. As Barack Obama articulated in his speech to the White House Correspondents Dinner in May 2009, the very presence of followers, as represented by the press, enabled him to do his job better. He said,

> A government without a tough and vibrant media is not an option for the United States of America. I may not always agree with everything you write or report on, and from time to time I may complain about your methods . . . [but] When you are at your best, you help me be at my best. You help all of us who serve at the pleasure of the American people to do our jobs better – by holding us accountable, by demanding honesty, by preventing us from taking the shortcuts or falling into easy political games that people are so desperately tired of.[1]

Although Obama is talking specifically about the role of media within the democratic process, I think his sentiments speak equally well to the vital role of followers in helping to shape leadership. Merleau-Ponty's notion of 'flesh' introduces the idea that leader and follower identities are created by perceptions interwoven to such an extent that one cannot exist without the other. Whether subtly through their gaze or more overtly through exercising dissent, followers are implicated and have influence within the leadership dynamic.

The 'flesh' analogy also reminds us that leadership has an embodied, physical aspect. As such, it provokes a visceral, felt response from those engaged in it. A question not often asked by leadership scholars concerns the quality of such felt apprehensions. How do we know leadership is occurring? We have already discussed the difficulties associated with seeing leadership. Is there any more traction gained by posing the question, 'How does leadership feel?'

HOW DOES LEADERSHIP FEEL?

Chapter 4 introduced the lens of aesthetic knowing by focusing primarily on the experience of charisma. However, I would like to suggest that aesthetic philosophy can expand our appreciation of the felt dimension of leadership beyond 'the charismatic' to include other qualitative aspects of leadership as it is experienced, including the 'beautiful', the 'comic', the 'tragic' or a range of other aesthetic categories. The aesthetic dimension of leadership performance is an area receiving increasing interest by leadership scholars. For instance, in the article 'The Aesthetics of Leadership', Hans Hansen and colleagues (Hansen et al. 2007) brings our attention to the qualitative aspects of leadership experience. In a number of articles Arja Ropo and her colleagues have attended to the embodied nature of leadership and the aesthetic qualities inherent in leadership performance (Ropo and Parviainen 2001; Ropo et al. 2002; Ropo and Sauer 2008) and the recently published book *Aesthetic Leadership* (Guillet de Monthoux et al. 2007) provide a range of case studies in which organizations and their leaders are analysed from the aesthetic perspective.

My own research into the contribution aesthetic appreciation brings to this field has focused primarily on what might constitute 'beautiful leadership' (Ladkin 2008). Drawing from Plato and the Plotinus, I suggest that constructing leader performances which can be apprehended as 'beautiful' involves combining mastery, coherence and purpose in the way in which the leader role is enacted. These categories are helpful but are still only proxies that point to the invisible, yet powerful aspect of leader performance that I am trying to capture.

Being aware of the aesthetic dimension of leadership entails attending to the immediate, visceral response one has to a particular individual or situation. It involves letting yourself become aware of the 'yuck' reaction a particular individual evokes when they invoke declarative power in a certain way or the raising of the hairs on the back of your neck when a different individual takes the stage. Attending to this dimension requires noticing the quality of a group's activity; is it buzzing or is it sluggish? What is the pace at which collective action is being undertaken, what is its rhythm and flow? What does its 'feel' tell us about the way leadership is being enacted? What kind of intervention might alter the aesthetic in a helpful way or how might collective action which is clicking along be sustained?

Paying attention to the aesthetic qualities of collective action provide new possibilities for those working within a leadership dynamic. It also calls for the asking of different questions. Instead of 'What is the goal we want to reach?', the question, 'What is the quality of the journey we want to create which will take us there?' might be asked. Given a certain aspiration, what are the implications for how leader and follower roles are enacted? Those taking up the leader role themselves might ask themselves, 'What is the quality of the aesthetic impression I would like to create in this circumstance?' rather than, 'How do I get people to do what I want them to do?' I am not arguing that the latter question is unimportant, rather that it might be helpfully augmented by questions concerning the desired qualities with which a leadership intervention might be imbued.

WHAT ARE THE IMPLICATIONS FOR RESEARCHING LEADERSHIP?

The analysis offered here goes some way to construct leadership as a phenomenon which is virtually impossible to research. As a starting point, it is always moving. It is not located in one place but rather flows between the different 'pieces' which constitute it. Where might a researcher look for it? Furthermore, it exists in the experiences of those who would attribute it. At any one moment, some people will see leadership while others perceive coercion. This is not a phenomenon which lends itself to positivistic deconstruction, measurement and logical analysis. Does that mean it cannot be studied? No. However, it does suggest that methods more suited to analysing entities which are materially present will have severe limitations when applied to the investigation of leadership.

Chapter 3 offered some suggestions about how leadership might most appropriately be explored. It is worth revisiting those in light of the ground covered since then. First, a point which I hope will be obvious now is the importance of attending to the questions posed at the start of any inquiry. I hope the book has amply demonstrated the extent to which the questions we ask drive the knowledge we discover. Perhaps even more crucial than paying attention to the particular questions being posed is recognizing the purpose behind them. The purpose towards which an inquiry is directed needs to guide the question posed. Whose knowledge will the question augment and how will they use the answers generated? What is the context in which the question is being generated? What purpose does the knowledge which will be generated aim to serve? These considerations are critical to the framing of questions which will yield useful responses.

Following from this, the analysis here suggests that anyone researching leadership must be very cognisant of the specific angle from which they are doing so. Phenomenology tells us that the perceiver is completely implicated in what is perceived and this is very true for a phenomenon such as leadership. As well as asking what a particular question is for, the researcher is encouraged to note why he or she is asking it and how they themselves might be implicated in it. Critically examining the viewpoint which colours questions may suggest alternative or more appropriate questions and approaches.

Additionally, researchers are encouraged to experiment with and devise new methods which might be sensitive enough to detect the invisible, absent aspects of leadership. Attending to the felt sense of those engaged in leadership dynamics, including their emotional as well as intellectual responses, are largely unexplored yet rich potential areas for further study. Similarly, highly textured accounts which seek to uncover the way people make sense of their experiences might provide further insights into the 'middle space' of leadership and extend the notion of the 'flesh' of leadership. Longitudinally-based studies which attend to the role context plays in creating the leadership moment could equally bring new insight to its emergent and highly particularized nature.

Finally, as stressed in the concept of 'identity' offered by phenomenology, those researching leadership might bear in mind that pronouncing a final, definitive account of this phenomenon is not possible. According to phenomenology, the identity of leadership can never be fully known. Any insights research can offer are therefore necessarily limited. However, that does not mean that such insights, particularly if they arise from research appreciative of the richly textured and fleeting nature of the phenomenon, would not be important. I would suggest that such accounts may provide particularly noteworthy insights about the experience of leading and leadership, rather than its apparent 'traces'. Certainly, for a phenomenon which is so difficult to know, leadership continues to hold a high degree of fascination for many of us in the West, whether as its students or merely as members of communities and nations.

This observation brings me to revisit one final question which was initially raised in Chapter 1. That is: what does our preoccupation with leadership tell us about ourselves and our own particular socio-historic moment?

WHAT DOES OUR FASCINATION WITH LEADERSHIP TELL US ABOUT OURSELVES?

Although I routinely encounter the question 'What is leadership?', I rarely stumble upon the query, 'What is leadership *for*?' This question raises issues of purpose and meaning and perhaps provides an apt final question to ponder. What does leadership 'mean' for our culture[2] at this point in time and what does our preoccupation with it reveal about us?

This question is posed against the backdrop of having been reminded that far from being a universally sought after phenomenon, leadership, as it is conceptualized and focused on in Western nations, does not hold such a central role in other cultures. When advising the World Association of

Girl Guides and Girl Scouts on the creation of their own leadership development programme, I was struck by the reaction of a number of women involved in that process who live in countries in which the concept of 'leadership' does not hold the same significance. They could not understand the power the notion held for those of us from North America and Europe. They spoke of how in their cultures far greater emphasis was placed on collective forms of activity without focusing so heavily on 'leaders' who could be seen to 'make a difference'. Of course their interpretation could be equated with the argument drawn throughout the book that leadership is more than leaders. Even so, the idea of leadership itself seemed to hold far less grip on the collective consciousness of the cultures from which these women came.

Their perspective prompted me to review the relationship we in the West have with the concept and to notice the often ambivalent way in which we approach it. The writing of this book has been conducted in the wake of two historic events which both have implications for exploring this territory; the election of the first mixed-race man as President of the United States of America and the slowdown in the financial markets resulting in the most significant world recession since the 1930s. In the first case, as I write, Barack Obama has been in office for less than six months and already the daggers are drawn to expose the mistakes he has made and the way in which, in such a short time, he has already not lived up to his promise. How can such an assessment be made so early in his Presidency? Does the capacity to be so critical so soon reveal something important about the place leaders hold for us within the twenty-first century Western world?

The ambivalence, if not anomy, which I am sensing is indicated by a headline in the UKs *Guardian* newspaper announcing: 'Lost Leaders': Which world leader messed up most comprehensively this week? Read Simon Tisdall's summary and see if you agree – from UN Secretary General Ban Ki-moon to Dmitry Medvedev of Russia' (Tisdall 2009, p. 23).

On the site, Ban Ki-moon is castigated for 'rejecting a further inquiry into the allegation that war crimes were committed by Israel and Palestine during the uprising in Gaza during January 2009' (despite the initial inquiry finding Israel had acted 'recklessly') and Medvedev was called to account for asserting Russia's military control of unrecognized borders of Georgia's regions in South Ossetia and Abkazia (Tisdall 2009, p. 23).

Are these leaders actually 'lost' for making these decisions? I am not suggesting that either Ban Ki-moon or Dmitry Medvedev is acting with great wisdom in the actions they have taken. I equally do not find Simon Tisdall's framing particularly sophisticated in its analysis or generative in its purpose. It does, however, seem representative of the kind of relationship many of us have with those who take up highly visible leader roles.

Although Obama, Ban Ki-moon and Medvedev are high-profile leaders and it could be argued that political interests will always colour people's responses to their actions, I am not certain that lower-profile organizational leaders are regarded with greater generosity. Blaming leaders for the failures and short-comings of collective action – be that action saving people from storm-induced floods or predicting financial collapse – seems to be common practice.

One explanation for this is offered by the critical theorist and dramatist Kenneth Burke who has looked carefully at the role guilt and blame play in Western cultures. He argues that in Western, individualistic cultures, having someone to blame when things go wrong is important (Burke 1965). Thus, leaders serve both as our saviours and as the ones we can call to account when messes are not sorted or prizes not won. If Burke's analysis is correct, perhaps part of our fascination with leadership is to have 'leaders' who we can blame when things go wrong. This interpretation would also support our continued love affair with 'leaders' rather than more fulsomely exploring and trying to discover ways of enacting 'leadership'.

Taking the notion of 'leadership' as presented here seriously has significant implications for our ability to continue to blame leaders. In accepting the notion that leadership is a dynamic in which followers are also implicated, failures of leadership are followers' responsibility as well. 'Leadership' demands a level of attention from all of those involved in its enactment which is not recognized from a 'leader-centric' viewpoint. The notion of the flesh of leadership implies that leaders and followers are together implicated in the enactment of leadership which successfully achieves mobilization towards desired purposes.

From this analysis, even the labels 'followers' and 'leaders' become potentially redundant. As so elegantly articulated by a fellow leadership scholar colleague, 'What we are talking about when we talk about leadership is more than the space between "leaders" and "followers", but our enactment together in concert and in community' (Bathurst 2009, personal communication). This statement seems to capture something of the essence of a phenomenological rendering of leadership which speaks to the lived, purposeful experience of it which perhaps can be known only in fleeting, ephemeral moments.

If this is the case, how in fact might this phenomenon be studied in any meaningful way? Perhaps this is the gift of exploring it through the lens of philosophy. For, as Bertrand Russell suggests in the quote (1946 [1996]) which opened this chapter, philosophy teaches us to live with uncertainty without becoming paralyzed. The difficulties associated with studying leadership should not deter the persistent inquirer. However, those researching it need to be very transparent about the angle from which they approach it and be clear about the purposes informing the questions they pose. They need to be mindful of the nature of the phenomenon being investigated and recognize the limitations of any method used to examine it.

One way philosophers keep themselves from becoming paralyzed is by asking questions, an approach which this book has set out to illustrate. The power of good questions is that they can expand well-worn territories and reveal new possibilities for thought and action. I hope this book has demonstrated the importance of attending to the questions we ask about leadership as well as the power of pursuing new ones. Perhaps living the questions, as Rilke (1929 [2000]) urged at the very beginning of the book, is the best advice for all of us aspiring to study, teach or enact our part of the leadership moment.

NOTES

1. Obama, B. (2009), 'Annual Dinner for the White House Press Corps', http://www.government.com (accessed 19 May 2009).
2. By 'our' I mean those of us for whom leadership holds a particular place within our way of understanding the world. Specifically, I am referring to Western and Western-influenced cultures which generally emphasise individualism over more collectively based approaches.

Bibliography

Alimo-Metcalfe, B. and R.J. Alban-Betcalfe (2001), 'The development of a new Transformational Leadership Questionnaire', *Journal of Occupational and Organizational Psychology*, **74** (1), 1–28.

Alvesson, M. and S. Sveningsson (2003), 'The great disappearing act: difficulties in doing "leadership"', *Leadership Quarterly*, **14** (3), 359–81.

Appelbaum, S.H., J. Berke, J. Taylor and J.A. Vazquez (2008), 'The role of leadership during large scale organizational transitions: lessons from six empirical studies', *Journal of American Academy of Business* **13** (1), 16–24.

Aristotle (1976), *The Nicomachean Ethics*, translated by J. Thomson, revised with note and appendices by H. Tredennick, introduction and bibliography by J. Barnes, London: Penguin.

Armstrong, D. (1968), *A Materialist Theory of Mind*, London: Routledge and Kegan Paul.

Balkundi, P. and M. Kilduff (2005), 'The ties that lead: a social-network approach to leadership', *Leadership Quarterly*, **16** (6), 941–61.

Barbaras, R. (2004), *The Being of the Phenomenon: Merleau-Ponty's Ontology*, translated by T. Toadvine and L. Lawlor, Indianapolis, IN: Indiana University Press.

Bass, Bernard M. (1985), *Leadership and Performance Beyond Expectations*, New York: Free Press.

Beer, M. and N. Nohria (2000), 'Cracking the code of change', *Harvard Business Review*, **78** (3), 133.

Berger, P. and T. Luckman (1966), *The Social Construction of Reality: A Treatise on the Sociology of Knowledge*, Garden City, NJ: Doubleday.

Bergson, H. (1912), *An Introduction to Metaphysics*, translated by T.E. Hulme and introduction by T.A. Goudge, Indianapolis, IN: Hackett Publishing Co.

Bergson, H. (1983), *Creative Evolution*, translated by A. Mitchell, Lanham, MD: University Press of America.

Beyer, J.M. (1999), 'Taming and promoting charisma to change organisations', *Leadership Quarterly*, **10** (2), 307–31.

Birnbaum, R. (2000), *Management Fads in Higher Education: Where they Come From, What they Do, Why They Fail*, San Francisco, CA: Jossey-Bass.

Buck Morss, S. (1992), 'Aesthetics and anaesthetics: Walter Benjamin's artwork essay reconsidered', *October*, **62**, 3–41.

Burke, K. (ed.) (1958 [1992]), *Permanence and Change: An Anatomy of Purpose*, 3rd edn, Los Angeles, CA: University of California Press.

Burns, J.M. (1978), *Leadership*, New York: Harper and Row.

Burns, J.M. (2004), 'Foreword', in J. Ciulla (ed.), *Ethics, the Heart of Leadership* (2nd edn), Westport, CT: Praeger, pp. ix–xii.

Cataldi, S.L. (1993), *Emotion, Depth, and Flesh: A Study of Sensitive Space*, Albany, NY: State University of New York Press.

Cheney, J. (2002), 'Truth, knowledge and the wild world', accessed 17 September 2003 at, www.waukesha.uwc.edu/phil/jcheney.

Cheney, J. and A. Weston (1999), 'Environmental ethics as environmental etiquette: towards an ethics-based epistemology', *Environmental Ethics*, **21** (2) 115–34.

Ciulla, J.B. (2004), *Ethics, the Heart of Leadership* (2nd edn), Westport, CT: Praeger.

Ciulla, J.B. (2008), 'Leadership studies and the "fusion of horizons"', *Leadership Quarterly*, **19** (4), 393–5.

Cohan, W. (2009), *House of Cards: A Tale of Hubris and Wretched Excess on Wall Street*, New York: Random House.

Conger, J.A. and R.N. Kanungo (1988), *Charismatic Leadership: The Elusive Factor in Organizational Effectiveness*, San Francisco, CA: Jossey Bass.

Conger J.A. and R.N. Kanungo (1987), 'Toward a theory of charismatic leadership in organisational settings', *Academy of Management Review*, **12** (4), 637–47.

Deleuze, G. (1993), *The Fold: Leibniz and the Baroque*, foreword and translation by T. Conley, Minneapolis, MN: University of Minnesota Press

Deleuze, G. (1994), *Difference and Repetition,* translated by P. Patton, London: Athlone Press.

Descartes, R. (1988), 'Meditations on first philosophy', translated by John Cottingham, in *Descartes: Selected Philosophical Writings*, New York: Cambridge University Press, pp. 73–122.

Dillon, M.C. (1997), *Merleau-Ponty's Ontology* (2nd edn), Evanston, IL: Northwestern University Press.

Donaldson, T. and P. Werhane (1999), *Ethical Issues in Business: A Philosophical Approach*, 6th edn, Upper Saddle River, NJ: Prentice Hall.

Drath, W.H. and C.J. Palus (1994), *Making Common Sense: Leadership as Meaning Making in Communities of Practice*, Greensboro, NC: Center for Creative Leadership Press.

Dunphy, D. and D. Stace (1993), 'The strategic management of corporate change', *Human Relations*, **46** (8), 905–20.

Elkington, J. (1998), *Cannibals with Forks: The Triple Bottom Line for 21st Century Business*, Oxford: Capstone.

Evans, F. and L. Lawlor (2000), *Chiasms: Merleau-Ponty's Notion of Flesh*, Albany, NY: State University of New York Press.

Fletcher, J. (2004), 'The paradox of post heroic leadership: an essay on gender, power and transformational change', *Leadership Quarterly*, **15** (5), 647–61.

Foldy, E.G., L. Goldman and S. Ospina (2008), 'Sensegiving and the role of cognitive shifts in the work of leadership', *Leadership Quarterly*, **19** (5), 514–29.

Follett, M.P. (1949 [1987]), 'The essentials of leadership', in L. Urwick (ed.), *Freedom and Co-ordination: Lectures in Business and Organization*, New York: Garland Publishers.

Gadamer, H.G. (1975 [2004]), *Truth and Method*, London: Continuum.

Gadamer, H.G. (1976), *Philosophical Hermeneutics*, translated by David Linge, Berkeley, CA: University of California Press.

Gemmil, G. and J. Oakley (1997), 'Leadership: an alienating social myth', in Keith Grint (ed.), *Leadership: Classical, Contemporary and Critical Approaches*, Oxford: Oxford University Press, pp. 272–88.

Gerstner, C.R. and D.V. Day (1997), 'Meta-analytic review of leader-member exchange theory: correlates and construct issues', *Journal of Applied Psychology*, **82** (6), 827–44.

Gibb, C. (1954), 'Leadership', in G. Lindzey (ed.), *Handbook of Social Psychology*, vol 2, Reading, MA: Addison-Wesley, pp. 877–917.

Graen, G.B., M.A. Novak and P. Sommerkamp (1982), 'The effects of leader-member exchange and job design on productivity and satisfaction: testing the dual attachment model', *Organization Behaviour and Human Performance*, **30** (1), 109–31.

Graen, G. and M. Uhl-Bien (1995), 'Relationship-based approach to leadership: development of leader-member exchange (LMX) theory of leadership over 25 years: applying a multi-level multi-domain perspective', *Leadership Quarterly*, **6** (2), 219–47.

Grewal, D. and E. Grewal (2008), 'Clinton battles bias against strong women', *Truthout*, accessed 16 March 2009 at www.truthout.org/article/daisy-grewal-and-elena-grewal-clinton-battles-bias-against-strong-women.

Grey, M. (2008), 'A Short History of Text Messaging', accessed 17 June 2009 at http://e-articles.info/e/a/title/A-short-history-of-text-messaging/.

Grint, K. (1997), *Leadership: Classical, Contemporary and Critical Approaches*, Oxford: Oxford University press.

Grint, K. (2001), *The Arts of Leadership*, Oxford: Oxford University Press.

Grint, K. (2005a), 'Problems, problems, problems: the social construction of leadership', *Human Relations*, **58** (11), 1467–94.

Grint, K. (2005b), *Leadership: Limits and Possibilities*, New York: Palgrave Macmillan.

Gronn, P. (2000), 'Distributed properties: a new architecture for leadership', *Educational Management and Administration*, **28** (3), 317–38.

Gronn, P. (2002), 'Distributed leadership as a unit of analysis', *The Leadership Quarterly*, **13** (4) 423–51.

Guillet de Monthoux, P., C. Gustafsson and S.E. Sjostrand (2007), *Aesthetic Leadership: Managing Fields of Flow in Art and Business*, Basingstoke: Palgrave Macmillan.

Hansen, H., A. Ropo and E. Sauer (2007), 'Aesthetic leadership', *Leadership Quarterly*, **18** (6) 544–60.

Hartman, E.M. (2006), Can we teach character? An Aristotelian answer, *Academy of Management Learning and Education*, **5** (1) 68–81.

Haslam, S.A. and S.D. Reicher (2007), 'Identity, entrepreneurship and the consequences of identity failure', *Social Psychology Quarterly*, **70** (1) 125–47.

Heidegger, M. (1962), *Being and Time*, translated by John Macquarrie and Edward Robinson, Oxford: Blackwell Publishers.

Heidegger, M. (1971), 'Building dwelling thinking', translated by Alfred Hofstadter, in *Poetry, Language, Thought*, New York: Haper Colophon, pp. 145–61.

Heifetz, R. (1998) *Leadership Without Easy Answers*, Cambridge, MA: Harvard University Press.

Heifetz, R. and D. Laurie (1997), 'The work of leadership', *Harvard Business Review*, **75** (1) (Jan/Feb), 124–34.

House, R., W.D. Spangler and J. Woycke (1991), 'Personality and charisma in the US Presidency: a psychological theory of leader effectiveness', *Administrative Science Quarterly*, **36** (3), 364–96.

Howell, J.M. (1988), 'Two faces of charisma: socialized and personalized leadership in organizations', in J.A. Conger and R.N. Kanungo (eds), *Charismatic Leadership: The Elusive Factor in Organizational Effectiveness*, San Francisco CA: Jossey Bass, pp. 213–36.

Howell, J.M. and B. Shamir (2005), 'The role of followers in the charismatic leadership process: relationships and consequences', *Academy of Management Review*, **30** (1), 96–112.

Howell, J.M. and B.J. Avolio (1992), 'The ethics of charismatic leadership: subversive or liberating?', *Academy of Management Executive*, **6** (2), 43–54.

Husserl, E. (1900 [2001]), *Logical Investigations Vol. 1*, translated by N. Findlay, London: Routledge.

Husserl, E. (1901 [2001]), *Logical Investigations Vol. 2,* translated by N. Findlay, London: Routledge.

Husserl, E. (1931 [1994]), *Briefwechsel Karl Schuhmann* in collaboration with Elizabeth Schuhmann, 10 vols, Dordrecht: Kluwer.

Husserl, E. (1937 [1970]), *The Crisis of European Science and Transcendental Phenomenology*, translated by D. Carr, Evanston, IL: Northwestern University Press.

Husserl, E. (1967), *Cartesian Meditations*, translated by D. Cairns, The Hague: Nijhoff.

International Monetary Fund (2009), 'Report', accessed 13 June 2009 at www.inf.org/external/dat.htm.

James, W (1909 [1996]), *A Pluralistic Universe, Hibbert Lectures*, Omaha, NE: University of Nebraska press.

James, W. (1975), *Pragmatism and the Meaning of Truth,* F. Bowers and I.K. Skrupskelis (eds), with an introduction by H.S. Thayer, Cambridge, MA: Harvard University Press.

James, W. (1979), *Some Problems of Philosophy,* F.H. Burkhardt, F. Bowers and I.K. Skrupskelis (eds), with an introduction by P.H. Hare, Cambridge, MA: Harvard University Press.

Kant, I. (1790 [2005]), *Critique of Judgement*, translated by J.H. Bernard, Mineola, NY: Dover.

Kets de Vries M.R.F. (1989), *Prisoners of Leadership*, New York: Wiley.

Kets de Vries M.R.F. (2004), *Lessons on Leadership by Terror: Finding Shaka Zulu in the Attic,* Cheltenham, UK and Northampton, MA, USA: Edward Elgar.

Kets de Vries, M.R.F. and D. Miller (1986), 'Personality, culture and organisation', *Academy of Management Review*, **11** (2), 266–79.

Kotter, J. (1996), *Leading Change*, Boston, MA: Harvard University Press.

Ladkin, D. (2005), 'The enchantment of the charismatic leader: charisma reconsidered as aesthetic encounter', *Leadership*, **2** (2) 165–79.

Ladkin, D. (2006), 'When deontology and utilitarianism are not enough: how Heidegger's notion of "dwelling" might help organisational leaders resolve ethical issues', *Journal of Business Ethics*, **65** (2), 87–98.

Ladkin, D. (2008), 'Leading beautifully: how mastery, congruence and form contribute to inspirational leadership performance', *Leadership Quarterly*, **19** (1), 31–41.

Lewin, K. (1951), *Field Theory in Social Science*, New York: Harper and Row.

Linstead, S. and T. Thanem (2007), 'Multiplicity, virtuality and organization: the contribution of Gilles Deleuze', *Organization Studies*, **28** (10), 1438–501.

Linge, D. (1976), 'Editor's introduction', in H.G. Gadamer (ed.), *Philosophical Hermeneutics*, translated by D. Linge, Berkeley CA: University of California Press, pp xi-xlviii.

Macalister, T. (2009), 'FSA speaks about crisis', *Guardian*, London, 16 February, p. 7.

MacIntyre, A. (1985), *After Virtue*, 2nd edn, London: Duckworth.

Meindl, J.R. (1993), 'Re-inventing leadership: a radical social-psychological approach', in J.K. Murnigham (ed.), *Social Psychological Organizations*, Englewood Cliffs, NJ: Prentice Hall, pp. 89–118.

Meindl, J.R. (1995), 'The romance of leadership as a follower-centric theory: a social constructionist approach', *Leadership Quarterly*, **6** (3), 329–41.

Meindl, J.R., S. Ehrlich and J. Durkerich (1985), 'The romance of leadership', *Administrative Science Quarterly*, **30** (1), 78–102.

Merleau-Ponty, M. (1945 [1962]), *The Phenomenology of Perception*, translated by Colin Smith, London: Routledge Classics.

Merleau-Ponty, M. (1968), *The Visible and the Invisible*, Claude Lefort (ed.), translated by Alphonso Lingis, Evanston, IL: Northwestern University Press.

Midgley, M. (1992), *Science as Salvation: A Modern Myth and its Meaning*, London: Routledge.

Mintzberg, Henry (2004), 'Enough leadership', *Harvard Business Review*, **82** (11), 22.

Moran, D. (2000), *Introduction to Phenomenology*, London and New York: Routledge.

Muta Maathai, W. (2008), *Unbowed: A Memoir*, London: Arrow Books.

Nietzsche, F. (1884 [1995], *Thus Spoke Zarathustra*, translated by W. Kaufmann, New York: The Modern Library.

Nightingale, B. (2008), 'A more perfect union', *The Times, 20 March*, pp. 34–35.

Obama, B. (2009), 'Annual dinner for the White House Press Corps', accessed 19 May 2009 at www.government.com.

Organizing for America (2008), 'Barack Obama', accessed 15 November 2008 at www.barackobama.com/index/.php.

Pfeffer, Jeffrey (1977), 'The ambiguity of leadership', *Academy of Management Review* **2** (1), 104–12.

Pillay, J. and A. Braganza (2008), 'The architectonics of transformational change: towards a dialogic theory of corporate turnaround', proceedings of the 2008 British Academy of Management Conference, Harrogate.

Place, U. (1988), 'Thirty years on – is consciousness still a brain process?', *British Journal of Psychology,* **47** (1) 44–50.

Plato (380 BCE [1992]), *The Republic,* translated by G.M.A. Grube, Indianapolis, IN: Hackett.

Quinn, R.E. (2000), *Change the World: How Ordinary People can Accomplish Extraordinary Results,* San Francisco, CA: Jossey Bass.

Raelin, J. (2003), *Creating Leaderful Organizations,* San Francisco, CA: Berrett-Koehler Publishers.

Raelin, J. (2006), 'Finding meaning in the organization', *MIT Sloan Manaagement Review,* **47** (3), 64–8.

Rescher, N. (1996), *Process Metaphysics: An Introduction to Process Philosophy,* Albany, NY: State University of New York Press.

Rilke, R.M. (1929 [2000]), *Letters to a Young Poet,* translated by J.M. Burnham: Novaro, CA: New World Library, p. 35.

Rittell, H. and M. Webber (1973), 'Dilemmas in a general theory of planning', *Policy Sciences,* **4** (1) 155–69.

Ropo, A. and J. Parviainen (2001), 'Leadership and bodily knowledge in expert organisations: epistemological rethinking', *Scandinavian Journal of Management,* **17** (1), 1–18.

Ropo, A. and E. Sauer (2008), 'Corporeal leaders', in D. Barry and H. Hansen (eds), *The Sage Handbook on New Approaches in Management and Organization Studies,* London: Sage, pp. 469–78.

Ropo, A., J. Parviainen and N. Koivunen (2002), 'Aesthetics in leadership. From absent bodies to social bodily presence', in J. Meindl and K. Parry (eds), *Grounding Leadership Theory and Research: Issues and Perspectives,* Greenwich, CT: Information Age Publishing.

Rost, J.C. (1993), *Leadership for the Twenty-First Century,* Westport, CT: Praeger.

Russell, B. (1946 [1996]), *History of Western Philosophy,* London: George Unwin Ltd.

Sartre, J.P. (1943 [2002]), *Being and Nothingness,* translated by Hazel Barnes, London: Routledge.

Schleiermacher, F. (1838 [1998]), *Hermeneutics and Criticism and Other Writings,* Andrew Bowie (ed.), Cambridge: Cambridge University Press.

Schmidt, L.K. (2006), *Understanding Hermeneutics,* Stocksfield: Acumen Publishing.

Scott-Villiers, P. (2009), 'A question of understanding: hermeneutics and the Play of history, distance and dialogue in development practice in East Africa', PhD thesis, School of Management, University of Bath, UK.

Shamir, B. (1999), 'Taming charisma for better understanding and greater usefulness: a response to Beyer', *Leadership Quarterly,* **10** (4), 555–62.

Sinclair, A. (1994), *Doing Leadership Differently: Gender, Power and Sexuality in a Changing Business Culture*, Melbourne, VIC: Melbourne University Press.

Sinclair, A. (2005), 'Body possibilities in leadership', *Leadership*, **1** (4), 387–406.

Sjostrand, S.E., J. Sandberg and M. Tyrstrup (eds) (2001), *Invisible Management: The Social Construction of Leadership*, London: Thompson Leary.

Smircich, L. and G. Morgan (1982), 'Leadership: the management of meaning', *Journal of Applied Behavioural Science*, **18** (3), 257–73.

Smit, T. (2001), *Eden*, London: Corgi Books.

Sokolowski, R. (2000), *Introduction to Phenomenology*, Cambridge, UK: Cambridge University Press.

The History Place (2009), 'John F. Kennedy "We choose to go to the Moon . . ."', accessed 16 March at www.historyplace.com/speeches/jfk-space. htm.

The New York Times (2008), 'Barack Obama's New Hampshire primary speech', accessed 16 March 2009 at www.nytimes.com/2008/01/08/us/politics/08text-obama.html?_r=1.

The New York Times (2008), 'Hillary Clinton's New Hampshire primary speech', accessed 28 December 2009 at www.nytimes.com /2008/01/08/ US/politics08/text-clinton, html.

Tisdall, S. (2009), 'Lost leaders', *Guardian*, London, 8 May, p. 23.

Townsend, Frances Fragos (2006), 'The federal response to Hurricane Katrina: lessons learned', Washington DC Office of the Assistant to the President for Homeland Security and Counterterrorism, accessed 15 September 2008 at www.whitehouse.gov/reports/katrina-lessons-learned.

Tsoukas, H. and R. Chia (2002), 'On organizational becoming: rethinking organizational change', *Organization Science*, **13** (5), 567–82.

Tushman, M.L. and E. Romanelli (1985), 'Organizational evolution: a metamorphosis mode of convergence and reorientation', *Research in Organizational Behavior*, **7** (2), 171–222.

Uhl-Bien, M. (2006), 'Relational leadership theory: exploring the social processes of leadership and organizing', *Leadership Quarterly*, **17** (6) 654–76.

US House Select Bipartisan Committee to Investigate the Preparation for and Response to Hurricane Katrina (2006), *A Failure of Initiative*, Washington, DC: US Government Printing Office, accessed 16 March 2009 at http://katrina.house.gov/full_katrina_report.htm.

van Heerden, I. and M. Bryan (2006), *The Storm*, New York: Penguin.

van Knippenberg, D. and M.A. Hogg (2000), *Leadership and Power: Identity Processes in Groups and Organizations*, London: Sage.

Waldersee, R. and A. Griffiths (2003), 'Implementing change: matching implementation and change type', *Leadership and Organizational Development Journal*, **25** (5), 424–34.

Wang, Lake (forthcoming), 'The development of national leaders in China', DBA study, Cranfield School of Management, Cranfield University.

Weber, M. (1922 [1968]), *Economy and Society: An Outline of Interpretive Sociology*, G. Roth and C. Wittich (eds.), New York: Bedminster Press.

Weber, M. (1924 [1947]), *The Theory of Social and Economic Organisation*, translated by T. Parsons, New York: Free Press.

Weierter, S.J.M. (1997), 'Who wants to play follow-the-leader?: a theory of charismatic relationships based on routinised charisma and follower characteristics', *Leadership Quarterly*, **8** (2) 171–94.

Whitehead, A.N. (1920), *The Concept of Nature*, London: Cambridge University Press.

Whitehead, A.N. (1927), *Symbolism: Its Meaning and Effect*, New York: Forham University Press.

Whitehead, A.N. (1967), *Science and the Modern World*, New York: Free Press.

Whitehead, A.N. (1978), *Process and Reality*, D.R. Griffin and D.W. Sherburne (eds), New York: Free Press.

Willner, A.R. (1984), *The Spell Binders*, New Haven, CT: Yale University Press.

Wood, M. (2005), 'The fallacy of misplaced leadership', *Journal of Management Studies*, **42** (6), 1101–21.

Index